THE CLASSIC
NORTHERN
ITALY

ANNA DEL CONTE

THE CLASSIC FOOD OF
NORTHERN ITALY

PAVILION

FOR ELEANOR

First published in Great Britain in 1995 by
Pavilion Books Limited
London House
Great Eastern Wharf Parkgate Road
London SW11 4NQ

This paperback edition published in 1999

Text and recipes copyright © 1995 by Anna Del Conte
The moral right of the author has been asserted
Foreword copyright © 1995 by Delia Smith
Recipe photographs copyright © by Roger Stowell
Home economist: Caroline Liddell
Stylist: Helen Payne
Map artworks by Alec Hurzer

(V) Indicates recipes suitable for vegetarians

Designed by Andrew Barron and Collis Clements Associates

A CIP catalogue record for this book is available from the British Library

ISBN 1 86205 218 2

Typeset in Galliard
Printed and bound in Singapore by Kyodo

10 9 8 7 6 5 4 3 2 1

This book may be ordered by post direct from the publisher.
Please contact the Marketing Department. But try your bookshop first.

CONTENTS

Merano

TRENTINO
ALTO
ADIGE

FRIULI
VENEZIA
GIULIA
Udine

VALTELLINA

Trento

Cormons

Lake
Maggiore

Lake Como

Bassano

Treviso

Trieste

Aosta
VALLE D'AOSTA

Bergamo

LOMBARDIA

Lake Garda

VENETO

Padova

Venezia

Milano

Torino

Po

Pavia

Mantova

Po

Goro

PIEMONTE

Asti

Parma

Ferrara

Adriatic Sea

Alba

EMILIA ROMAGNA

Reggio nell'Emilia

Modena

Bologna

LIGURIA

Genova

Aulla

Cesenatico

Lerici

MARCHE

Bordighera

Lucca

Firenze

Ancona

TOSCANA

Arezzo

Siena

Perugia

Pedaso

UMBRIA

San Benedetto
del Tronto

Montefalco

Norcia

MAREMMA

Pitigliano

Todi

Mediterranean
Sea

N

| 0 | 25 | 50 | 75 | 100 Miles |
| 0 | 50 | 100 | 150 Kilometres |

FOREWORD

It is England's good fortune that an accomplished Italian food writer fell in love with, and married, an Englishman. Anna Del Conte was born and reared a Milanese and is a true daughter of that special breed of Northern Italians who share an innate and intense passion on the subject of food.

Living in this country, but keeping strong links with Italy and her family, Anna's writing and culinary enthusiasm have been a beacon of true light among greyer shades of the misrepresentations that predominate in cookbooks and magazines under the heading *Italian*.

Anna is a purist. She will not countenance anything that isn't in the strictest sense authentic. So, with this in mind, I am here to recommend to you what surely must be the best researched and presented book on Northern Italian food yet published. If you want to grasp and understand the <u>real</u> thing, it is here on every page. With this book you will not only be able to cook authentic Italian food, you will also be able to go on an exciting journey of discovery throughout the whole of Northern Italy.

I personally have been waiting for this book for some time. Thank you, Anna, for all the hard work and research that has gone into it, and for making real Italian cooking and eating accessible to all of us.

Delia Smith

INTRODUCTION

History and geography have both played their part in making the cooking of Italy so strongly regional. For all the hundreds of years between the fall of the Roman Empire and the middle of the last century (1861 to be precise) the Italian peninsula was divided into independent, sovereign – and often hostile – states. That these states were frequently under foreign domination was another factor that pitted one state against another.

The degree to which this regionality still exists today can hardly be exaggerated. 'Where are you from?' is the first thing one Italian asks another when they meet for the first time. Before my husband had grown used to this *campanilismo*, he was struck by hearing me say, in surprised tones, 'She's from Florence . . . but she's very nice.' The Florentines have never been bosom friends of the Lombards!

It is only natural that this regionality, and the foreign domination, should have had a profound effect on Italian cooking. After the Napoleonic débâcle, for instance, the Spanish Bourbons returned to Naples and Sicily, the Vatican continued to govern central Italy, and the Hapsburgs were sitting happily all over Veneto and Lombardy. Meanwhile the Dukes of Savoia (the future kings of Italy) were becoming more and more powerful in Piedmont, and the charming Grand Duchess Marie Louise, Napoleon's widow, was teaching her subjects in Parma how to make cakes à l'Autrichienne.

So it is that, to this day, Parma boasts some of the best dolci in Italy, Venetian cooking has strong Hungarian and Eastern influences, the cooking of Lombardy prides itself on some of the best dishes of braised meat which the Austrians brought south, while the French taught the Milanese the use of butter and cream.

Although the same basic ingredients are used throughout northern Italy, they are cooked in different ways in each region. A fish soup from Ancona on the Adriatic, delicately flavoured with saffron, would be very different from the fish soup of Tuscany, a fiery cacciucco, and specifically from Livorno, on the Mediterranean, whose cooking has been strongly influenced by its spice trade with North Africa.

Another excellent example concerns the various ways of cooking *baccalà* and *stoccafisso* – salt cod and stockfish. This preserved fish was first brought to Sicily at the beginning of the millennium by the Normans. In the old days fish could not be kept or transported and, during some months of the year, could not even be caught. Thus, because of the Italians' partiality for fish, this preserved cod became very popular all over the peninsula. It was always available, was plentiful and – unlike now – was cheap.

There are a great number of recipes for baccalà or stoccafisso in any regional cookery book. The same fish, yes, but cooked with local flavourings and local methods. Liguria offers baccalà with spinach or Swiss chard, while in Tuscany baccalà is coated with flour, fried first and then *insaporito* – made tasty – in a tomato sauce, as are the Tuscans' red mullet and their cardoons. But it is in Veneto that the most famous recipes for stoccafisso have been created. The stockfish, succulent with melting onions, is cooked in milk with local potatoes and plenty of garlic and parsley, but never with the southern tomatoes. There and in Lombardy, baccalà and stoccafisso are always served with the Alpine staple, polenta.

Polenta and rice illustrate another aspect of the regionality of Italian food. They are both grown in northern Italy, and it is there that recipes for them abound. The risotti are lavishly dressed with butter, the local fat. Indeed, one used to talk of the 'butter line', which ran from west to east, to the north of Tuscany and south of Emilia-Romagna. North of this line, butter was the cooking fat, to the south it was oil.

These divisions result from the country's geography and climate, and they are sharpened by the contrast between the sea and the mountains. The northern part of the 1200 kilometre-long peninsula is fastened to continental Europe by the uninterrupted chain of the Alps. The country's only plain is here in the North, the huge Po valley, rich and fertile, where cattle graze and rice grows. Another massive chain cuts the country across vertically, the Apennines, from which countless valleys run down to the Adriatic sea on the eastern side and the Tyrrenian on the western.

Up to the Second World War these valleys, dotted with olive trees and covered with vines, were not connected by roads, and their inhabitants pursued their cultures and cooking unaware of what was going on 20 kilometres away on the other side of the mountains. Two such valleys, which run south almost next to each other, from Liguria into Tuscany, are the Lunigiana and the Garfagnana. I have found that many of the dishes of one of these valleys are quite unknown in the other. Another example from my own experience: when in a restaurant near Siena recently I suggested to the chef that I would like a soup of *farro* – emmer wheat. He told me that to have the best farro soup I should go to the nearby province of Lucca. '*Lì, sì che la fanno buona.*' (That is where they make it well.) And why? Because that is where the best farro is grown.

But there are two vital factors that are present throughout all Italian cooking, in all regions. The first and foremost is the importance always given to using only top quality ingredients, which are respected and appreciated for what they are. What Italians want when they eat is for the flavour of the main ingredient to come through loud and clear. All the other ingredients are there to help this aim. In a soup, a risotto, a stew, a dish of vegetables or even a sauce for pasta, a basis of flavours supports and enhances the main ingredient.

The second factor, a direct consequence of the first, is the love Italians have for home cooking. There is no haute cuisine in Italy, only *cucina casalinga* (home cooking), and this obviously means *cucina regionale*. Even recipes developed by the greatest chefs can be traced back to home cooking. For instance, sauces are only used to dress staple foods such as pasta and polenta. They are not, as in the French cuisine, used as an addition to meat or fish. The precept of Italian cooking is that the ingredient must always be respected and appreciated in its own right.

This respect for the ingredients is common to most Mediterranean cooking. It is also ancient, as can be seen by reading the Sicilian cookery writer Archestratus, who lived in the fourth century BC, when Sicily was part of the Greek empire. He writes: 'Sauces of cheese or pickled herbs are added to inferior fish, but in general this cooking is not based on sauces, the preference being for the addition of oil and light herbs to the fish juices. Meats are prepared with equal simplicity. Ingredients are cooked with few flavourings.' Such flavouring as there is comes from the beginning of the cooking, often in the form of a *battuto* or a *soffritto*, which together form the point of departure of most dishes. Many dishes from these northern regions are 'slow food', cooked at length to suit the long cold evenings by the fire.

You might be surprised to see how very few pasta dishes there are in this book, but pasta – apart from the home-made egg pasta of Emilia-Romagna – is not part of the traditional cooking of most of these regions. No sun-dried tomatoes, no rocket or arugula, few aubergines [US eggplants] and even fewer mozzarella dishes. Here we are in the North where the palpable influences often come from beyond the Alps.

The book is divided into ten regions, of which seven are the real northern Italian regions. To these I have added three regions which geographically are part of central Italy; they are Tuscany, Umbria and Marche. These regions, plus Liguria, bring in the Mediterranean kind of food which is traditionally lacking in the northern regions. It is here that pasta and olive oil have prevailed over rice and butter, not only in the past 20 years of health-conscious eating, but for many centuries.

With the 160 recipes collected here I wanted to give an idea of the enormous variety of northern Italian cooking. All the recipes represent the cooking of the regions they belong to. Some are classic recipes, like the ossobuco alla milanese and the Genoese cappon magro, while others are less well known, given to me by local cooks and friends. I have also been careful to choose recipes that can be reproduced successfully in this country, bearing in mind the availability of ingredients and the fact that some dishes do not export as well as others. But mostly these are recipes for dishes I like, collected for this personal book. My remarks concerning the presentation of the dishes reflect the way dishes are served in an Italian family, each dish being brought to the table on a large platter for the diners to help themselves.

What I have also set out to do is to throw some light, through the food and the cooking of these northern regions, on the less obvious aspects of this part of Italy, which I understand so well and love so much.

AFTERTHOUGHTS, ADVICE, HINTS AND TIPS

My English friends have suggested that I should include some of the little points that crop up in my conversation with them and which, they say, are often unfamiliar to the non-professional cook. So I start by giving an explanation of some of the Italian culinary terms I use.

Battuto is a pounded mixture (the word comes from *battere* – to beat or pound). The battuto is the basis of most dishes, from a pasta sauce to a bean soup. In the old days, when people were blissfully unaware of cholesterol and the furring-up of arteries, a battuto always contained salted pork fat – *lardo* – which was pounded with onion, celery, carrot, parsley and other herbs, and sometimes garlic. Nowadays olive oil and butter is used instead of pork fat, with possibly a little pancetta (see below) or prosciutto. When I add pancetta or prosciutto I use a food processor, which does an excellent job in a whizz.

A battuto usually becomes a soffritto (see below), except when it is added *a crudo* (in the raw state) to a sauce or a soup.

Soffritto is the battuto which has been fried, or actually 'under-fried', which is what the word means. The battuto is sautéed in a saucepan or a frying pan over a gentle heat until the onion is soft. When using garlic, this should be added to the onion later, when the onion is nearly done, or the garlic will become too dark by the time the onion is soft. Only when the battuto contains pancetta or fatty prosciutto can the garlic be added at the same time.

A well-made soffritto is fundamental to the final taste of the dish.

Insaporire is to let the ingredients take up the flavour of the soffritto or of the sauce. This is a very important step in the making of a dish, and one to which the right amount of time should be devoted. In the making of a bolognese ragù, for instance, the minced meat added to the soffritto must be well *insaporito* on a lively heat, while turning it over and over, before the wine, stock or milk is added for the slow cooking that follows.

Now, here are some afterthoughts and tips, arranged in alphabetical order.

BUTTER

I always use unsalted butter because it has a more delicate flavour and it can be heated to a higher temperature. Salted butter contains impurities which turn black at a high temperature and give the dish a coarse taste. Salted butter is also totally unsuitable in pastry, cakes and desserts, and delicate sauces.

I never clarify butter, because it removes its character. When I need to heat butter to a higher temperature, I add some olive oil. The oil can be heated to a high temperature without burning.

CHILLI

In the northern regions of Italy chillies are used very little, if ever. They appear in Tuscany, Umbria and Marche. The kind used there are the small dried ones, reputedly among the hottest of them all. Even these vary, however, so I suggest that you experiment with what you buy, keeping in mind that Italian dishes are never very hot, the chilli being considered a flavouring to blend with others and not to provide an overriding fire.

DRIED PORCINI

I suggest that they should be soaked for about 1 hour. This may be longer than they need, but it depends on the porcini. If they are beautiful, large fresh-looking slices they will only need 20 minutes or so, but if they are small dried-up bits you must give them longer in the soaking water.

EGGS

To see whether your eggs are fresh, place them in a bowl of salted water. If they fall to the bottom and stay there, they are fresh and suitable to be used raw or with a minimum of cooking. If you keep your eggs in the fridge, remove them from it in good time and bring them back to room temperature before using them.

FISH

Wash any fish in a mixture of water and and wine vinegar to freshen it up. When you add boiling water or stock to a fish which is stewing, pour it gently into the side of the pan to avoid breaking the fish's skin

FLOUR

In all the recipes I suggest using Italian 00 flour, which is available in Italian specialist food shops and in some of the best supermarkets. It is a flour which is easier to knead when used for cakes, pastry, pasta-making etc. and it has a more fragrant flavour.

FORK VERSUS SPOON
Use a fork to stir sautéeing potatoes, carrots, courgettes etc. Spoons tend to break them.

GARLIC
To keep the garlic you brought back from Italy or France, peel it and put it in a jar. Cover with extra virgin olive oil and refrigerate. You can use the oil as well; it will be garlic-flavoured oil.

LEMON
Add a few drops of lemon juice to prevent the sugar from crystalising when you make caramel, and to egg whites to stabilise them before beating.

LEMONS AND ORANGES
In any recipe that calls for orange or lemon rind I strongly advise you to use unwaxed fruits. The wax sprayed on the fruit is toxic, and it does not wash off easily. If you cannot find unwaxed fruits, put your lemons or oranges in a sink of very hot water and scrub hard.

MEAT
Remove meat from the fridge in good time before cooking, so that it reaches room temperature.

OLIVE OIL
When you use olive oil as a base for a soffritto together with butter, you do not need to use an extra virgin olive oil. A plain olive oil will do, because it has less flavour and it is lighter.

Whenever necessary I have suggested which kind of extra virgin olive oil you should use in a recipe. Some of the Tuscan *fruttati* olive oils, for instance, are too strong to dress sea bass or a plate of seafood. These oils are also not suitable as cooking oils.

I use plain olive oil or groundnut oil [US peanut oil] for deep frying. These two oils can be heated to the high temperature needed for deep frying. I never re-use oil after frying, because with prolonged heating oil develops toxic substances.

ONIONS AND LEEKS

If your onions, spring onions or leeks are too strong, cut them in half and soak them for a couple of hours in salted water. Squeeze out, rinse and dry.

PANCETTA

Pancetta, from the belly of a pig, is a similar cut to streaky bacon, but is differently cured. In some supermarkets you can buy pancetta, smoked or unsmoked, already diced, in vacuum packs. This is ideal for a battuto. If you cannot find this, buy pancetta *stesa*, which is better for cooking than the sausage-shaped version called pancetta *arrotolata*. This latter is less fatty and can be eaten instead of salame or prosciutto.

PROSCIUTTO

If you have a friendly Italian shop-keeper, ask for the knuckle of a prosciutto, which you can usually get at half the price of the prosciutto itself. This end piece has the right proportion of lean meat to fat, necessary for battuti, sauce bases or for stuffing or larding. Ask the shop-keeper to cut all the rind off the knuckle (keep this for flavouring a pulse soup or a stew), and then you should cut the meat into chunks and keep them in the freezer.

For cooking I prefer to use prosciutto di San Daniele rather than prosciutto di Parma because it has a stronger flavour.

PULSES

Apart from lentils, all pulses need soaking overnight before cooking. Cook the pulses, covered with fresh water by at least 5cm/2in, on a very low heat or in a low oven. Add the salt at the end of the cooking because salt tends to crack the skin.

Chick-peas take longer to cook than any other pulses. Their skin is tougher, and in order to soften it I mix a paste made with 1 tablespoon of flour and 1 tablespoon of bicarbonate of soda [US baking soda] into the soaking water. Rinse thoroughly before cooking.

RISOTTO

With each recipe I have suggested the best kind of rice to use. Whatever the kind, however, it must be Italian because only Italian rice has the right combination of starches to allow the grain to absorb the liquid.

The amount of stock given in each risotto recipe is as close as possible to what you will need. But you might find that you have finished the stock before the risotto is ready. Do not despair – just add boiling water.

SALT

An unfashionable ingredient, alas, in spite of being essential in the diet of all animals. Salt is unfashionable because it is said to be bad for those with high blood pressure and heart disease.

Salt enhances the flavour of food. The right amount of salt – a personal choice – should be added at the beginning or during the cooking, in time for it to dissolve properly and flavour all the dish. If added at the table, not only is the result unsatisfactory, but also more salt usually has to be added to achieve the right seasoning. Always add salt to the water before you add pasta, rice or vegetables.

Good sea salt, such as Maldon, is best for cooking and for your health.

STOCK

Add the outside leaf of an onion to impart a lovely golden colour to your chicken stock.

STOCK OR BOUILLON CUBES

Italian cooks use stock cubes in quite a few dishes. This is not an aberration. Stock cubes in Italy are less strong than those sold in this country. However, some stock cubes are now available here that contain a minimum of monosodium glutamate or none at all, and they are really quite good. Remember that stock cubes are salty, so add less salt.

Having said that, I must stress that a good, traditional, well-flavoured home-made stock is invaluable, unsurpassable and totally necessary for clear soups and delicate risotti.

TOMATOES

Keep tomatoes out of the fridge, preferably on a sunny windowsill. They will become tastier and their all-too-often leathery skins will soften.

VEGETABLES

This is one of my hobby horses. When I came to England in the '50s the vegetables were cooked, and that meant boiled, to a mush. Then came the nouvelle cuisine revolution, and now the vegetables served in many restaurants are simply raw. For us Italians, crunchy French beans or al dente asparagus are anathema, and even worse are crunchy turnips, lentils or artichokes.

It is not possible to give a precise cooking time for vegetables, since it depends on their quality and freshness. It also depends on whether the vegetable has been grown in proper earth or in a hydroponic culture, in which case it will cook very quickly indeed. Also remember that the cooking time for stewing vegetables, in very little liquid, is longer than for boiling in plenty of water or for frying. Carrots, for instance, will be cooked in 20 minutes maximum in boiling water, but will take longer, even cut into sticks, if you cook them in oil and/or butter with a little stock or water added gradually.

VINEGAR

I am always surprised that so much has been written about the finer points of olive oils, and so little has been written about the importance of good wine vinegar. A salad dressed even with the best extra virgin olive oil can be ruined by a second-rate vinegar.

You will know a vinegar is good by its price – good vinegar is not cheap, because a good vinegar comes from a decent wine. The process of making the vinegar must not be accelerated by the addition of chemicals.

Wine vinegar is the only one traditionally used in Italy. Red and white wine vinegar differ mainly in colour, the flavour being similar.

WATER

Water plays an important part in Italian cooking. It is the added ingredient that allows a piece of meat or a dish of vegetables to cook for the right amount of time without burning, drying up or becoming too concentrated.

Water must be added very gradually so that it can be absorbed slowly, allowing the food to cook. Do not drown any ingredient in water, but use it to develop the flavour and to achieve the right point of 'doneness'.

WINE

I only suggest the use of a particular wine when that wine is crucial to the final taste of the dish. Otherwise I leave the choice to you. When you use red wine, use one with body but not too much tannin, as this would come out in the taste of the dish.

Use good wine. Any wine that is not good enough for drinking is not good enough for cooking. When you use poor wine you ruin the dish, something that is worse than when you are just drinking it.

Batteria di Cucina

I am always fascinated by what a cook – and by this I mean a person who likes cooking, not a professional – uses in his or her kitchen. Some people can produce a perfect dinner with only a few utensils and a minimum of space. These I admire. I need space, although I use few utensils, and even fewer gadgets, but I also need the right saucepan. Here are my suggestions for a *batteria di cucina* suitable for Italian cooking, to be added to a normal kitchen batterie.

The right saucepan is fundamental to the success of many dishes. First you will need one large saucepan with lid, for pasta, of at least 41/6pt [USA 4 qt] capacity, plus a large colander with feet. The saucepan does not need to be heavy. But you need a large heavy-based saucepan, or a flameproof casserole, for risotto, which can double up for making polenta. Two sauté pans with lids, a large and a medium, will come in handy for many dishes from meat to apples, as will an oval casserole for braising meat, and a heavy ridged cast-iron pan for grilling vegetables.

I also recommend two earthenware pots of the kind you can put directly on the heat – a large deep one for soups and pulses and a shallow one for stews and fish.

Now the gadgets. I could not cook without my *mezzaluna* (half-moon knife) for chopping, but maybe you can chop well and fast with a heavy, well-sharpened knife. Nor could I cook without my food mill, which I find essential for puréeing vegetables, sauces etc. I also use my food processor a lot, but not for puréeing. A flame diffuser and an electric carving knife are also invaluable.

That's all.

THE RECIPES

After an introduction to each region, the recipes are arranged in the order in which a meal is served in Italy: antipasti, primi (1st course), secondi (2nd course) and desserts, cakes and biscuits or cookies. But of course you can serve a traditional primo such as a risotto as a secondo, an antipasto as a primo or a secondo . . . and so on.

The recipes are usually for four persons. However, some recipes are for more because the dish can only be made successfully in larger quantities, for example a piece of braised meat, a cappon magro (page 138) or a cake. Do not try to reduce these. Prepare the lot and eat it in two or more sittings.

On the other hand you can always increase the quantities, and here is a rule to follow. You do not need to increase the quantity of the cooking fat in the same proportion as the other ingredients. Some of the fat, say 1 tablespoon of the oil or of the butter, is there 'for the pan'. This rule does not apply, of course, when for capacity reasons you have to use two saucepans.

MEASURES AND QUANTITIES

When you follow a recipe, use just one system of measures – metric, imperial or American cups – all through the recipe.

All spoons are meant to be level, and 1 tablespoon=15ml, 1 teaspoon=5ml. A set of measuring spoons is a great help to a cook. A set includes 5 spoons which measure from 'a pinch' to 1 tablespoon.

I have given specific egg sizes in some recipes. Where no size is specified you can use size 2 or 3 (US extra large or large), whichever is in your refrigerator.

It is important to pay attention to the proportions of the various ingredients used. This will teach you to achieve the 'Italian flavour', and having learnt that, you will no longer need to follow a recipe slavishly. However, I would also stress that good cooking requires precision, care and patience. Creativity comes later, just as in any other art or craft.

LOMBARDIA

G astronomically speaking, I am convinced that Lombardy is the most interesting region of Italy. You might well think, 'She would say that, being Milanese,' but I have tried to dispel any feelings of chauvinism before coming to this conclusion. And, after all, 'interesting' does not necessarily mean 'best'.

There are nine provinces in Lombardy, and there are nine different cuisines. In the two years prior to finishing this book I have been all over Lombardy, visiting various towns, many food producers and, of course, eating my way from Valtellina in the North to the river Po in the South, and from the eastern bank of the Ticino river in the West to the western bank of Lake Garda in the East. The rustic *polenta taragna* from the mountains behind Bergamo in the North is miles away from the aristocratic elegance of the ravioli di zucca of Mantua, ravioli stuffed with pumpkin, amaretti and mostarda di Cremona and heightened by a splash of Grappa. The *bresaola* cured in the caves of Valtellina, with its clean taste of beef, redolent of the German heritage, is another example of the characteristics of that northern area, as is the smoked salame made from venison and beef.

Valtellina is the longest Alpine valley, stretching eastwards from the northern shores of Lake Como to the Stelvio peak, 3500 metres high. This spectacular valley was loved by Leonardo da Vinci, who even mentioned the good *osterie* (inns) you can find along the route. As in other northern valleys the food is that of mountain people. The home-made pasta, pizzoccheri (see page 25), is made with buckwheat flour, a grain that grows strongly up to 800 metres. The pasta is layered with potatoes and cabbage, locally grown, and dressed with *bitto*, a local cheese, and the magnificent local butter.

Another local cheese used a lot in cooking is *casera*, a semi-hard cheese with that unmistakable flavour of the cow-shed. With it the locals prepare *sciatt*, a sort of fritter made with buckwheat and white flour to which shredded casera and Grappa are added. The best sciatt I ate were made at the delightful Hotel della Posta in Sondrio, the capital of Valtellina, where with Philippa Davenport I spent a gastronomic week as guests of the local Chamber of Commerce. The most enjoyable thing, after the sciatt, was the time spent with the owner of the hotel, Renato Sozzani, talking food and eating the splendid meals he provided. He is the author of a book on the food of the valley, a real connoisseur, the sort who muses with nostalgia over past meals such as the pizzoccheri eaten on, say the 6th November 1975, which were better than the ones he had on the 14th January 1984. The Italian author Prezzolini compares the gastronomic memories of the Italians to the theatrical memories of the British, who can compare the production of a 1959 *Hamlet* with that of 20 years later.

The dairy products of Valtellina are especially good because of the pasture on which the cows graze, and also because of the particular breed of cows. They are the least cow-like cows I know; they are small, strong, nervous and quick as they move uphill from the valleys, where they spend the winter, to the Alpeggi, the meadows high in the mountains where they stay from June to September.

In fact, all Lombardy is renowned for its dairy products. The list of local cheeses is long and varied, from a soft sweet *stracchino* (one of my favourite cheeses, especially when eaten with mostarda di Cremona) to the piquant gorgonzola di montagna, the old-fashioned gorgonzola beloved of cheese connoisseurs. The creamy mascarpone from south Lombardy has conquered the world under the ubiquitous guise of tiramisù. But the real mascarpone, and not the UHT long-life product that travels the world, bought in situ and available only during the winter, must be enjoyed neat, just as it is, in all its virgin purity. That was how I enjoyed the mascarpone and the ricotta piemontese that a woman brought to our flat in Milan every Tuesday during the autumn. She was dressed all in black, which contrasted sharply with the whiteness of her wares, wrapped in immaculate muslin on a large flat wicker basket. The mascarpone and ricotta we bought were weighed on her steelyard, placed on a plate and carried to the kitchen to be served and finished that same day.

The flavour of these cheeses lingers in my memory, as does that of the herbs and wild greens brought to the house during the spring by Lina. Lina came from nearby Segrate, now a spaghetti junction of motorways next to the asphalt jungle of Linate airport. Lina's baskets were overflowing with borage, sage, dandelions, nettles, sorrel, and masses and masses of parsley.

As the best basil comes from Liguria, so the best parsley comes from Lombardy. I can still remember the taste of the salsa verde made every Monday to go with the *lesso* (boiled beef). I hardly touched the beef, but gorged myself first on the deliciously tangy salsa verde and then went on to savour the sweet piquancy of the mostarda di Cremona, the other accompaniment to the lesso.

Up to last year I was sure that the best local dishes were all to be enjoyed in winter, probably because I have spent more time in Lombardy during the winter months. But then, in 1993, I was in Pavia, Mantua and the vicinity in

August and September, and I discovered a world I had forgotten. The beautiful large yellow sweet peppers of Voghera are served grilled in an antipasto or used to make one of the freshest and most colourful risotti. The river shrimps are also used in a risotto, or just boiled and eaten like that, with lemon juice. And the frogs, fried whole (headless of course), make the most succulent and crunchy antipasto I know. Alas, they are rapidly disappearing, along with the river shrimps, which survive only in some private estates.

I watched frog fishing one hot August afternoon, alongside the canals of the rice paddies in that flat country, geometrically divided by lines of Lombard plane trees that remind one of a Mondrian painting. It is a still, hazy countryside, silent apart from the continuous screeching of the cicadas and the buzzing of insects. Men with very long rods stood silently on the banks of these tiny canals, looking at me disapprovingly in fear that my presence would frighten away their prey. But the catch was small, hardly enough even for a risotto, one of the men told me disconsolately.

The fishermen fishing in the lakes usually have better luck. I was told that the lakes are less polluted now than they were a few years ago. At the trattorie beside the lakes perch and tench have come back, to be served in many ways, the traditional being *a cotoletta* – breaded and fried in butter. Butter, which Julius Caesar is said to have eaten for the first time in the Po valley on his return from the Gallic wars, is still the right cooking fat for traditional dishes. I felt very humbled when in Casteggio, near Voghera, at the Trattoria Da Lina I asked if their delicious risotto coi peperoni was made with olive oil. Lina, the attractive owner-chef, looked at me in bewilderment. 'Oil? Certainly not. This is an old local recipe.' I didn't dare to tell her that I, a Lombard, make an excellent risotto coi peperoni with oil.

Olive oil, up to the Second World War, was only used by well-to-do families to dress salad, instead of the more plebeian rape-seed oil or walnut oil, which was otherwise used to polish furniture. After this, the walnut trees of Lombardy were all felled to make enough furniture to replace that destroyed during the war. Because of this the Lombards began to use olive oil more extensively.

Another strong influence was given after the war by the Tuscan restaurateurs, who opened their trattorie, with the flask of Chianti on the table, just as they did in the '50s in London. Then, in the '60s, the southern labourers came north with their Mediterranean diet, and the Lombards began to eat and enjoy the food of southern Italy – healthier, yes, but less varied. Some took up aubergines [US eggplant] and rocket [US arugula] and forgot the sweet onions of Brianza, the deep-flavoured Savoy cabbages, the rich pumpkins of

Mantua and even the earthy-tasting potatoes that Alessandro Volta – he of voltage fame – had brought from France and grown first on his land in Brianza.

But these good things are not totally forgotten. Italians are too chauvinistic where food is concerned. Lombards still believe that the best salame is the salame of Varzi in southern Lombardy, and that the best luganega is made in and around Monza. Not long ago I visited an artisanal factory making pork sausages where the luganega was still flavoured with wine and Parmesan, as in the old days.

In Milan you can enjoy some of the best Lombard cooking. After years when the local cooking seemed to be swamped by the invasion of chefs from Tuscany, Naples, Bologna and Puglia, I find that now Milanese and Lombard cooking, with its rich *cassoeula* (page 40), its *polpette* (page 42) and its risotti, is triumphantly back on the menu.

My good friend and mentor, the octogenarian food historian Massimo Alberini, feels very encouraged by the turn taken by the cooking in restaurants. He is quite sure that there is a strong renaissance of traditional regional cooking which is going to stay. The lovely thing about Alberini is that in spite of his long memory of the food of the past, he has good words to say about the present state of affairs. He pointed out to me the wealth of exotic ingredients available now and on display in the Milanese food shops. Japanese-inspired dishes sit next to *calzoni* from Puglia, *gravad lax* from Sweden or *caponata* from Sicily.

Yet the bulk of the most popular dishes are from old Lombardy, very similar to the dishes that were sold in Zanocco, our local delicatessen, now defunct, whose prosciutto was reputed to be even better than that of Peck. I remember the ritual of the daily shopping with my mother, who unlike most of her contemporaries used to go herself *a fare la spesa*. She used to say that, 'un buon pranzo comincia nel negozio' (a good dinner begins in the shop), and off we went to be fêted by the local shops. To me it was just like stepping on to a stage. First, Signora Bianchi in Via Montenapoleone (just opposite where we lived in Via Gesù) who presided, with her crinkly hair à la Queen Mother, over her bread, sweet breads, biscotti, focaccie and tortelli. Then Zanocco, where chubby Arturo always gave me a slice of prosciutto, and then to Pasini the grocer, my favourite stop. In those days, when food was not prepacked, a grocer's shop was the most intense experience for the sense of smell. The greengrocer in Via Borgospesso, on the other hand, was a delight to the eyes with its assortment of fruit and vegetables which quickly told you which month it was. And just further on at the corner of Via Spiga there was the man selling *calde arrosto* (roast chestnuts). I am sure I learnt how to shop from those early days. As the late Jane Grigson so aptly puts it in her *Fish Cookery*, 'Children are coloured indelibly by their mother's expertise – or lack of it. Conversations with butcher, baker, nurseryman, are picked up by a pair of ears at counter level and stored in the infant lumber room.'

Somehow my fondest memories of Milan are all autumnal, unlike those of Stendhal, who has described Lombardy mostly in the summer. Let me borrow some lines from Stendhal, who loved Lombardy, its food and its women, lines that are very evocative of the varied appeal of this region. 'We are at the top of the hill; to the right a splendid view: fertile planes and two or three lakes; to the left another splendid view, which in detail is the opposite of the other. . . This beautiful Lombardy, with all the luxurious appeal of its greenery, its riches and its endless horizons.'

PIZZOCCHERI Ⓥ
Buckwheat Pasta with Potato and Cabbage

Until 10 years ago pizzoccheri were only eaten in Valtellina, an Alpine valley running east from Lake Como. Although they were mainly eaten by the locals, pizzoccheri were also consumed by the hordes of skiers who, every weekend, go up the slopes and down again, thus burning up the energy derived from the huge quantities of pizzoccheri ingested at every meal. But now pizzoccheri appear at smart hostesses' dinners, on the menu in restaurants in Milan and further afield, and are even produced industrially.

Pizzoccheri are made from the only cereal, buckwheat, which can grow in mountainous regions. The acrid-smokey flavour of buckwheat, which used to be despised by our grandparents because of its association with poverty, has now become an emblem of the good earthy food appreciated by gourmets.

Centuries ago buckwheat was grown in all the Alpine regions and both pasta and polenta were made with it. Then maize arrived from the New World and supplanted the old staple. Soon polenta was being made with maize, and pasta, imported from further south, was made with white flour. Nowadays buckwheat is only grown in Valtellina and Carnia, in the eastern Alps.

Recently I saw pizzoccheri being made in the ideal setting and by the ideal maker. Laura, the pizzoccheri-maker in question, is a dark local Ceres, living in a house surrounded by fields where cats, dogs and horses roam happily around. On the way there we drove through some fields of buckwheat. It is an unimpressive plant, with heart-shaped leaves and a tall reddish stem carrying the dark seeds. Laura had just had a baby, so she seemed to knead and roll the dough with an even more gentle and loving movement.

In the local tradition the dinner consisted of a large platter of different local salami, and then an ever larger platter of pizzoccheri, followed by a crostata – a jam tart, the most usual country sweet. Perfect. We could gorge ourselves on pizzoccheri, which oddly enough are not over-filling; nourishing, yes, but you certainly do not feel blown up after two serious helpings. I had many excellent plates of pizzoccheri after that, but none so perfect as those made by Laura. And I was set to wondering how much the atmosphere can influence the palate.

THE RECIPE

The cheese traditionally used in this dish is *bitto*, a local cows' milk cheese which has a complex herby flavour and which melts very well. After a certain amount of trial and error I have decided that a good substitute is fontina. Fontina can be bought in specialist Italian shops or top supermarkets. If you cannot get it, buy a French St Paulin which has good melting properties and a not too dissimilar flavour.

Buckwheat flour is sold in most health-food shops, though I have noticed that it varies considerably from one brand to another. Some buckwheat flours are easier to knead than others, so you might have to vary the amount of white wheat flour. The pasta here is made with a dough enriched with egg and milk, whereas originally the flours were only blended with water.

Pizzoccheri are made with Savoy cabbage, Swiss chard or green beans, whichever are in season at the time. I have also successfully used Brussels sprout tops and spring greens, whose bitterness is a good match for the smokey earthiness of the pasta. You can also use a mixture of these vegetables.

SERVES 6

FOR THE PASTA

200g/7oz [US 2 cups] buckwheat flour
100g/3½oz [US scant 1 cup] flour, preferably
Italian 00, approximate weight
1 tsp salt
1 size-2 egg [US extra-large egg]
120ml/4fl oz warm milk, approximately

FOR THE DRESSING

225g/8oz potato, cut into cubes
salt and freshly ground black pepper
300g/10oz Savoy cabbage, cut into 1cm/½in strips
75g/2½oz [US 5 tbsp] unsalted butter
1 small onion, very finely chopped
1 garlic clove, very finely chopped
6 fresh sage leaves, torn into pieces
150g/5oz fontina, cut into slivers
75g/2½oz [US ½ cup + 2 tbsp] freshly grated
Parmesan

First make the dough. Mix together the two
flours and the salt on the work surface. Make a
well in the middle and break the egg into it.
Using a fork, begin to bring in the flour from the
wall, while slowly adding the milk. Do not add all
the milk at once, since you may not need all of it.
Or, depending on the absorbency of the flour and
the humidity of the atmosphere, you may need to
add a little warm water as well, or a couple of
tablespoons of white flour. The dough should be
soft and elastic, although it is much stickier and
wetter than a dough made with only white flour
and eggs. Knead for 5 minutes and then wrap the
dough in a linen towel or cling film and let it rest
for a minimum of 1 hour. I have sometimes made
my dough the day before and kept it overnight in
the fridge.

When the time comes to cook the dish, roll
out the dough, either by hand to a thickness of
about 2mm/¹⁄₁₂in, or using a hand-cranked pasta
machine, pushing the strips through the rollers up
to the last but two notches. You have to flour the
strips quite often when rolling them out. Cut the
rolled-out pasta into pappardelle-size noodles,
about 2 × 10cm/¾ × 4in. Lay the strips out on
clean cloths, not letting them touch each other.
(You can prepare all this a day in advance. The
next day the pizzoccheri will be dried, but just as
good.)

Put a large saucepan containing about 4l/7pt
[US 4qt] of water on the heat. Add 1½ tablespoons of salt and the potato and bring to the
boil. After 10 minutes or so, when the potato
cubes begin to soften at the edges, throw in the
cabbage and continue cooking for about 5
minutes, until the cabbage has lost its crunchiness. Now it is time to slide in the pizzoccheri.
Mix well and cook for 5 minutes after the water
has come back to the boil.

While all this preparation is going on, put the
butter, onion, garlic and sage in a small heavy-
based pan and cook gently, stirring very often and
letting the onion became pale gold. Fish out the
sage.

Heat the oven to 180°C/350°F/Gas Mark 4.

Butter a shallow oven dish. When the pizzoccheri are done, drain the whole mixture in a
colander. Spoon a ladleful or two of the pasta
mixture over the bottom of the dish and add a
little of the two cheeses, a little of the onion-
butter sauce and plenty of pepper. Add more
pasta and dress it again in the same way until the
whole lot is dressed. Toss thoroughly. Cover with
foil and put in the oven for 5 minutes, so that the
cheese will melt properly.

Serve with plenty of red wine from the
Valtellina, such as a Sassella or a marvellous
Inferno, if you can find them!

RISOTTO ALLA MILANESE
Risotto with Saffron

In my previous books I have written at length about this favourite dish of mine, one of the pillars of Milanese cooking. So here I'll skip the preamble and go straight to the recipe.

Like all over-popular dishes, risotto alla milanese (known in its native city as risotto giallo, or yellow risotto) has been the subject of endless variations. This is my recipe, which has been in use in my family for generations, or at least for as long as my father (who would now be 104) could remember. He insisted that risotto giallo was made like this. The only liberty I am taking is to suggest the use of pancetta instead of bone-marrow, which is difficult to come by these days. It is not the same, but a nice fatty unsmoked pancetta is quite a good substitute. Prosciutto can also be used, but it must be fatty and not the fatless, and far less tasty, prosciutto one usually gets in this country. (See my tips on prosciutto on page 15.)

If you can, use Carnaroli rice. Otherwise use a good quality Arborio. The better the rice, the longer it takes to cook. In Italy we cook Carnaroli for 18 minutes from the time you begin to add the stock. Arborio will take 1 or 2 minutes less.

SERVES 4

1.2l/2pt [US 5 cups] home-made meat stock (page 230)

1 shallot or ½ small onion, very finely chopped

60g/2oz beef-marrow, unsmoked pancetta or fatty prosciutto, very finely chopped

75g/2½oz [US 5 tbsp] butter

350g/12oz [US 1¾ cups] Italian rice, preferably Carnaroli

120ml/4fl oz red wine

⅓ tsp powdered saffron of 1 tsp saffron strands

salt and freshly ground pepper

60g/2oz [US ½ cup] freshly grated Parmesan

Bring the stock to simmering point and keep it at a very low simmer.

Put the shallot, beef-marrow (or the substitutes) and 60g/2oz [US 4 tbsp] of the butter in a saucepan and sauté until the shallot is soft and translucent. Add the rice and stir until well coated with fat. Pour in the wine, boil for 2 minutes, stirring constantly, and then pour in 200ml/7fl oz of the simmering stock. Cook until nearly all the stock has been absorbed and then add another 150ml/5fl oz of stock. The risotto should cook at a steady lively simmer. Continue adding the stock in small quantities like this, waiting for one to be nearly all absorbed before adding the next.

About half-way through the cooking add the saffron dissolved in a little hot stock. When the rice is ready – it should be soft and creamy, not mushy or runny – taste and adjust the seasoning.

Draw off the heat and add the rest of the butter and 3 tablespoons of the Parmesan. Leave to rest for a minute or two and then give the risotto a good stir. This is what we call the *mantecatura*, the final touch, to make the risotto even creamier. Serve immediately, with the rest of the cheese handed separately.

RISOTTO AL GORGONZOLA Ⓥ
Risotto with Gorgonzola

This old recipe from Lombardy is for the quintessential creamy risotto, yet the flavour is unexpectedly piquant. The cheese used must be real gorgonzola and not Dolcelatte, a new type of cheese created by Galbani for the British market, which does not have enough oomph. Parmesan is never served with this risotto.

SERVES 4 AS A FIRST COURSE OR 3 AS A MAIN COURSE

4 shallots, very finely chopped
60g/2oz [US 4 tbsp] unsalted butter
salt and freshly ground black pepper
1.2l/2pt [US 5 cups] vegetable or light meat stock (pages 230–1)
300g/10oz [US 1½ cups] Italian rice, preferably Carnaroli
150ml/5fl oz dry white wine
250g/9oz gorgonzola piccante or di montagna, cut into small pieces
a lovely bunch of fresh flat-leaf parsley, chopped

Put the shallots and the butter in a large, heavy-based saucepan. Add a pinch of salt to release the moisture in the shallots, thus preventing them from browning, and sauté gently for about 7 minutes or until soft and translucent, stirring frequently.

Meanwhile, heat the stock in a separate saucepan to simmering point. Keep it simmering all through the cooking of the rice.

Add the rice to the shallots and stir well, coating the grains in the butter. Sauté until the rice is partly translucent. Turn the heat up and pour over the wine. Let it bubble away, stirring constantly, and then begin to add the simmering stock little by little, in the usual way for a risotto.

After 15 minutes, mix in the Gorgonzola. Stir constantly until the cheese has melted and then continue cooking the rice, adding the rest of the simmering stock little by little. If you have used up all the stock use a little boiling water to finish the cooking.

When the rice is al dente, season with plenty of pepper. Taste and if necessary season also with salt, although the saltiness in the cheese and stock may be enough.

Transfer to a heated bowl and sprinkle with the parsley. Serve immediately.

TORTELLI DI CREMA Ⓥ
Ravioli from Crema

Crema, a small town in south-east Lombardy, boasts two things, and rightly so: a splendid square with the Duomo and a Renaissance arcade, and these tortelli. For years I had wanted to go to Crema, more for the tortelli, which are made nowhere else, than for the square, the likes of which are two a penny in provincial Italian towns. The best tortelli, I was told, were made by Maria Pia Triassi at her restaurant, the Cral Ferriera, in the outskirts of the town. And so that is precisely where I went, and I was certainly not disappointed.

The tortelli di Crema are typical of the best in the cooking of southern Lombardy, where the flavours of the Renaissance are still strongly discernible. People there seem to keep the gastronomic glories of the past in their repertoire more than anywhere else. The subtle taste resulting from the combination of sweet and savoury is very well defined in this dish.

Maria Pia uses a special kind of amaretti that contain a small amount of chocolate. Being a perfectionist she warned me against using other kinds of amaretti, but I liked the tortelli di Crema so much that I was prepared to experiment with other amaretti. And this is my adaptation of her recipe.

THE RECIPE

This is not a dish you can prepare in half an hour, nor is it a dish you can serve to anyone. It has an unusual flavour that some people might not appreciate.

I make small ravioli, which is the traditional way to make them. Nowadays most restaurants, especially in Britain, serve very large ravioli, 2 or 3 per person. This is to save labour, but the taste of the ravioli changes, often for the worse, due to the difference in proportion between stuffing and pasta.

The pasta for the tortelli di Crema is a 'poor man's' pasta, i.e. made with eggs and water. Because it is very soft it goes better with the stuffing. But if you are more familiar with the more common *pasta emiliana* containing only eggs, make this by all means. Use amaretti di Saronno; they have the right amount of bitter almonds for this dish.

MAKES ABOUT 60 RAVIOLI, ENOUGH FOR 5 TO 6 PEOPLE

FOR THE PASTA

400g/14oz [US 3½ cups] Italian 00 flour
1 tsp salt
2 size-2 eggs [US extra-large eggs]
1 tbsp oil

FOR THE STUFFING

1 tbsp sultanas [US golden raisins]
1 tbsp chopped candied citron
2 tbsp dry Marsala or dry sherry
100g/3½oz amaretti di Saronno
1 tsp grated dark chocolate
75g/2½oz [US ½ cup + 2 tbsp] freshly grated Parmesan
1 size-2 egg [US extra-large egg]
3 tbsp fine white breadcrumbs
4 tbsp mascarpone
salt and freshly ground black pepper

FOR THE DRESSING

75g/2½oz [US 5 tbsp] unsalted butter
1 fresh sage sprig
60g/2oz [US ½ cup] freshly grated Parmesan

First prepare the stuffing. Soak the sultanas and the citron in the Marsala for 20 minutes or so.

Put the amaretti in the food processor and process to fine crumbs. Turn into a bowl and add all the other ingredients. Mix very thoroughly – a job best done with your hands. Add also the sultanas, citron peel and Marsala. Season with salt and pepper to taste. Cover the bowl with cling film and put in the fridge to chill. (It is much easier to work on chilled stuffing.)

While the stuffing is chilling make the pasta. Put the flour and the salt on the work surface. Make a well and break the eggs into it. Add about 7 to 8 tablespoons of lukewarm water. Beat with a fork, gradually drawing the flour in from the walls of the well. When most of the flour is incorporated, begin to knead with your hands. (You can do all the foregoing in a food processor.) When you have properly kneaded the dough, wrap it in cling film and leave aside to rest for at least half an hour.

After a rest for the dough (and for you, perhaps) give the dough a good kneading, and cut off about one eighth to begin work on. Keep the rest of the dough well wrapped in cling film. Roll out a sheet of dough up to the last but one notch of the hand-cranked pasta machine, or, if you are making the pasta by hand, to a thickness of about ½mm/⅕₀in.

Trim the dough to a strip 10cm/4in wide. Dot with generous teaspoons of stuffing, at intervals of 5cm/2in, all down the strip, setting the stuffing 2.5cm/1in back from one of the long edges in a line parallel to the edge. Fold the other long edge over the stuffing to join the first edge. Trim the joined edges with a fluted pastry wheel and then, with the same wheel, cut across between each mound of stuffing. Separate the squares, squeeze out any air and seal the ravioli all around. If necessary, moisten your fingers to seal the edges better. Spread the ravioli out on clean dry linen towels, making sure they do not touch, to prevent them sticking. Making ravioli sounds very difficult when you read the instructions, but it is quite easy once you are actually making them.

Proceed to work on the next eighth of the dough, and then the next, until you have no stuffing, or pasta, left. If you are not cooking the ravioli straight away, leave them to dry, turning them over two or three times so that they dry evenly.

Put a large, wide saucepan full of water on the heat. Bring to the boil and then add 1 tablespoon of oil and 1½ tablespoons of salt. Gently drop in the ravioli. Stir gently and bring the water back to the boil. Lower the heat so that the water does not boil too fiercely – otherwise the ravioli might break – and cook until al dente, about 2 to 5 minutes depending on the thickness of the dough and the dryness of the ravioli. The best way to tell if they are done is to cut a bit off the edge and taste it.

While the ravioli are cooking, melt the butter for the dressing with the sage in a small saucepan.

Lift the ravioli out of the water with a slotted spoon, pat dry gently with kitchen paper towel and transfer them to a heated shallow dish. Pour some melted butter and sprinkle some cheese on each ladleful of ravioli, so that they will all be well dressed. This is the only and the best dressing for these extraordinary tortelli.

Rotolo di Spinaci Ⓥ
Spinach Roll

There is a more usual rotolo di spinaci made in Emilia-Romagna with pasta dough. My mother used to make her rotolo with potato dough, which I think is much nicer, and here is her recipe.

You can also dress the rotolo with a good tomato sauce (see page 228), or with the fontina sauce on page 65, all perfect in their different ways.

SERVES 8

800g/1¾lb floury potatoes, such as King Edwards, as nearly the same size as possible
40g/1½oz shallots, finely chopped
150g/5oz [US 10 tbsp] unsalted butter
1.2kg/2½lb spinach, cooked, very thoroughly drained and chopped
180g/6oz [US ¾ cup] ricotta cheese
125g/4oz [US 1 cup] freshly grated Parmesan
a large pinch of grated nutmeg
1 size-2 egg plus 2 egg yolks [US extra-large eggs]
salt and freshly ground black pepper
1½ tsp baking powder
200g/7oz [US 1¾ cups] Italian 00 flour
1 tbsp coarsely chopped fresh sage leaves
2 garlic cloves, bruised

Scrub the potatoes and boil them in their skins in plenty of lightly salted water until tender, about 25 minutes.

While the potatoes are cooking, prepare the filling. Sauté the shallots in a third of the butter for 4 to 5 minutes, until soft. Add the spinach and cook for a further 2 minutes, stirring constantly. Transfer the spinach mixture to a bowl and add the ricotta, half the Parmesan, the nutmeg, one egg yolk, and some salt and pepper. Mix very thoroughly.

When the potatoes are cooked, drain them thoroughly. As soon as they are cool enough to handle, peel them and push through the small disc of a food mill, or a potato ricer, straight on to a work surface. (Do not use a blender or a food processor because these will not incorporate air into the purée, to make it light.) Make a well in the centre of the potato purée, drop in the whole egg and the second egg yolk and add a little salt, the baking powder and most of the flour. Knead for about 5 minutes, adding more flour if necessary: the dough should be soft, smooth and slightly sticky. Shape the dough into a ball.

Flour your work surface and roll out the potato dough into a rectangle about 35 × 30cm/14 × 12in. Spread the spinach filling over it evenly, leaving a 2cm/¾in border all around. Roll up the potato dough into a Swiss roll [US jelly roll] shape. Wrap the roll tightly in muslin or cheesecloth and tie at each end.

Fill a fish kettle or oval-shaped flameproof casserole three-quarters full of water and bring to the boil. Add salt, and gently lower the roll into the water. Return the water to the boil and simmer, partly covered, for 30 to 40 minutes. See that the water keeps a constant simmer. Remove the roll from the water, unwrap and leave to cool.

Heat the oven to 200°C/400°F/Gas Mark 6.

Cut the roll into 2cm/¾in slices and place them, slightly overlapping, in an ovenproof dish. Melt the remaining butter and add the chopped sage leaves and the garlic. When the butter begins to turn golden, draw the pan off the heat. Fish out and discard the garlic. Pour the butter mixture over the slices. Bake in the oven for 15 minutes. About 5 minutes before the reheating is finished, sprinkle with half of the remaining Parmesan.

Let the dish rest for a couple of minutes before serving, with the remainder of the cheese.

Polenta Taragna Ⓥ
Buckwheat Polenta with Butter and Cheese

This is a speciality of the Valtellina and the other Alpine valleys that run between Bergamo in Lombardy and Merano in Alto Adige. A certain amount of buckwheat flour is substituted for maize (polenta) flour, thus producing a sweeter, nuttier polenta. Laced with cheese and butter, it makes a magnificent dish that is served by itself as a first course. The cheese used should ideally be a local soft cheese called scimud. I have also used Caerphilly, Wensleydale and Lancashire, all of which have a similar texture and just a little of that tangy flavour needed in a good polenta taragna.

I use two-thirds maize (polenta) flour to one-third buckwheat, but you could make it half and half for an earthier, nuttier flavour. As with the usual polenta, you must use a deep but wide saucepan.

SERVES 4 TO 5

250g/9oz maize (polenta) flour [US 2 cups coarse cornmeal]

125g/4oz [US 1¼ cups] buckwheat flour

2 tsp salt

100g/3½oz [US 7 tbsp] unsalted butter, cut into pieces

100g/3½oz cheese (see introduction), cut into slices

Heat the oven to 180°C/350°F/Gas Mark 4.

Heat 2l/3½pt [US 2qt] of water to just boiling point. (I find that the flours are less likely to form lumps if you add them when the water is not yet boiling.)

Meanwhile, mix the two flours and the salt together. When the water is nearly simmering – it will begin to form bubbles at the edge – draw the pan off the heat and add the flour, letting it fall between your closed fingers, fistful by fistful, while you beat the mixture in the pan hard with the other hand. When all the flour has been added, put the pan back on the heat and cook, beating constantly, until the mixture is bubbling hard like an erupting vulcano. Buckwheat polenta needs longer cooking than plain polenta, so I advise you to use the method for 'polenta made in the oven' described on page 234.

Butter an oven dish very well and pour the polenta mixture into it. Place a piece of buttered foil on the top and bake for at least 1½ hours.

When done, beat in the butter pieces and then the cheese. Continue to stir hard until the cheese and the butter have melted. Serve immediately in a heated large bowl.

Razza in Salsa d'Acciuga
Skate with Anchovy Sauce

All I know of the origins of this recipe is that it comes from my family, and my family comes – almost entirely – from northern Italy. Skate is mainly eaten in the north of Italy, and in fact the way this dish is cooked points to a French influence. Thus, the fish is poached in a French court-bouillon, and the sauce, which contains no tomatoes, is thickened with flour.

Skate is easy to find on the market and it is usually fresh and good. I was very pleased to read in Alastair Little's excellent book *Keep It Simple* that he, like me, finds that the ammonia smell, sometimes detectable in a piece of skate, remains through the cooking and ruins the taste of the fish. This is contrary to what some experts say, which is that this unpleasant smell is a sign of the freshness of the fish and will disappear when the fish is cooked. My advice is to smell your skate before you buy it!

SERVES 4

900g/2lb skate, cut into 4 portions by the fishmonger
1.2l/2pt [US 5 cups] fish stock (page 231)

FOR THE SAUCE

30g/1oz [US 2 tbsp] unsalted butter
2 tbsp olive oil
1 garlic clove, bruised
1 layer of sweet onion
60g/2oz canned anchovy fillets, drained and chopped
2 tsp flour
3 tbsp capers
2 tbsp chopped fresh flat-leaf parsley
1 tbsp lemon juice
freshly ground black pepper

Poach the fish in the simmering fish stock for 8 to 10 minutes. When the fish is done, drain it and keep warm. Reserve the cooking liquid.

To make the sauce, choose a sauté pan large enough to hold the fish later in a single layer. Heat the butter and the oil and throw in the garlic and the onion layer. When you begin to smell the aroma of the garlic and onion, fish them out and discard them. Turn the heat down and add the anchovies. Press them against the bottom of the pan to reduce them to a mash.

Mix in the flour and then add 150ml/5fl oz of the fish cooking liquid. Cook over gentle heat for about 5 minutes, stirring constantly and adding, if necessary, a little more fish liquid until you get a fluid sauce, like single cream [US light cream].

Rinse the capers and add to the pan together with the parsley, lemon juice and plenty of pepper. Taste and correct seasoning. Carefully transfer the fish to the pan and heat it up in the sauce, while you spoon the sauce over it. Five minutes should be enough.

Now that the dish is ready you can divide it among the individual plates. As fish is not easy to transfer, it may be an idea to do this in the calm of the kitchen with the right tool, rather than at the table with everybody watching. But if it is family, and your pan is attractive, bring this to the table. It is always more convivial and homely to serve food from a single large container.

COSTE AL GRATIN Ⓥ
Gratin of Swiss Chard Stalks

Although a gratin of vegetables might be considered a French dish, it is also a very familiar feature of Lombard cooking. Very often, during my youth in Milan, our dinner consisted of a soup, a gratin dish and fruit to finish. The gratin could be of fennel, spinach or courgettes [US zucchini], or – the best to my mind – of Swiss chard, as in this recipe.

The amount of Swiss chard you have to buy depends on the size of the stalks. As a guide, you should buy twice the weight you need for the recipe. The delicious leaves can be used in the same way as spinach, as a vegetable or in a filling, or to make the dish on page 135.

SERVES 3 TO 4

enough Swiss chard to yield about 700g/1½lb of stalks

salt and freshly ground black pepper

a béchamel sauce (page 228), made with 60g/2oz [US 4 tbsp] unsalted butter, 40g/1½oz [US ¼ cup] flour and 450ml/15fl oz full fat milk

4 tbsp freshly grated Parmesan

grated nutmeg

butter for the dish

1 tbsp dried breadcrumbs

15g/½oz [US 1 tbsp] unsalted butter

Wash the Swiss chard stalks thoroughly and cut into 5cm/2in pieces.

Make the béchamel as usual, and keep it cooking gently over a flame diffuser or in a bain-marie for about 30 minutes, stirring occasionally. Then mix in the Parmesan, plenty of pepper, and salt and nutmeg to taste.

While the béchamel is gently cooking, cook the Swiss chard stalks in plenty of salted boiling water for about 10 minutes, until they are soft. Drain and dry with kitchen paper towel.

Heat the oven to 180°C/350°F/Gas Mark 4.

Butter a shallow oven dish. Spread 2 tablespoons of the béchamel over the bottom. Cover with the Swiss chards and spread with the remaining béchamel. Sprinkle with the breadcrumbs and dot with the butter. Bake until golden on top, about 15 minutes.

Take the dish from the oven and allow to rest for 5 minutes before serving it.

CIPOLLE RIPIENE
Stuffed Onions

I think that every cook in northern Italy has his or her favourite way of stuffing onions. This is how onions were usually stuffed in my home in Milan. The sweetness and crunchiness of the onion cups are a pleasantly contrasting foil to the rich stuffing.

SERVES 4

4 Spanish onions, about 225g/8oz each
salt and freshly ground black pepper
60g/2oz [US 4 tbsp] unsalted butter
180g/6oz minced veal [US ground veal]
30g/1oz mortadella, finely chopped
4 tbsp freshly grated Parmesan
1 egg
2 tbsp Marsala
2 tbsp dried white breadcrumbs
120ml/4fl oz meat stock (page 230)

Wash the onions and plunge them into a large saucepan of salted boiling water. Boil for about 20 minutes, until you can easily pierce the onion with the point of a knife. Drain and leave to cool a little.

Peel the onions; you usually have to remove two or three layers of skin as well. Cut each onion in half around its 'equator' and remove the centre. Make 12 cups with the larger onion halves and arrange them side by side in a buttered oven dish.

Now prepare the stuffing. Chop the inside of the onions to the size of grains of rice. I suggest you do this by hand and not in a food processor, which would reduce the onion to a pulp and extract all the juices.

Heat half the butter in a smallish frying pan. Add the veal and sauté until the meat has lost its raw colour. Add 8 tablespoons of the chopped onion and stir well (keep the rest for another dish). Now mix in the mortadella, season with salt and pepper to taste and fry the lovely mixture for 2 minutes or so. Transfer the mixture to a bowl and add all the other ingredients, except the stock and remaining butter. Mix thoroughly and then taste to check if you need to add a little more salt and pepper.

Heat the oven to 200°C/400°F/Gas Mark 6.

Fill the onion cups with the mixture and place a nugget of the remaining butter on top of each onion. Pour the stock over and around the onions. Bake for 15 minutes, then turn the heat down to 180°C/350°F/Gas Mark 4. Baste the onions with the juices, cover the dish with foil and bake for a further 30 minutes or so. Serve warm or at room temperature.

FARAONE AL MASCARPONE
Guinea Fowl with Mascarpone

It is notable that in Italy even a town has its own style of cooking, and is proud of it. This recipe comes from a book called *La Cucina Lodigiana* (The Cooking of Lodi). Lodi is a town in southern Lombardy, the area where rich pastures nourish fat cows.

Mascarpone is a local cream cheese, which is now also available abroad in its UHT form. Although UHT mascarpone is not as good as the fresh product eaten in Lombardy, it is good enough to use in this excellent recipe. The mascarpone keeps the bird moist during the cooking, oozing out of the cavity and mixing with the cooking juices.

SERVES 3 OR 4
1 guinea fowl
salt and freshly ground pepper
2 tbsp mascarpone
60g/2oz [US 4 tbsp] unsalted butter
1 small onion, cut into pieces
1 carrot, cut into pieces
2 celery stalks, cut into pieces
3 or 4 cloves
a pinch of ground cinnamon
120ml/4fl oz dry white wine
2 tbsp white rum

Heat the oven to 200°C/400°F/Gas Mark 6.

Singe the guinea fowl and remove as many of the stubborn quills as you can. (As they are now plucked by machine, pheasants and guinea fowl need a lot of attention before being cooked.) Wash and dry it thoroughly inside and out. Season with salt and pepper and spoon the mascarpone into the cavity.

Choose an oval flameproof casserole in which the bird will sit snugly. Put the butter, onion, carrot, celery, cloves and cinnamon into it and sprinkle with salt. Place the guinea fowl on the vegetables and pour over the wine and the rum.

Place the casserole on the heat and bring the liquid slowly to the boil. Cover the pan and place in the oven. Cook for about 1 to 1¼ hours, until the bird is tender.

Cut the bird into small pieces. Place them on a dish and keep them warm, well covered with foil.

Remove and discard the cloves, then process the cooking vegetables and all the juices to a purée. Taste and adjust seasoning. Spoon some of the sauce over the pieces of guinea fowl and hand around the rest in a sauce boat.

CAPPONE RIPIENO DI NOCI
Poached Chicken Stuffed with Walnuts, Ricotta and Parmesan

Capon is the original Christmas bird of northern Italy. A capon is a cock that has been castrated at around 2 months. The bird grows larger than a cock and has a white, delicately tasty meat. All through the history of cooking, capon has been a favourite on court tables, and many old recipes are dedicated to this bird. In Italy you can still find capons raised in farms, ready for Christmas, and they are a very different bird from the mass-produced battery chicken. In this country capons do not exist any longer; they are illegal because the cocks were being 'caponized' with hormones.

In Italy capons are sometimes cooked on the spit, flavoured with black truffles – a method no longer so popular since 120g/4oz of truffles are needed for one bird – and sometimes boiled, particularly in Lombardy. Roasted capon is traditional in Tuscany, Umbria and Marche. In grand Christmas dinners or country feasts, boiled capons precede the roast, which nowadays is often turkey. The advantage over turkey is that capon makes the best meat stock, which is used to prepare the risotto giallo (saffron risotto), the traditional Christmas first course in Lombard homes.

The recipe I give here calls for the bird to be stuffed. The stuffing is quite delicious and unexpected with its nutty flavour and texture relieved by the delicate milky ricotta, while the Parmesan brings that wonderful flavour that no other cheese can give. The use of walnuts in the stuffing is definitely a Lombard tradition.

Up to the Second World War there were many walnut trees in Lombardy. The fruit was not as good as that from the walnut trees of southern Italy, being smaller and less sweet. So it was used in stuffings, while the *noci di Sorrento* (Sorrento walnuts) were, and still are, the most highly prized for eating at table. After the War most of the walnut trees in northern Italy were felled to be used for furniture. Walnut trees are now rare in Lombardy, but the traditional stuffing for capon, or walnut sauces for pasta as made in Liguria and Piedmont, are still very popular.

THE RECIPE

Here, in the absence of capons, I buy a large chicken from my excellent butcher. It cooks much quicker than a farmyard capon, but the texture of the meat and its flavour is quite good. Be careful not to overcook it or it will become dry.

Buy the very best walnut kernels or, better still, buy walnuts in their shells and crack them yourself.

SERVES 10

a fresh free-range chicken of about 2.5–3kg/6–7lb
salt and freshly ground black pepper
2l/3½pt [US 2qt] chicken stock
150ml/5fl oz dry white wine

FOR THE STUFFING

200g/7oz [US 2 cups] walnut kernels (see above)
a large bunch of fresh flat-leaf parsley
40g/1½oz celery leaves
2 eggs
100ml/3½fl oz double cream [US heavy cream]
150g/5oz [US ⅔ cup] ricotta
90g/3oz [US ¾ cup] freshly grated Parmesan
salt and freshly ground black pepper
grated nutmeg

FOR THE SAUCE

90g/3oz [US 6 tbsp] unsalted butter
100g/3½oz [US ⅔ cup] flour
1–1½ tbsp chopped fresh tarragon
4 tbsp double cream [US heavy cream]
salt and freshly ground pepper, white if available

First prepare the stuffing. Put the walnut pieces in a small saucepan of boiling water and boil for 20 seconds. Lift out a few pieces at a time and remove as much as you can of the bitter skin. This is quite a time-consuming job. The walnuts are undoubtedly sweeter and nicer without the skin; however, if you do not have the time, or the inclination, to spend something like 40 minutes doing this, forget it. Dry the walnuts if you have peeled them, and chop them in a food processor together with the parsley and the celery leaves. Put the mixture in a bowl and add all the other ingredients for the stuffing. Mix very thoroughly and set aside.

Wipe the chicken inside and out and season the inside with salt and pepper. Push the stuffing into the cavity of the chicken and sew up the hole with thick cotton thread.

Put the chicken on a wire rack in a large deep pan or a heavy roasting tin. Pour in enough stock to come level with the top of the chicken. Put the pan on the heat and bring to the boil.

Heat the wine in a small saucepan and as soon as it is bubbling pour it over the chicken. Taste the stock and add a little salt if necessary. Bring to the boil again. Cover the pan tightly with its lid or with a double sheet of foil and simmer very gently for about 1½ hours. Test if the bird is ready by inserting the point of a knife in the thickest part of the thigh. The knife should penetrate very easily.

Lift out the chicken and place on a dish. Cover with foil and keep warm in a cool oven. Strain the stock and measure about 1.2l/2pt [US 5 cups] for the sauce.

Melt the butter in a heavy-based saucepan. Mix in the flour and, as soon as the butter has absorbed it, begin to add the measured hot stock gradually, while whisking constantly. Return the saucepan to the heat and cook very gently, stirring constantly, until the sauce begins to bubble. Now put the sauce over a flame diffuser and continue cooking for about 10 minutes. Mix in the tarragon and the cream just before transferring the sauce to a heated sauceboat. Taste and add salt and pepper if needed.

Cut the chicken into pieces and lay them on a heated dish. Fish the stuffing out of the cavity with a metal spoon and place in blobs around the chicken. Pour over 3 or 4 tablespoons of the stock to keep the chicken and stuffing nicely moist and then coat the chicken pieces with a little of the sauce. Serve the rest of the sauce alongside in a heated sauceboat.

Ossobuco alla Milanese
Milanese Ossobuco

I get very annoyed when I read recipes for ossobuco alla milanese containing tomatoes. Oddly enough, even some of the Italian writers I respect, and who should know, include tomatoes in their recipes for ossobuco.

The traditional ossobuco alla milanese does not contain tomatoes. In fact, few Milanese dishes contain tomatoes or tomato sauce. As with Veneto or Piedmontese cooking, tomato hardly ever became part of the traditional repertoire. The reason is obvious – no tomatoes grow in these most northerly regions of Italy.

And then think of the traditional accompaniment to ossobuco alla milanese. It is risotto alla milanese – risotto with saffron (page 27). Saffron and rich tomato sauce do not go together, nor does tomato sauce go with the delicious *gremolada* added at the end of the cooking, the taste of which must come through loud and clear against the winey flavour of the meat, and nothing else.

I am afraid another reason for ossobuco alla milanese containing tomatoes is that it has been the habit of Italian restaurants outside Italy to put tomato sauce with everything. For them it has been the signature of traditional Italian cooking, no matter if the dish comes from Milan, Valle d'Aosta or Naples.

There is an ossobuco cooked in a tomato sauce, and this originated in Emilia-Romagna. It is not served with risotto and it is not finished off with the magical gremolada.

Let me finish this diatribe by quoting the 'Italian Mrs Beeton' Pellegrino Artusi, who includes tomatoes in his recipe for ossobuco, without specifying 'alla milanese', however. 'This is a dish to be made by the Milanese because it is a Lombard speciality. I only want to describe it, without any pretensions, in fear of being laughed at.'

THE RECIPE

Ossobuchi come from the hind leg of a calf, and ideally should be no more than 4cm/1½in thick. Buy ossobuchi all of the same size so that they take the same amount of time to cook.

SERVES 4

4 ossobuchi, about 250g/9oz each

2 tbsp olive oil

flour for dusting

salt and freshly ground pepper

40g/1½oz [US 3 tbsp] butter

1 small onion, finely chopped

½ celery stalk, finely chopped

150ml/5fl oz dry white wine

300ml/10fl oz meat stock (page 230)

FOR THE GREMOLADA

1 tsp grated rind from an unwaxed lemon

½ garlic clove, very finely chopped

2 tbsp chopped fresh flat-leaf parsley

Tie the ossobuchi around and across with string as you would a parcel. Choose a heavy sauté pan, with a tight-fitting lid, large enough to hold the ossobuchi in a single layer. Heat the oil, and meanwhile lightly coat the ossobuchi with some flour in which you have mixed a teaspoon of salt. Brown the ossobuchi on both sides and then remove to a side dish.

Add 30g/1oz [US 2 tbsp] of the butter to the sauté pan together with the onion and the celery. Sprinkle with a little salt, which will help the onion to release its liquid so that it gets soft without browning. When the vegetables are soft – after about 10 minutes – return the meat to the pan along with the juice that will have accumulated.

Heat the wine and pour over the meat. Turn the heat up and boil to reduce by half, while scraping the bottom of the pan with a metal spoon.

Heat the stock in the pan you used to heat the wine and pour about half over the ossobuchi. Turn the heat down to very low and cover the pan. Cook for 1½ to 2 hours, until the meat has begun to come away from the bone. Carefully turn the ossobuchi over every 20 minutes or so, taking care not to damage the marrow in the bone. If necessary, add more stock during the cooking, but very gradually – not more than 3 or 4 tablespoons at a time. If, by the time the meat is cooked, the sauce is too thin, remove the meat from the pan and reduce the liquid by boiling briskly.

Transfer the ossobuchi to a heated dish and remove the string. Keep warm in a cool oven.

Cut the remaining butter into 3 or 4 pieces and add gradually to the sauce. As soon as the butter has melted, remove from the heat, as the sauce should not boil. This addition of the butter will give the sauce a glossy shine and a delicate taste.

Mix the ingredients for the gremolada together, stir into the sauce and leave for a minute or two. After that, just spoon the sauce over the ossobuchi and serve immediately.

CAZZOEULA
Stewed Pork with Cabbage

'*L'ha de vess trachenta e minga sbrodolona e sbrodolenta*' (it must be thick and not watery and soupy). Thus goes the saying in Milanese dialect about this great Lombard dish. Its name obviously has the same etymological origin as the French cassoulet, and the two dishes are in fact similar. But it is thought that the dish was actually brought to Lombardy by the Spaniards who were lords of this region for several centuries.

Whatever its origin, cazzoeula is now one of the dishes mainly associated with Milan and the Brianza, the hilly area between the city and the lakes where, once upon a time, the Milanese aristocracy used to spend their summers.

When I was very young my family, too, spent the month of September in Brianza, staying with friends named Grossi, in Erba, a little town between Como and Lecco. I found this recipe in my mother's recipe book, with the note 'Nina's recipe – the local cook in the Grossi's house'. I remember nothing about Nina or the Grossi, who seem to have disappeared from my mother's life long ago. But I do know that my mother's cazzoeula was delectable. She was often asked to prepare cazzoeula for my younger brother and all his friends on All Souls' Day, 2nd November, a day when this dish was traditionally eaten in most Milanese homes.

THE RECIPE

Cazzoeula is one of the recipes that can be produced in this country without searching too far for ingredients. Luganega is the only ingredient that is not available everywhere, although a good Toulouse, or coarse ground pork sausage with 100% meat content and no flavouring, would do.

Cazzoeula can be served with polenta, or just with lots of bread.

SERVES 6

2 pig's trotters, split into quarters
250g/9oz pork rind
2 tbsp olive oil
30g/1oz [US 2 tbsp] butter
2 large onions, chopped
700g/1½lb meaty pork spare ribs, cut into 2- or 3-rib pieces
2 large carrots, chopped
2 celery stalks, chopped
1.3kg/3lb Savoy cabbage, shredded into 2.5cm/1in pieces
450g/1lb luganega, or other coarse ground pure pork sausage, cut into 5cm/2in pieces
salt and freshly ground black pepper

Cover the trotters and the pork rind with 1l/ 1¾pt [US 1qt] of water, bring to the boil and cook for 45 minutes. Remove the trotters and the rind, cut off the excess fat and chop the rind into 5cm/2in squares; set aside. Allow the stock to cool, then refrigerate; when the fat has solidified on the surface, remove it and discard. (I have found that removing the fat makes the dish lighter, but if you haven't got time, you can omit this step and proceed.)

Put the oil, butter and onions in a large 4l/7pt [US 4qt] heavy-based saucepan or stockpot and fry for 5 to 10 minutes, until the onion is soft but not brown. Add the trotters and the rind and sauté for 30 seconds. Add the spare ribs and cook for 10 minutes, stirring frequently. Add the carrots and celery and sauté for a further 2 minutes, then cover with the stock from the trotters.

Cook, covered, over a very low heat for 3 hours, stirring every now and then and adding some hot water if the stew gets too dry.

Blanch the cabbage for 2 minutes and drain very well. Add it and the luganega to the saucepan, mix well and cook for a further 30 minutes. Taste and adjust the seasonings before serving straight from the heat, preferably in the stockpot.

FRICANDO
Rich Braised Beef

'Fricandeau' is the subject of an entry in *Larousse Gastronomique*. It is very similar to the Italian fricandò. So was it originally French or Italian? Here, as often elsewhere in the gastronomic arena, France and Italy compete. Many historians maintain that the dish originated in Italy and went to France, as did many other sophisticated dishes during the Renaissance when Italy was the leader in culinary matters. It then came back to Milan with Napoleon or, more precisely, with his Egyptian chef, who, when Napoleon's fortunes turned sour, stayed on in Milan to open a restaurant.

I feel sure that the dish was made in both countries, being a typical method of braising a piece of meat, but in Italy in the 19th century, it took the French name when it became fashionable to eat 'a la française'. The Italian version, however, has assumed the characteristic trademarks of its country. Thus it is larded with prosciutto, and celery is usually one of the braising vegetables.

THE RECIPE

The original fricandò is made with *noix de veau*. Because veal is unpopular and/or not easily available in this country, I suggest replacing it with a young but well-hung piece of beef. A piece of chuck or the eye of the silverside are the best cuts. Topside is not suitable for braising. The piece should be about 10cm/4in in diameter. Ask your butcher to tie it in a neat roll, so that it will keep its shape while cooking. Remember to remove the meat from the fridge at least 2 hours before you begin to cook it.

The prosciutto should be thickly sliced – about 3mm/⅛in. I buy prosciutto from the end of the ham, as it has more fat. It is also much cheaper. Your Italian food shop will keep the knuckle for you and slice it thickly. I prefer San Daniele prosciutto for larding and stuffing because it has a stronger flavour than Parma.

The traditional accompaniment to fricandò is potato purée.

SERVES 8

200g/7oz fatty prosciutto, thickly sliced
a 1.3–1.5kg/3–3½lb piece of beef (see above), securely tied in a roll
salt and freshly ground pepper
60g/2oz [US 4 tbsp] unsalted butter
2 tbsp olive oil
100g/3½oz Italian or Spanish onion
4 cloves
30g/1oz fresh flat-leaf parsley, leaves only
60g/2oz carrot, cut into chunks
30g/1oz celery, preferably the leaves of a stalk
150ml/5fl oz meat stock (page 230)

Cut the prosciutto roughly into large pieces. Put the pieces in a food processor and whizz for a few seconds until it is very coarsely chopped. Scoop it out on to a board.

Take the meat and stand it on one of its extremities. With a sharp, pointed knife – I use a boning knife which is long and narrow – make a deep incision in the roll of meat, along the grain, i.e. along the length of the roll. Take a lump of minced prosciutto between your fingers and push it into the cut. Push it down to the bottom of the cut, using a round chopstick or a round pencil. Make 4 or 5 incisions and then turn the meat over and repeat the operation. If your incisions are deep enough you will be able to lard half the meat from one end and the other half from the other end.

Put 1 tablespoon or so of salt on the board and mix it with plenty of freshly ground pepper. Roll the meat in the mixture and pat the seasoning hard into the meat. Pat in also any bits of leftover prosciutto.

Choose a heavy flameproof casserole in which the meat will fit fairly tightly. Heat the butter and oil and, when the foam of the butter begins to subside, lower the meat into the pan. Brown the meat on all sides on a lively heat. Let one side get lovely and brown before you turn the meat over. This operation is very important for the final result: caramelizing the outside of the meat gives the dish the right flavour. To do it properly takes about 10 minutes.

Heat the oven to 150°C/300°F/Gas Mark 2.

Cut the onion in half, or into quarters, depending on its size, and stick it with the cloves. Throw it into the casserole together with the parsley, carrot and celery. Give the vegetables a good stir and then pour in the stock. Put the lid on and place the casserole in the oven. Cook for 3 to 3½ hours. Keep an eye on it and turn the meat over every 20 minutes or so.

When the meat is tender, i.e. when the prongs of a fork can penetrate it easily, lift it out, loosely cover it with foil and set it aside. Let the juices rest for a couple of minutes and then skim as much fat as you can from the top. (Do not throw this fat away; it's mainly butter. Put it into a bowl and keep it in the fridge to be used for braising potatoes or cabbage or for meat sauces and ragù.) Transfer the juices to a food processor or a blender and blend until smooth.

Carve the meat into fairly thick slices – about 1cm/⅜in. If you were to carve it any thinner it would crumble. You need a very sharp knife or, an invaluable tool, an electric carving knife. Carve as many slices as you think you will need. Place the unsliced end piece at one end of a heated oval dish and lay the slices all the way down the dish, slightly overlapping.

Reheat the sauce and spoon a little over the carved meat. Pour the rest into a heated sauce-boat to hand round separately.

Note: You can cook the meat and prepare the sauce in advance. Put everything back in the casserole to be reheated in a moderate oven when the time comes.

POLPETTE
Meat Rissoles

'Polpette are the quintessential Italian food, or rather I should say, a particularly Lombard food. The real motherland of polpette is Milan, where a great many are eaten, and where I remember years ago having heard an old aristocrat saying "If one could gather all the polpette that I have eaten during my life, one could pave the city from Piazza del Duomo to Porta Orientale"' . . . which is 1½ kilometres. I have translated that passage from *L'Arte di Convitare* by Giovanni Raiberti, published in 1939.

Polpette, however, are very much older than 1939. Cristoforo Messisbugo's book *Libro Novo* was published in 1557, and in it he has three different kinds of polpette. Although he was the chef of the wealthy Don Hippolito d'Este, polpette were mainly food of the poor. And the northern regions of Italy were indeed poor up to the end of the last century.

Old-fashioned polpette are made mainly with left-over meat – any meat, whether chicken, beef or veal – which could have been boiled, braised or roasted. But in the old days that was never enough for another meal, so bread, cheese, mortadella or other pork products were added to make the meat go further. Nowadays, when meat is everyday food for anyone who wants it, polpette are usually made with raw meat.

'Polpette', writes Elizabeth David in her *Italian Food*, 'are not at all dull; in fact they make a most excellent little luncheon dish.' Well, I think they make an ideal family dish for lunch or dinner.

THE RECIPE
These are the polpette of my childhood, as made by our cook Maria. Maria came from Friuli, a region that had the reputation of supplying the best cooks for private houses. The poverty of Friuli sharpened the wits of its inhabitants, who

learned to embellish the most humble ingredients – just what family cooks need to do. A case in point is to be found in these polpette. During the autumn Maria used to put a little morsel of truffle in each polpetta, a small gem to be discovered within the unpretentiousness of minced meat.

The ricotta adds lightness to the meat, which could otherwise be heavy and stodgy. I prefer to buy good braising meat rather than meat already minced; then I know what's there. Ask your butcher to cut off the fat before mincing the meat.

SERVES 4

450g/1lb lean minced beef [US ground round]
125g/4oz [US ½ cup] fresh ricotta
1 egg
a small bunch of parsley sprigs, leaves only, chopped
1 garlic clove, very finely chopped
3 tbsp freshly grated Parmesan
salt and freshly ground pepper
about 2 tbsp flour
1 tbsp olive oil
15g/½oz [US 1 tbsp] butter

Put the meat in a bowl and mix in the ricotta. Lightly beat the egg and then incorporate it into the meat mixture together with the parsley, garlic and Parmesan. Now season with salt and pepper according to your taste. But do remember that salt brings out the flavour of the ingredients; be wise, but not mean. Mix everything together very thoroughly. I use my hands because I find them the best tool for breaking up the nuggets of meat.

Pull away some of the mixture the size of a golf ball. Roll it in your hands quickly and without squeezing too hard. (It is easier if you moisten your hands.) Flatten the balls at opposite poles to shape the polpette, which ideally should be about 2cm/¾in thick. Continue making polpette until you have used up all the meat. If you have time, place the polpette in the fridge for at least 30 minutes, to firm them up.

When you are ready to cook, put the flour on a plate and lightly coat each polpetta with flour. Heat the oil and butter in a frying pan. When the fat is golden, slide in the polpette and cook them for 2 minutes. Turn them over and cook the other side. How long you cook them depends on how you like your meat. I prefer polpette like these to be pink inside, and that takes about 5 to 7 minutes over lively heat. A sign to look out for is when the reddish juices begin to trickle through to the surface. If you like your polpette cooked through, turn the heat down a little and let them cook for a few more minutes.

This is the basic recipe. Now you can vary your polpette by transferring them, without the cooking juices, into another frying pan containing a good tomato sauce. Let them *insaporire* – take up the flavour of – the sauce for about 15 minutes, turning them over once, and then serve. Another excellent way to finish polpette comes from Artusi's book, *La Scienza in Cucina e l'Arte di Mangiar Bene*. He suggests adding at the end a little mixture of egg yolk and lemon juice.

UCCELLI SCAPPATI
Pork Bundles with Pancetta and Herbs

The name of this recipe means 'birds that have flown away'. The explanation of this curious name is that the pork bundles are cooked in the same way as little birds. Small birds, eaten with polenta, are a traditional dish of northern Lombardy and many other regions. In his *Voyages dans la Brianza*, Stendhal wrote that Milanese ladies were very fond of this peasant dish, as he was too: 'In the evening the delights and joy of the dinner with the uccelletti, polenta and the general gaiety.'

The prepared pork escalopes sold in good supermarkets are ideal for this recipe. They are thin, and all more or less of the same neat shape. This is one of the few cuts of meat which I prefer to buy in a supermarket. If you go to a butcher, buy thin slices of loin of pork and ask the butcher to trim them to a neat rectangle and to beat them thin.

It is a very simple, quick and easy dish that I am sure you will like.

SERVES 4

12 thin pork escalopes, about 450g/1lb total weight
salt and freshly ground pepper
12 slices of unsmoked pancetta, about 150g/5oz total weight
3 fresh rosemary sprigs
2 dozen fresh sage leaves
40g/1½oz [US 3 tbsp] unsalted butter
1 layer of onion
4 tbsp dry white wine

Put the escalopes on a board and season them with salt and pepper on both sides. Cover each of them with a slice of pancetta, cut a little smaller than the escalope. Scatter a few rosemary needles over and then roll up the escalopes from a long side. Thread one sage leaf, one bundle, one sage leaf, one bundle, then another sage leaf and the last bundle plus the last sage leaf on to a short metal skewer. Repeat with three more skewers. Thus you have three bundles on each skewer, each enough for one person.

When all the skewers are ready, heat the butter with the onion layer in a large frying pan. When the foam begins to subside and the butter begins to take on a lovely hazelnut colour, place the skewers in the pan. Sauté at a lively heat for 2 or 3 minutes, then turn the skewers over and sauté the other side of the bundles for about 2 minutes.

Pour over the wine and cook at a lively heat for 2 more minutes, then turn the heat down and finish cooking for a couple of minutes. Taste and adjust seasonings. Draw the pan off the heat and let the meat rest for 5 minutes before serving. During this time the meat juices will be released and mix in with the winey liquid. Uccelli scappati should not have much cooking liquid; just about 1 tablespoon per serving.

POLLO BRUSCO DI ANNAMARIA
Poached Chicken in a Vinegary Sauce

Annamaria de'Pedrini is a fine cook and a generous friend. She gave me the recipe for this excellent dish, which has been served at Christmas in the de'Pedrini household in Lombardy for generations. The chicken forms part of the antipasti, together with lobster, prawns, pâté de foie gras and *affettato* – mixed cured meats.

You can often see a similar dish in the windows of the best Milanese *salumerie* (delicatessens). It is an easy dish, ideal for a buffet party or for a dinner in the summer.

SERVES 4 TO 6

1 carrot
1 onion, stuck with 2 cloves
1 celery stalk
2 meat bouillon cubes
2 black peppercorns
2 bay leaves
a few parsley stalks
300ml/10fl oz dry white wine
salt and freshly ground pepper
a free-range chicken of about 1.5kg/3½lb

FOR THE SAUCE

150ml/5fl oz extra virgin olive oil
150ml/5fl oz white wine vinegar
2 tbsp capers, rinsed and dried
4 garlic cloves
60g/2oz anchovy fillets
2 tbsp flour
180g/6oz porcini under oil, drained
150g/5oz artichokes under oil, drained

Put the carrot, onion, celery, bouillon cubes, peppercorns, bay leaves, parsley stalks, wine and a little salt in a stockpot. Add the chicken and fill with cold water up to the level of the chicken. Now remove the chicken from the pan and set aside. Bring the water to the boil and then put the chicken back in the pot. When the water has come back to the boil, turn the heat down so that the water just trembles, but does not really boil. The secret of successful poaching lies in keeping the water just under the simmering point. The temperature of the water should be maintained so that only an occasional bubble breaks slowly to the surface. Cook until the chicken is done, about 1¼ hours. Leave in the stock while you prepare the sauce.

Put the oil and vinegar in a small saucepan. Chop together the capers, garlic and anchovies and add to the pan. Heat the mixture and, when bubbles begin to appear at the edges, throw in all the flour while you whisk hard with a small wire balloon whisk. Cook gently for 2 or 3 minutes and then add 6 tablespoons of the chicken stock. Continue cooking for a further 2 or 3 minutes, whisking constantly. Draw off the heat.

If the porcini pieces are large, cut them into about 2.5cm/1in pieces; cut the artichokes in half. Mix into the sauce, which should be quite thick. Taste, add salt and pepper and set aside.

Skin the chicken and cut into small portions: 2 pieces from each breast cut across, 2 drumsticks and 2 thighs. Put into a container and coat each piece with a little of the sauce, keeping some back for the final coating. Cover the container and refrigerate for 2 or 3 days. Also refrigerate the sauce that has been set aside.

Transfer the chicken pieces to a serving dish and spoon the remaining sauce over them to give them a fresh and glossy look.

LA TERRINA DI POLLO DELLA
TRATTORIA ALL'ANTICA
Chicken Terrine

When I am in Milan, my home town, I rarely go out to dine in restaurants. I am either asked by friends and relations to their homes, or, when staying with my brother, I like to cook and try out recipes, so that I can compare different foods and ingredients with what I can get in England. But on one of my last visits I decided I must reconfirm my old dictum that you eat better in Milan than in any other Italian city. So I asked Marco, my brother, to book a table at a very typical Milanese restaurant, and the Trattoria all'Antica, in one of the oldest parts of the city, could not have been a better choice.

We were welcomed by the elegant Maria, and by an enchanting Chinese waitress speaking perfect Italian. A large figure in white with his chef's hat poised at a rakish angle was hovering in the background. He came to meet us at the table and simply said that the food would arrive soon. No menu, and that was that. It was a perfect meal, redolent of the aromas and flavours of the Milanese cooking of my youth, with no concession to sun-dried tomatoes or any other southern Italian intrusions.

I was torn between asking for the recipe for the superb crespelle with cheese or this terrine, but then I opted for the terrine because I realized that the crespelle could be made in this country only in London, and in Edinburgh thanks to Valvona & Crolla, and only by hunting around in search of the right cheeses.

THE RECIPE
Domenico Passera, he of the chef's hat, suggests serving the terrine on a bed of *insalatina*. This could be mâche, frisée or watercress, but not rocket [US arugula] which would jar with the delicate flavour of the terrine and would not be in keeping with Lombard traditions, having been unknown there until the '60s.

I buy chicken thighs with the bone in because the bone adds a lot of flavour to the meat.

SERVES 8

800g/1¾lb fresh chicken thighs
3 tbsp olive oil
2 garlic cloves, bruised
salt and freshly ground pepper
1 fresh rosemary sprig
200g/7oz chicken livers
200g/7oz [US 14 tbsp] unsalted butter
100g/3½oz [US ½ cup] very finely chopped onion
1 bay leaf
6 tbsp brandy

Heat the oven to 200°C/400°F/Gas Mark 6.

Skin the chicken thighs, remove and discard the fat attached to them, and place in a roasting tin.

In a bowl mix together the oil, garlic, 2 teaspoons of salt and a good grinding of pepper. Brush the thighs all over with the seasoned oil using the rosemary sprig. Throw the rosemary, the garlic and any left-over oil into the tin and place the tin in the oven. After 5 minutes remove and discard the garlic. Cook, basting once or twice, for about 20 minutes. The chicken should no longer be bloody though still undercooked. Leave to cool while you cook the chicken liver. Leave the oven on.

Trim the fat and gristle off the chicken livers and cut the livers into pieces. Heat 60g/2oz [US 4 tbsp] of the butter, the onion, bay leaf and 1 teaspoon of salt in a frying pan and cook to soften the onion. As soon as the onion is soft add the chicken livers. Fry for 5 minutes, then splash with the brandy. Finally, cook rapidly for 2 or 3 minutes.

Go back to the chicken thighs. Remove the bone and cut the meat into pieces. Put the meat, the chicken livers with all the cooking juices, and the remaining butter cut into pieces in a food processor and give it a whizz for 2 or 3 seconds. Add salt and pepper. (I add 1 teaspoon of salt and ½ teaspoon of ground pepper, because any pâté or terrine that is served chilled needs a lot of seasoning.) Whizz again to a very coarse texture – not a smooth pâté-like consistency. Taste and check seasoning.

Line a 1l/1¾pt [US 1qt] loaf tin with foil and spoon the mixture into it, pushing it down and banging the tin hard on the work surface to eliminate any air pockets. Cover with cling film.

Now you must cook the terrine in a bain-marie in the oven. To do that, place the terrine in a roasting tin and pour some boiling water into the tin to come half to three-quarters of the way up the side of the tin. Bake for 20 minutes.

When the terrine is cold, refrigerate for at least 3 hours.

You can serve the whole terrine in a dish, surrounding it with a little salad, drizzled with a few drops of extra virgin olive oil, or you can slice the terrine and put it on individual plates on a bed of lightly dressed salad.

ANIMELLE

Sweetbreads

All kinds of offal [US variety meats] are popular in Italy, but I am including only sweetbreads, for the simple reason that they are the offal I like best. They are delicate in flavour and texture and can be cooked in many interesting ways.

First let me tell you what sweetbreads are, in case you don't know. They are the thymus glands in the upper chest of a young animal, and they disappear as soon as it becomes adult. A sweetbread is formed of two parts attached to each other, called the heart, and the throat. The heart is large, lean and regular in shape, while the throat consists of little pieces, because the inedible bits have been removed from around the edible ones. These latter sweetbreads are particularly suited for going into stuffings, while the heart is used for proper sweetbread dishes.

Both calf's sweetbreads and lamb's sweetbreads are available in most butchers, or can be ordered. The calf's are much larger and sweeter and are more highly regarded. But lamb's sweetbreads are good too and should not be underestimated. They are also much cheaper and more easily available.

THE RECIPES

All sweetbreads need some preparation before you proceed to follow a recipe. First you must soak them in cold water for about 2 hours to let the blood run out. After that, bring to the boil a saucepan of water containing a slice of onion and a small stalk of celery. Add 1 tablespoon of wine vinegar and some salt. When the water is boiling throw in the sweetbreads and simmer gently for 5 minutes if calf's heart sweetbreads, but only for 2 minutes if they are the throat ones or if they are lamb's sweetbreads. Having blanched them in this way, drain and rinse them, then peel off the membrane and remove any bits of fat or hardened blood.

And now you can proceed to cook them in your favourite way. These are mine.

ANIMELLE A COTOLETTA
Breaded Calf Sweetbreads

In Lombardy this is a traditional way of cooking a number of different ingredients, such as veal escalopes, cèpe caps, brains and fish fillets, as well as these sweetbreads.

This recipe should be made with the heart part of a calf's sweetbread, which you can cut into neat slices. Having said that, I have also made it with lamb's sweetbread, which has the characteristic stronger flavour of lamb's meat.

Instead of using clarified butter, I replace some of the butter with olive oil, which allows the butter to heat to a higher temperature without burning.

SERVES 4
600g/1¼lb calf's sweetbreads
2 eggs
salt and freshly ground pepper
about 100g/3½oz [US 1 cup] dried white breadcrumbs, spread on a board
75g/2½oz [US 5 tbsp] unsalted butter
1 tbsp olive oil
lemon wedges

Prepare the sweetbreads as described in the introduction and then cut them into neat pieces.

Lightly beat the eggs in a soup plate and season with salt and pepper.

Coat both sides of the sweetbread pieces in the eggs and then let the excess egg flow back into the plate. Now coat the pieces with the breadcrumbs, patting firmly with your hands.

Heat the butter and the oil in a frying pan, which must be large enough to contain the sweetbreads without crowding them. When the butter foam begins to subside, slip in the sweetbreads and cook for 3 minutes, then flip them over and cook for 2 minutes, until deeply gilded. Make sure you keep the heat high enough to cook the sweetbreads, but not so hot as to burn the butter.

Transfer to a heated dish and serve straight away, surrounded by lemon wedges.

ANIMELLE IN FRITTURA PICCATA
Sautéed Sweetbreads with Lemon and Parsley

This is another way of cooking veal that is also used for cooking sweetbreads. You can use calf's throat sweetbreads, or lamb's sweetbreads which I find very suitable for this preparation. Use a pan that you can bring to the table, if you have one.

SERVES 4

700g/1½lb sweetbreads

60g/2oz [US 4 tbsp] unsalted butter

1 garlic clove, bruised

100g/3½oz [US ⅔ cup] flour

about 5 tbsp meat stock (page 230)

salt and freshly ground pepper

the juice of 1 lemon

3 tbsp chopped fresh flat-leaf parsley

Prepare the sweetbreads as described in the introduction.

Heat the butter and the garlic in a frying pan.

Quickly flour the sweetbreads and throw them into the pan as soon as the butter foam begins to subside. Sauté for 2 minutes over moderate heat, shaking the pan frequently but not constantly, so that the sweetbreads can brown. Add the stock and cook for a further minute or so. Season with salt and pepper, pour over the lemon juice and sprinkle with the parsley. Mix quickly and serve at once.

LA TORTA PARADISO
Paradise Cake

After considering various alternatives for the English name of this cake (Heavenly Cake?) I decided that only a literal translation of the Italian does it justice. Torta paradiso is synonymous with Pavia, a city to the south of Milan, where it was created by Enrico Vigoni at the end of the last century. Pavia is a delightful city which boasts a noble past and one of the oldest universities in Europe. It is a city where the sleepy habits of the surrounding misty countryside mingle with the lively entrepreneurial spirit of the Lombards.

As my son Guy lives there, I am often in Pavia and I love it. One of the treats when I'm there is to go to the Pasticceria Vigoni in the Strada Nuova, to have an espresso or a cappuccino with one of their exquisite *paste* (small cakes) and buy a piece of torta paradiso to take home.

When I was preparing this book I went to talk to the manager of Vigoni, Pietro Grecchi. I immediately told him that I was not there to ask for the recipe of the torta paradiso, since I knew it was a well-guarded secret. But Grecchi refuted this by saying that the only secret lies in the quality of the ingredients. The flour is the best flour produced specifically for cakes and biscuits [US cookies] the eggs are supplied by local breeders who give their hens plenty of space and feed them with the best food, while the butter is made by the old churning method, using the whole cream and not the whey of the cream used for cheese-making. Sadly, this butter cannot be bought in shops in Italy.

Grecchi told me that, to the Pavesi, torta paradiso means their city. At Christmas he sends thousands of the cakes to the Pavesi dotted around the world, accompanied by a bottle of Santa Maria della Versa, a spumante Brut produced with local grapes. Grecchi also assured me that torta paradiso is a most nourishing food, so much so, in fact, that he runs the Milan-Pavia race (32 kilometres) on nothing more than 50g of torta paradiso and a glass of milk!

Well, a lot of fascinating information, but I came out of the beautiful art nouveau shop without the recipe. However, a few days later I was given a very similar and excellent recipe by a kind lady who has a pasta shop in a small town near by. And this is her recipe, which I call La Torta Paradiso di Wilma Magagnato. Apart from being utterly delicious, the cake has the added benefit of being suitable for people who are allergic to wheat flour. Serve it, as in Pavia, with sparkling wine at the end of a dinner, although it is also good as an accompaniment to poached fruit, or taken at tea time . . . coffee time . . . any time.

THE RECIPE
Potato flour is available in good supermarkets, specialist food shops and health-food shops.

SERVES 10 TO 12
325g/11oz [US 3 sticks less 2 tbsp] best unsalted butter, at room temperature
325g/11oz caster sugar [US 1½ cups granulated sugar]
3 size-2 very fresh eggs [US extra-large eggs]
325g/11oz [US 2⅓ cups] potato flour
3g/a generous ½ tsp cream of tartar
3g/a generous ½ tsp bicarbonate of soda [US baking soda]
3g/a generous ½ tsp salt
1 unwaxed lemon
butter and dried breadcrumbs for the tin
icing sugar [US confectioners' sugar], to finish

Heat the oven to 170°C/350°F/Gas Mark 3.

Cut the butter into small pieces and put them in a bowl. Add the sugar and mix together until wholly blended. (I use my hands, because it's easier and quicker than a spoon.) Add one egg at a time to the butter-sugar cream, while beating constantly. For this operation I use a hand-held electric mixer. Do not add a second egg until the previous one is totally incorporated.

Sift the potato flour with the cream of tartar, bicarbonate of soda and salt, and sprinkle large spoonfuls over the surface of the butter-cream. Incorporate each spoonful of flour with a large metal spoon and a high movement to incorporate some air as well.

Wash and dry the lemon and, using a zester or a small grater, grate the rind – only the yellow part – into the mixture. Mix well.

Prepare a 25cm/10in spring-clip tin by buttering the inside very generously and sprinkling the surface with dried breadcrumbs. Turn the tin upside-down and tap out all excess crumbs. Spoon the cake mixture into the tin, give the tin a jerk or two to settle the mixture and bake for 45 minutes or thereabouts, until the cake is dry inside and has shrunk from the edge.

Unmould the cake and leave on a wire rack to cool. Use great care when you transfer this very fragile cake. Before serving, sprinkle the top with a thick layer of icing sugar.

You can keep the cake, well wrapped in foil, for . . . how long? You may well ask. I'm afraid I don't know because in my house a torta paradiso is likely to be polished off in 2 or 3 days. But you can keep it for a week or so, although it will lose its fragrance.

FETTINE DI MELE ALL'ANTICA
Sautéed Sliced Apples

La Cucina Mantovana is a very informative book on the cooking of Mantua. Cia Eramo, its author, claims that the recipe on which the following is based is by the great Bartolomeo Stefani (although I could not find it in his book). Stefani was chef to Ottavio Gonzaga and wrote *L'Arte di Ben Cucinare*, published in 1662. He was the first chef to reject the over-elaborate cooking of the Renaissance, and to approach food and cooking in a more workaday fashion. His recipes are never extravagant and his influence is still felt to this day.

The liqueurs suggested in Eramo's book are Calvados and Grand Marnier. I prefer to use only Calvados. I have tried the dish with and without cream and I am sure it is better on its own, as in its original version. Eramo concludes her recipe by writing, 'A dessert which is a genuine delicacy'.

SERVES 4

4 crisp dessert apples

45g/1¾oz [US 3 tbsp] unsalted butter

150–180g/5–6oz caster sugar [US ¾–1 cup granulated sugar], depending on the sweetness of the apples

2 unwaxed lemons

4 tbsp fresh orange juice

4 tbsp Calvados

Peel the apples and remove the core, leaving the apples whole. Cut them across into slices about 1cm/½in thick.

Choose a large frying pan into which the apple slices will fit in a single layer. If you don't have a large enough pan use two frying pans, increasing the amount of butter to 30g/1oz [US 2 tbsp] per pan. Melt the butter and add 4 or 5 tablespoons of the sugar. Let it caramelize a little and then add the apple slices. Sauté on one side over a lively heat until golden, then gently turn the slices over and add another 2 or 3 tablespoons of sugar.

Wash one of the lemons, grate the rind and add to the pan. Squeeze both lemons and add 6 tablespoons of the juice to the pan together with the orange juice. Continue cooking, while gradually adding the remaining sugar, until the apple slices can be easily pierced by the point of a small knife.

Now heat the Calvados in a metal ladle. Pour it into the pan while you put a match to it. Let the flame die down, then transfer the apples to a heated dish and spoon over that delicious buttery syrup. Serve at once.

You can prepare the dish in advance and reheat it in the oven. Flame it just before serving.

Il Gelato di Limone
Lemon Ice-cream

Charles, my English son-in-law, came back to this country recently after living in Italy for a year. The other day, while eating this ice-cream approvingly, he asked me if I could explain why ice-creams are always so much better in Italy. 'Easy,' I said, 'the fruit ripens in the hot Italian sun and it's only picked when it's properly ripe.' But then he pointed out that all ice-creams are better, not only the fruit ones. And my answer to that was that in Italy ice-creams are made with eggs as well as cream or milk, not only with cream. It is the egg yolk that gives the ice-cream that silky smooth texture and delicate yet positive flavour.

I wonder if this lemon ice-cream is the one that Stendhal refers to in his diary for 4th October 1816. After an evening at La Scala in Milan, he writes, 'Half way through the evening it is the normal duty of the escorting gallant to regale his mistress with ices, which are served in the box. These sorbets are divine; they may be of three kinds: gelati, crepé and pezzi duri, and no one should fail to make so rewarding an acquaintance. I am still undecided which of the three species is the most exquisite; and so, every evening, I resort to experiment.'

THE RECIPE
If you use waxed lemons you should scrub them very hard under hot water. You will feel a greasy substance coming off the lemon. Not very pleasant. So try to get unwaxed lemons, which you must wash and dry.

SERVES 4 OR 5
3 unwaxed lemons
150g/5oz [US ¾ cup] sugar
2 size-2 egg yolks [US extra-large egg yolks]
150ml/5fl oz double cream [US heavy cream]

Remove the zest from 2 of the lemons with a vegetable peeler, leaving the white pith behind as this would give the ice-cream a bitter flavour. Put the zest in a small saucepan and add 150ml/5fl oz of water and the sugar.

Squeeze all the 3 lemons and pour the juice into the saucepan. Bring the mixture very slowly to the boil and simmer for 5 minutes, stirring the whole time to help the sugar to dissolve. Strain the syrup.

Beat the egg yolks in another saucepan, which should have a heavy base. Pour in the syrup while you beat. I use a hand-held electric mixer for this. The mixture will become very light and bubbly. Put the saucepan on a very low heat and heat until the mixture begins to thicken. Stir constantly with a wooden spoon, no longer with the electric mixer. Draw off the heat and put the pan in a sink of cold water. Continue to stir for a couple of minutes until the saucepan has cooled down, otherwise the custard might still curdle at the bottom. Stir in the cream.

When the mixture is cold, pour it into an ice-cream maker and freeze, following the manufacturer's instructions.

If you have kept the ice-cream in the freezer, don't forget to transfer it to the fridge about 30 to 40 minutes before you want to serve it. Ice-cream is nicer a little sloppy rather than solid.

Pan con l'Uva
Bread with Raisins

Nothing brings back my early schooldays more vividly than pan con l'uva. Opposite the entrance to our primary school in Milan's Via della Spiga there was a tiny baker's shop, and all the way down the narrow street one could smell the most delicious breads being baked. Before gathering in the school hall for assembly we all queued for our favourite bread – pan con l'uva. A piece, about

5cm/2in long, just out of the oven at the back of the shop, was handed to us wrapped in thick yellow absorbent paper. We used to put this *merenda* in our desk, which meant that the classroom was pervaded by the best smell in the world, that of freshly baked bread plus the sweet smell of the *zibibbo* – large fat dried grapes. The zibibbo come from Sicily or Pantelleria. They are reconstituted in water before baking and, when hot, they exude the exhilarating smell of fresh grapes.

When my children started school in London and came back with descriptions of what they could buy in the tuck shop, I thought how lucky I had been to have had in my desk something I looked forward to so much that even the most boring lesson was part of the treat.

In her fascinating book *La Lombardia in Cucina*, Ottorina Perna Bozzi writes that the first pan con l'uga (its name in dialect) appeared in 1876 on a stall at Porta Venezia. This was at the terminus of the first tram line, the Milano– Monza, which had just been built. The bread was apparently made in Monza and brought to Milan by a clever entrepreneur. Eventually a baker opened a shop in Milan where the Milanese flocked to buy their beloved pan con l'uva before catching the tram. Ottorina Perna Bozzi goes on to say that this bread soon established itself as the favourite snack for children to take to school, as it certainly was up to my time.

THE RECIPE

The best dried grapes to use are the dried Muscatel, which you can find in a few specialist shops. They have a flavour and juiciness that is similar to the zibibbo. Other than those, I prefer raisins to sultanas [US golden raisins] because they have a more pronounced and slightly less sweet flavour.

This bread is best eaten when still warm. If you have made it in advance, reheat it in a low oven for 10 minutes or so.

SERVES 6-8

200g/7oz [US 1⅓ cups] dried Muscatels or raisins
225g/8oz [US 2 cups] white flour, preferably Italian 00
15g/½oz easy-blend dried yeast [US 2pkg rapid-rise yeast]
a pinch of salt
100ml/3½fl oz semi-skimmed milk [US low-fat milk]
40g/1½oz [US 3 tbsp] unsalted butter, melted
2–3 tbsp lukewarm water
2 tbsp dark Muscovado sugar

If you are using Muscatels, remove the grapes from the stalk. Soak the Muscatels or raisins in hot water for about 4 hours. Drain them and pat them dry with kitchen paper towel. Set aside.

Mix the dry ingredients together in a bowl and then add the milk and the butter. Knead, adding enough water to form an elastic, silky and smooth dough. Knead for about 5 minutes, then place the dough in an oiled bowl. Roll the dough to coat with oil all over, to prevent the surface becoming dry and crusty. Cover with a thick linen towel and let the dough rise in a warm place until it has doubled in volume, about 2 to 2½ hours.

Place the dough on a lightly floured work surface and pat or roll it into an oval shape, about 1cm/½in thick. This dough will be a little sticky.

Sprinkle about one-third of the raisins over the dough and pat them into the dough. Now do the same with another batch of raisins, and then again until all the raisins are embedded in the dough. Pat the raisins down with the palm of your hands and sprinkle with the brown sugar. Roll the dough up, Swiss-roll [US jelly-roll] fashion, tapering at each end. Tuck the ends of the dough roll under, and place the bread on a floured baking tray. Place the tray in a warm corner of the kitchen, cover with a linen towel and leave it for a second rising, until the dough has doubled, about 1 hour.

Heat the oven to 200°C/400°F/Gas Mark 6.

Place the bread in the oven and bake for 15 minutes. Turn the heat down to 180°C/350°F/Gas Mark 4 and bake for a further 30 minutes. Transfer the bread to a wire rack and allow to cool a little before serving. It is nicest when warm but can also be eaten cold.

Il Sandwich di Panettone
Panettone Sandwich

I am not giving a recipe for panettone, first because it is very difficult to make successfully, and secondly because the panettone you can buy in shops is better than any home-made panettone I have ever tasted.

Nowadays panettone comes in three versions, the plain old-fashioned one, one with chocolate chips, and a panettone stuffed with zabaione or with tiramisù. Some brands of panettone are better than others. A good one is made by Scarpato. It contains no additives, and the panettone is hand-made in the traditional way with good creamy butter and the right amount of dried fruit; it has a beautiful light texture. It is a plain panettone in the old-fashioned squat dome shape, and all these points commend it to an old-fashioned Milanese like me.

Panettone, which to me means a Milanese Christmas, has recently become the Christmas cake par excellence all over Italy. And now it is marching on to conquer the world. It is available all year round from Italian food shops, and it is always welcome, whether eaten with a cup of coffee for breakfast, with a cup of tea at tea-time, with a glass of Vinsanto at the end of a meal or just on its own at any time.

The origins of panettone go back to the Middle Ages, when a large loaf of bread, sometimes enriched with various ingredients – called *pan grande* – was made in every home; on the top the master of the house would mark a cross. Its name has probably come about through adding an affectionate diminutive (denoting sweetness) to *pane*, hence panetto, and then the suffix *-one*, which always indicates largeness.

THE RECIPE

In recent years panettone has been used in this country to make a kind of bread and butter pudding. Being light it lends itself to this treatment, and many chefs have created their own version. I find this one the best. It is a recipe by Vincenzo Bergonzoli of the Ristorante San Vicenzo in London, where I have always eaten well. Vincenzo serves the pudding on its own, in the real Italian tradition, but it also goes well with a jug of hot zabaione.

SERVES 8

450g/1lb panettone
1 unwaxed orange
1 unwaxed lemon
3 size-2 eggs [US extra-large eggs]
450g/1lb mascarpone
6 drops of vanilla extract
2 pinches of ground cinnamon
3 tbsp caster sugar [US granulated sugar]
40g/1½oz [US 3 tbsp] unsalted butter
4 tbsp sweet white vermouth
icing sugar [US confectioners' sugar], to finish

Cut half the panettone into slices just over 1cm/½in thick, and the other half into slightly thinner slices. Keep them separate. Leave the panettone to dry uncovered for 24 hours or so.

Wash the orange and the lemon and dry them. Grate the rind and then squeeze the juice. Strain the juice.

Heat the oven to 170°C/325°F/Gas Mark 3.

Beat the eggs in a large bowl. Add the mascarpone and beat until the eggs have been incorporated. Now beat in the vanilla, cinnamon, lemon and orange rind and juice, and sugar. (I use a hand-held electric mixer for the final whisking.) The mixture should be quite thick. Melt half the butter and add to the mixture.

Take a shallow oven dish in which the panettone will fit in two layers. (I use a rectangular metal dish measuring 22 × 17cm/9 × 7in.) Grease the dish with a little of the remaining butter and line with greaseproof paper [US wax paper]. Grease the paper too. Lay the thicker slices of panettone over the bottom, plugging any holes with pieces of panettone. Moisten with some vermouth using a pastry brush. Spread over the mascarpone cream and then cover with the thinner slices of panettone, moistening these slices also with the remaining vermouth. Dot with the rest of the butter and bake for half an hour.

Cut the pudding into slices or squares, depending on the shape of your oven dish. Release the pieces all around the edge with the help of a thin knife and transfer them to individual plates. Sprinkle with icing sugar just before serving.

PAN DI MIGLIO

Polenta and Elderflower Cake

In Lombardy this cake is eaten on St George's day, St George being regarded (for reasons that are totally obscure) as the patron saint of dairy farmers. I still remember the joy, as a child, of pouring rich Lombard cream into a soup plate and placing in the middle a small round of pan di miglio. The pan di miglio just softens in the cream and you get mouthfuls of a simple bready sweetness mellowed in the cream.

This traditional sweet bread used to be made with millet flour (*miglio*) before the arrival of maize from the New World, which has replaced it.

Pick the elderflowers when in full bloom, from bushes growing in full sunshine; they have more flavour. Pick the little white elderflowers off the stalks, trying to remove as many of the tiny stalks as you can.

You can make about 8 small (5cm/2in) buns, which will then spread and grow to about twice that size. Or you can put the dough in a 20–22cm/8–9in shallow tin, which I find easier and better.

SERVES 6

100g/3½oz [US 7 tbsp] unsalted butter
200g/7oz coarse-ground maize (polenta) flour [US 1¾ cups coarse cornmeal]
125g/4oz [US 1 cup] white flour, preferably Italian 00
1½ tsp baking powder
a pinch of salt
125g/4oz caster sugar [US ½ cup+2 tbsp granulated sugar]
1 egg
2 tbsp milk
6 level tbsp elderflowers
butter for the tin

Heat the oven to 180°C/350°F/Gas Mark 4.

Melt the butter very slowly in a small saucepan.

Mix the dry ingredients together in a bowl. Add the egg, melted butter and milk and mix well. Now mix in the elderflowers.

Generously butter a 20cm/8in tart tin and fill with the mixture. Spread it and level it with your hands. Bake for about 40 minutes or until the point of a sharp knife inserted in the middle of the pan di miglio comes out dry. Serve with thick pouring cream, or eat it as it is with tea, coffee or a glass of sweet wine.

VALLE D'AOSTA & PIEMONTE

When my children were young we used to drive to Italy for our summer holidays, rather than fly. We enjoyed the journey across France, the changing face of nature as we travelled south and the warming of the climate. But most of all we enjoyed the thought of getting closer to Italy. And then, at last, the crossing of the frontier; this was the exciting moment, France behind us, then no-man's-land and then l'Italia! I shall always remember once after parking near the Gran San Bernardo frontier post, looking behind me as we walked towards our first espresso and seeing my elder son, Paul, kneeling down and kissing the concrete of the petrol station.

The Mont Blanc tunnel was a favourite of ours. You got into the tunnel in France and, after 10 dark minutes, you came out in Italy, whose sun was usually there to greet us. But what my young children noticed with disappointment year after year was that, although we were in Italy, we seemed to be still in France. The language heard in the bars sounded like French, the names of the villages were French, the coins used were still French francs. Only when we eventually got to Aosta, the capital of the region, did we begin to feel safely home.

One thing, however, was a clear indication of where we were: the food. In the bars, pizze and focacce were lined up next to croissants and brioches; Baci Perugina and Pocket Coffee were there next to the cashier and, best of all, coffee was a proper espresso.

The food and cooking of Valle d'Aosta, while nominally Italian, is more northern European than Mediterranean, with its emphasis on dairy products and its lack of vegetables. No pasta, no olive oil, no tomatoes. There are nourishing soups based on bread, as well as sausages, rice and polenta and chestnuts dressed with butter and cream – a Teutonic type of cooking. The reason for this, of course, is the Germanic influence. Germanic peoples descended through Switzerland into the lateral valleys of Valle d'Aosta in the 13th century, and there they remained, isolated, speaking their language and keeping their traditions.

Years ago in Gressoney I met an old lady, Signora Martini, who could hardly speak Italian. She spoke a sort of German patois. Her cooking was the most valdostano I have ever tasted. In her cellar hung a *mocetta*, a local salame which was then made from the thigh of a wild goat, but now is usually made with domestic goat meat. Beautiful Reinette apples and Martin Sech pears were lined up next to jars containing all kinds of fungi under oil and even preserved meat, which this old woman was still making. Meat was preserved in salt and herbs for the winter months and used then to make carbonata, a direct descendant of the Flemish carbonade, the difference being that the beer is replaced by wine.

Signora Martini asked us to dinner the next day. We started with a glistening white mountain of *gnocchi alla bava* – potato gnocchi dressed with fontina, the best local cheese, now also available here, albeit in a mass-produced form that does not do justice to the flowery, herby and nutty flavour of the real product. After a magnificently generous bowl of carbonata, the meal was rounded off with caffè valdostano. This is coffee mixed with Grappa, red wine, sugar and lemon rind, and it is served in the *grolla*, a large earthenware container with six or eight spouts from which the coffee is drunk by the various guests while the grolla is handed around.

I am afraid that night was the scene of one of the more embarrassing episodes of my life. My son Guy, then aged six, wanted to have a sip too, in spite of my warnings that the drink contained spirits, which he hated. But the Martinis loved children and were ready to spoil him. '*Ma glielo lasci assaggiare!*' (but let him try it). And so Guy sipped, and the next moment the sip came out of his mouth in a perfect spray, spattering the previously immaculate white tablecloth with black spots. Guy was in tears, I was nearly in tears, but the Martinis seemed to enjoy the happening and laughed heartily. To be honest, I didn't like that coffee either and wished I could do the same as Guy, instead of having to swallow that nasty black concoction. The drinking of coffee in this way is a symbol of comradeship and hospitality, and Italians, I know, are touchy on that subject.

In Aosta the cooking begins to take a different shape. It becomes more complex and sophisticated, with vegetables to the fore, heralding the wealth of vegetables in Piedmont. Piedmontese cooking seems to me to be divided according to its topography. The lowland area next to Lombardy is mainly devoted to rice culture, the Alpine zone shares the characteristics of the cooking of Valle d'Aosta, and the rich hilly area is a mecca for the gourmet with its arrays of excellent dishes and famous produce. The prize of this area is the white truffle. And what a prize it is, one of which the locals are hugely proud, and rightly so.

I have been in or around Alba quite a few times during the truffle season. The last time was at the truffle fair in Moncalvo, an attractive town north of

Asti, to which I was invited by the great gastronome and author, Giovanni Goria. The square was packed with people and with stalls selling pumpkins, cheeses, honey, mushrooms and all sorts of those horrid ethnic knick-knacks that have become a fixture at any fair anywhere in the western world. The stalls with truffles, being the most important, were under the *loggiato* (arches), with the mayor and the judges standing at the central stall. The names of the winners were called out over a loudspeaker, to great applause from the bystanders, as up to the mayor went each winning *cavatore* (truffle hunter) leading his dog. These dogs are usually a cross between a mongrel and a hound. The hound provides the nose, while the less aristocratic parent contributes the intelligence! I was completely won over by Diana, a smallish sort of grey pointer. She was named 'best truffle dog of the year', but she was afflicted with stage-fright and kept hiding between her master's legs, trembling at the flashes from all the surrounding cameras. Her owner told me, however, that once free on the field, Diana became a different dog, courageous, adventurous and unyielding.

After the ceremony we all went to eat at the social club, which sounds awful, and I dare say was not Claridges, and yet the meal I had there was one of the best ever. The truffles, alas, appeared only, and with parsimony, in the risotto and in the *tajarin* – the local tagliatelle, which were simply dressed with melted butter, flavoured with garlic, herbs and plenty of grated Parmesan. But the nine courses were so good that one forgave the minimal appearance of the truffles. The meal ended with *la coppa di Seiràss* and lots of local biscuits such as brutti ma buoni (page 75) and melting-in-the-mouth soft amaretti. La coppa di Seiràss is a creamy pudding made with the magical ricotta piemontese, a softer richer ricotta than the romana, which is the sort you can buy here in Italian food shops. Ricotta piemontese is a by-product of cheeses made with cow's milk, while ricotta romana is a by-product of pecorino.

There are many other remarkable cheeses from Piedmont, the best being the toma and tomini, which can be eaten young, when still fresh, milky and soft, or aged, when they became robust and charmingly aggressive. Fresh tome are used a lot in antipasti, the range of which, in Piedmont, is infinite. Any decent Piedmontese meal will kick off with a minimum of five antipasti, the cold ones placed on the table and the hot brought in from the kitchen in quick succession. In these Lucullan antipasti the pride of place is given to the magnificent vegetables from the hilly areas: the asparagus of Santena, the small onions of Ivrea, the sweet peppers and leeks of the Valle del Tanaro, to mention but a few.

Equally rich and diverse is the last course. *Torte* (cakes), *cioccolatini*, *biscotti* and *budini* (puddings) are a feast to the eye and, of course, the palate. Turin, the capital, is the best place to enjoy all this. For the chocoholic, the Pasticceria Peyrano is the must of all musts. Even I, not a chocoholic and not even very keen on chocolate, cannot resist buying a tray of this and a tray of that whenever I set foot in the shop. My favourite *pasticceria*, however, is the Forneria Polo in Corso Dante, where the charming Sandra produces excellent breads and all sorts of cakes, biscuits and cookies, with her husband helping in the back of the kitchen by baking, rolling, stirring and filling. I used to go to Turin often when my older brother lived there. Now that he has retired to the country I think back with nostalgia to these two shops, the like of which it would be difficult to find anywhere in the world.

My appreciation of Piedmontese sweets is reflected in the fact that I have included more recipes for desserts and cakes from Piedmont than from any other region.

MINESTRA DI RISO E CASTAGNE Ⓥ

Rice and Chestnut Soup

A chestnut soup of one kind or another is made in nearly all Alpine towns. This one can be made with milk instead of stock, but I find that too thick and heavy and prefer the lighter touch of a good vegetable stock.

A word of warning about chestnuts. Buy good large, shining nuts. Peeling them is a bit of a bother, but however hard I have tried, I have not been able to find any simpler or quicker way. For this recipe you don't have to peel a great many chestnuts, so it is not too bad.

SERVES 4

450g/1lb chestnuts
1.2l/2pt [US 5 cups] vegetable stock (page 231)
125g/4oz [US ½ cup] Italian rice, preferably Vialone Nano
salt
20g/¾oz [US 1½ tbsp] unsalted butter
2 tbsp chopped fresh flat-leaf parsley

First rinse the chestnuts in cold water. Then, using a small pointed knife, slit the shell of each chestnut across the whole of the rounded side, being careful not to cut too deep and dig into the actual nut. Put the chestnuts in a saucepan, cover with cold water and bring to the boil. Boil for 15 to 20 minutes. The chestnuts will still be slightly undercooked, but do not worry; they will finish cooking later in the stock.

Now the boring job of peeling them, which means that you must remove not only the outer shell, which is easy enough, but also the brownish inner skin with its unpleasant bitter taste. You will need a small pointed knife. To peel, lift a few chestnuts from the water, leaving the rest in the hot water (warm chestnuts are easier to peel).

Throw away any bad nuts – you will notice them by the acrid smell they give off as soon as you begin to peel them.

Cut the chestnuts coarsely into pieces and put them in a clean saucepan. Cover with the stock and bring to the boil. Simmer gently, with the lid on, for 30 minutes. Mix in the rice and cook until al dente. Taste and check salt. No pepper should be added to this slightly sweet soup. Draw the pan off the heat and stir in the butter and the parsley. Ladle the soup as soon as the butter has melted.

MINESTRA DI RISO E SEDANO Ⓥ

Rice and Celery Soup

The best rice soups are from the more northerly regions of Piedmont, Lombardy and Veneto. This recipe is from the valley of the River Tanaro, which rises on the other side of the Alps from San Remo and runs North into the Po, crossing all the southern part of Piedmont. The valley is very fertile and produces some of the best vegetables in Italy.

Use green celery whenever in season as it has a stronger flavour than white celery.

SERVES 4 TO 5

450g/1lb celery, preferably green celery
125g/4oz floury potato
2.2l/4pt [US 2¼qt] vegetable stock (page 231)
4 tbsp extra virgin olive oil
30g/1oz [US 2 tbsp] unsalted butter
2 tbsp finely chopped onion
125g/4oz [US ½ cup] Italian rice, preferably Vialone Nano
freshly grated Parmesan

Remove the inside leaves from the celery. Wash and dry them and then chop them. Set them aside for the final touch.

Remove the strings from the outer celery stalks with a potato peeler. Wash the stalks and cut half of them into pieces.

Peel the potato and cut into similar pieces. Put both chopped vegetables in a heavy pot with half the stock and half the oil. Bring to the boil and simmer gently until the vegetables are cooked. Now pour the contents of the pan into the bowl . of a food processor and whizz until smooth, or put it through a food mill fitted with the small-hole disc. This second method might be slower but it certainly gives the best result, since the purée is more homogeneous.

Wash the saucepan and finish the soup. Put the remaining oil, the butter and onion into the pan and sauté the onion for about 10 minutes. Cut the remaining celery into thin sticks, about 2.5cm/1in long, and throw into the pan. Stir it around to *insaporire* – pick up the flavour – for 5 to 6 minutes.

Add the celery and potato purée to the pot. Mix well and then pour in the remaining stock gradually, while stirring with the other hand to incorporate the purée into the stock. Bring to the boil.

Now you must add the rice. Give a good stir and let it cook until tender, about 10 minutes.

Ladle the soup into soup bowls, sprinkle with the reserved celery leaves and serve with grated Parmesan. Some people will love to add it.

ZUPPA DI CECI ASTIGIANA
Chick-pea and Vegetable Soup

I recently bought an excellent book by one of the greatest Italian gastronomes, Giovanni Goria, who is the expert on Piedmontese cooking. The book gives a recipe for this soup, and I was fascinated to read in its introduction about the connection between chick-peas and All Souls' Day.

It reminded me of a superstition I was told as a child by our cook from Friuli. At her home, every year on the night of 1st November, her mother used to put two bowls of chick-peas on the kitchen table. One of the two was for them to eat the next day, while the other was *per i morti* – for those who had died, who were supposed to be allowed to come down (definitely not up!) to earth to eat them. The chick-peas always remained untouched, and to explain this, Maria would say, 'Well, I expect the good Lord needed them up there for something special.' Goria writes about this story though with slight variations, so it is evidently part of the common lore of peasant superstitions.

Chick-peas are humble, unpretentious food, but I cannot see why they should be food for the dead. Perhaps it is because they are so good that one hopes to be able to eat them in the next life!

THE RECIPE
Chick-peas are eaten all over northern Italy on All Saints' or All Souls' Day. The recipes differ quite considerably, the only constant ingredient being, of course, the chick-peas. This recipe is for a thick, nourishing soup from Asti in south-eastern Piedmont. It is a soup that I only discovered in 1993, when I went there for a truffle fair.

My recipe is based on that included in *La Cucina del Piemonte* by Giovanni Goria. The soup can also be ladled over slices of lightly toasted white country bread, such as Pugliese,

that has been rubbed with garlic. It then becomes
the ideal meal for a cold winter night. Buy chick-
peas from a reliable shop with a quick turnover. If
they have been stored for too long, chick-peas
never become tender no matter how long you
cook them. And there is nothing more unpleasant
than undercooked pulses.

SERVES 8

500g/1lb 2oz [US 2½ cups] best dried chick-peas
1 tbsp flour
1 tsp bicarbonate of soda [US baking soda]
1 tsp salt
1 onion, cut into pieces
a fresh bouquet garni, containing parsley, rosemary,
sage and bay leaf
2 garlic cloves
150g/5oz fresh pork rind
1 leek, both white and green part, cut into
matchsticks
2 carrots, cut into matchsticks
2 medium potatoes, cut into matchsticks
1 celery heart with its yellow leaves, cut into
matchsticks
2 or 3 outside leaves of cabbage, cut into strips
salt and freshly ground pepper

FOR THE SOFFRITTO

15g/½oz dried porcini
90g/3oz pancetta
2 garlic cloves
the needles of 1 fresh rosemary sprig
the leaves of 1 fresh sage sprig
2 tbsp extra virgin olive oil

The day before, put the chick-peas in a large bowl
and cover with lukewarm water. If you live in a
part of the country where the water is very hard,
use filtered water or, better still, rain water. Make
a paste with the flour, bicarbonate of soda, salt
and some water and mix it into the bowl. Leave
to soak for 24 hours or so.

The next day, drain the chick-peas and rinse
them quickly under cold water. Put them in a
large stockpot. I use an earthenware pot for
pulses and soups, earthenware being the best
material because it heats slowly and diffuses the
heat all over the container. It is, therefore, ideal
for slow cooking. Cover with 4.5–5l/8–9pt
[US 4½–5qt] of cold water and add the onion,
bouquet garni and peeled garlic cloves. Bring to a
simmer and cook for about 2 to 3 hours, setting
the lid slightly askew over the pot. This cooking,
as for all pulses, must be very gentle indeed.

While the chick-peas are cooking, blanch the
pork rind for 15 minutes in boiling water to rid it
of some of the fat. After that, cut it in 5mm/¼in
strips and throw it into the stockpot to cook with
the chick-peas.

To prepare the *soffritto* soak the dried porcini
for about 1 hour in hot water. I have found that
the recommended 30 minutes is often not long
enough, especially when the porcini are not very
good and have been dried too quickly to a leathery texture. After the hour, or less if you have
beautiful slices of dried porcini, lift them out. If
gritty, rinse them under cold water. Chop them
finely. Filter the liquid through a sieve lined with
muslin, cheesecloth or kitchen paper towel.

Add all the cut-up vegetables to the pot to
cook with the chick-peas for a further hour.
During this long slow cooking you might have to
add some water. Always add boiling water.

Chop finely the pancetta, garlic, rosemary and
sage and put in a small frying pan with the olive
oil. Sauté gently for 2 minutes and then add the
chopped porcini and a pinch of salt. Continue
cooking for about 10 minutes, keeping the heat
very low so that the whole mixture will sauté

gently and not fry. Add a couple of tablespoons of the porcini liquid if you see it getting too dry.

About 10 minutes before the soup is ready, scrape in the soffritto. Mix well and then taste. Check salt and add plenty of pepper.

When the soup is ready ladle it into individual bowls. Pass round a bottle of your best oil at the table for your family or guests to pour some into their soup.

RISO IN CAGNONE ALLA
PIEMONTESE Ⓥ

Rice Dressed with Fontina and Butter

'Everyone talked of the excellent table I kept . . . My macaroni al sughillo, my rice sometimes as pilau, sometimes in cagnone, my olla podridas were the talk of the town.' Thus wrote Casanova in his *Memorie.*

I wonder if his riso in cagnone was Lombard or Piedmontese, since there are two versions. The rice in the Lombard version is dressed with butter flavoured with sage leaves and garlic, a very traditional dressing for rice or pasta. This is the Piedmontese version, made with local fontina, a cheese from Valle d'Aosta, which is available in specialist cheese shops or Italian food shops.

THE RECIPE
If you cannot find Italian fontina, use raclette, a similar cheese from Switzerland.

SERVES 4 AS A FIRST COURSE OR 3 AS A MAIN COURSE
350g/12oz [US 1¾ cups] Italian rice (Carnaroli or Arborio)
salt
125g/4oz fontina
60g/2oz [US 4 tbsp] unsalted butter

Cook the rice in plenty of boiling salted water.

Meanwhile, cut the cheese into tiny cubes and put half in a serving bowl. Put the bowl in a low oven.

Melt the butter and let it become the deep golden colour of hazelnuts. Add half to the bowl in the oven.

When the rice is done, drain it, but leave it quite wet, and transfer it to the bowl with the cheese and butter. Mix thoroughly and then add the remaining cheese. Toss again very well until the cheese has melted completely. Pour over the rest of the melted butter and serve immediately.

Note: traditionally no pepper is added.

GNOCCHI DI PATATE Ⓥ
Potato Gnocchi

Whenever I make gnocchi in my kitchen in Barnes I am suddenly transported back to our family kitchen in Via Gesù in Milan, and I can still see my little fingers flipping gnocchi over a white linen napkin, while my beloved Maria, our cook, was saying, 'Brava, you make them even better than I do.' Flick, flip, first into the flour then down the prongs of the fork. I used to love making them, though I cannot remember if I was equally keen on eating them.

Now, 'forty years on', I love eating gnocchi, but I find the flipping rather boring. So I am looking forward to the day when my little grand-daughter will sit with me in the kitchen and flip gnocchi.

Gnocchi can be made with or without eggs. Broadly speaking, gnocchi with eggs are made in Veneto, while in Piedmont not only do they not use eggs but the best gnocchi makers manage to add only 100g of flour to 1kg of potatoes!

THE RECIPE
Potato gnocchi, like many traditional basic dishes, are not as easy to make as it seems. You have to know the right potatoes to use, to add just enough flour to hold the gnocchi together but not to make them heavy, and to boil them on the right heat, just enough for the flour to cook. Gnocchi containing eggs are easier to cook because they do not present the problem that '. . . faced the lady, who as soon as she had immersed the spoon in the saucepan to stir them around, found nothing in it; the gnocchi had disappeared.' This extract is from Artusi's book *La Scienza in Cucina e l'Arte di Mangiar Bene.* Artusi puts the blame on the lady not adding enough flour. But I have had it happen to me, when I've used the wrong sort of potatoes. So I advise you to start by cooking only 2 or 3 gnocchi. If they disintegrate, or stick to each

other in a gluey mess, add an egg and a little flour to the dough.

Once you find a variety of potato that makes good gnocchi, stick to it. I make egg-less gnocchi with waxy potatoes, Desirée or Estima, while I add an egg to the floury varieties. The flavour of gnocchi with egg or without is, of course, different. Those without egg are softer and lighter in the mouth and the potato flavour is more pronounced. Gnocchi with eggs have more 'spirit' and more body. I prefer gnocchi without eggs, simply dressed with butter and cheese, or with a fontina or a gorgonzola sauce, plus a shaving of truffle if I am in luck. The sturdier gnocchi with eggs I like dressed with a tomato sauce (page 228) or with a pesto alla genovese (page 131).

GNOCCHI WITHOUT EGGS

SERVES 4
900g/2lb waxy potatoes
1½ tsp salt
150–180g/5–6oz [US 1¼–1½ cups] flour, preferably Italian 00

Boil the potatoes in their skins. When the point of a small knife can easily be pushed through to the middle, the potatoes are ready. Drain and peel them as soon as you can handle them. Purée them through the smaller disc of a food mill, or a potato ricer, straight on to your work surface. Spread the purée around to cool it and then add the salt and some of the flour. Do not add all the flour at once. Stop as soon as you can knead the mixture into a dough, which should be soft, smooth and still slightly sticky. Shape the dough into sausages about 2.5cm/1in in diameter, and cut the sausages into 2cm/¾in chunks.

Now you have to put the grooves into the gnocchi, a more complicated operation. The grooves, by the way, are there for a reason, not just for beauty – they thin out the middle of the gnocchi, so that they will cook more evenly and, when cooked, will trap more sauce. Keeping your

CLOCKWISE FROM TOP LEFT:
BUCKWHEAT POLENTA WITH
BUTTER AND CHEESE (PAGE 32)
STEWED VENISON (PAGE 84)

POACHED CHICKEN
IN A VINEGARY SAUCE
(PAGE 45)

POTATO RAVIOLI, LEFT (PAGE 117);
BUCKWHEAT PASTA WITH POTATO AND
CABBAGE (PAGE 25)

PARADISE CAKE, LEFT (PAGE 49)
BUCKWHEAT CAKE (PAGE 86)

KNOBBLY NUTTY BISCUITS (PAGE 75);
BISCUITS WITH FENNEL (PAGE 121);
LITTLE RING BISCUITS (PAGE 227)

hands, the fork and any surface lightly floured, flip each dumpling against the prongs of the fork, without dragging it, letting it drop on to a clean linen towel. Some cooks flip the dumpling towards the handle; others, like me, go from the handle to the point of the prongs. You will find your favourite way.

When all the gnocchi are grooved, bring a large saucepan of salted water to the boil. Cook the gnocchi in 3 or 4 batches, not all at once. The gnocchi will first sink to the bottom of the pan, when you must give them a very gentle stir, and then very shortly after they will float up to the surface. Count to 10 and then retrieve them with a slotted spoon. Pat them dry quickly with a piece of kitchen paper towel and transfer them to a heated dish. Dress each batch with a little of whichever sauce you have chosen. When all the gnocchi are cooked, pour over all the remaining sauce and serve at once.

GNOCCHI WITH EGG

Add 1 egg to the potato purée and then add the flour. With the egg you might have to add a little more flour, up to 200g/7oz [US 1¾ cups].

GNOCCHI ALLA BAVA

This is the fontina dressing made in Piedmont. It is hardly a sauce. Each batch of drained gnocchi is layered with fresh butter and very thinly sliced fontina cheese. For 4 people you will need 60g/2oz [US 4 tbsp] of unsalted butter and 125g/4oz of fontina. Leave the dish in a pre-heated very hot oven for 5 minutes, enough for the cheese to melt. They are quite delicious.

TROTELLE AL VINO ROSSO
Trout Baked in Red Wine

Red wine is combined with fish in quite a few Italian dishes. Being more robust, red wine, rather than white, goes into squid, inkfish and octopus stews, as well as into fish soups. This recipe, however, is different in that it combines red wine with trout, a more delicate fish. The reason is surely that red wine is the Piedmontese wine par excellence, white wine being limited to far fewer zones. And this is a Piedmontese recipe.

As the sauce is robust, the addition of a little anchovy paste is needed to enhance the fish flavour, lacking in our new breed of farmed trout.

SERVES 4

4 trout, about 225g/8oz each
salt and freshly ground black pepper
1 small carrot
2 shallots
1 small celery stalk
1 garlic clove
2 bay leaves
a small bunch of parsley
4 fresh sage leaves
the leaves of 4 fresh thyme sprigs
2 tbsp olive oil
500ml/16fl oz red wine
30g/1oz [US 2 tbsp] butter
1 tbsp flour
6 anchovy fillets, drained and chopped

Wash and dry the trout and then season them inside and out with salt and pepper. Lightly oil a roasting tin and lay the trout in it.

Heat the oven to 200°C/400°F/Gas Mark 6.

Chop together finely the carrot, shallots, celery, garlic and herbs and put into a saucepan with the oil, 2 tablespoons of water and 1 tea-

65

spoon of salt. Cook gently for 5 minutes, stirring occasionally. Add the wine, bring to the boil and simmer for 10 minutes.

While the sauce is cooking, put the fish in the oven and bake for 5 minutes. Now spoon the sauce around the fish and bake for a further 10 minutes. The trout should be just right after this time. Lift them out of the tin and place them on individual plates. Keep them warm in the turned-off oven while you finish the sauce.

Pound together the butter, flour and anchovy fillets.

Strain the cooking juices into a small saucepan and, when it is just beginning to boil, add the anchovy butter a little at a time, while you whisk constantly with a small balloon whisk. Taste and check seasoning. Spoon a little sauce around each fish and serve at once.

TORTA DI PEPERONI
Sausage and Peppers Pie

The best sweet peppers in Italy come from an area that stretches from Voghera in southern Lombardy to Asti in the fertile valley of the Tanaro, a tributary of the Po in southern Piedmont. And in a way that happens so often in Italy, the best dishes with peppers are from the region where the best peppers grow.

The local pastry is made with water, flour and olive oil, and stretched very thin – not an easy task. I suggest using filo pastry, which is similar to the original.

Buy plain pork sausages with at least 90% meat content. They should have no flavourings, since that might clash with the flavour of the peppers.

SERVES 6 TO 8

225g/8oz Spanish onions
120ml/4fl oz extra virgin olive oil
salt and freshly ground black pepper
1 tsp brown sugar
120ml/4fl oz semi-skimmed milk [US low-fat milk]
700g/1½lb red and yellow sweet peppers
200g/7oz pure pork sausages
3 size-2 eggs [US extra-large eggs]
4 tbsp freshly grated Parmesan
1 packet filo pastry, about 225g/8oz, defrosted if frozen

Slice the onions very thinly and put them into a sauté pan with 2 or 3 tablespoons of the oil, a good pinch of salt and the sugar. Cook for about 5 minutes and then add 3 or 4 tablespoons of the milk. Mix and continue cooking, at the lowest heat, until the onions are very soft indeed, about 40 minutes. If the heat is a bit too high you might have to add a little more milk. Keep a watch on the pan.

Meanwhile, wash and dry the peppers. Quarter them and remove core, ribs and seeds. Once they are clean, cut them into very small pieces, about 1cm/½in. Add to the onion and cook at a higher heat for about 10 minutes.

Skin the sausages and crumble them or chop them, whichever you find easier. Add them to the pan too and sauté until the meat looks properly cooked, another 10 minutes or so. Stir often. Add seasonings to taste, remembering that this pie is served cold. (Food served cold needs a little more seasoning than when served hot.) When this is done, scoop the whole thing into a large bowl.

Beat the eggs together lightly and slide into the bowl. Add the cheese and mix very well. Set aside.

Heat the oven to 180°C/350°F/Gas Mark 4.

Take a 20cm/8in spring-clip tin and brush the inside with some of the remaining oil. Line it with a sheet of filo pastry, letting the surplus hang over the rim. Brush the filo with oil and then add

a further 3 sheets of filo, placing each sheet at a
slightly different angle and brushing each sheet
thoroughly with oil. Spoon the peppers and
sausage mixture into the tin. Turn the hanging
pastry sheets over the top, laying them loosely, all
lovely and wavy, and oiling each layer well. If the
folded-over pastry sheets are not long enough to
cover the top, place another sheet or two, still
loosely, as this makes the pie look very pretty
when baked. Don't forget to brush these with oil
as well.

Place the tin in the oven and bake for 30
minutes. Turn the heat up to 220°C/425°F/Gas
Mark 7 and bake at this higher temperature for
10 minutes to give the pie a rich brown colour.

Cool it in the tin and then unclip and
unmould it. Serve tepid or at room temperature.

POLLO AI FUNGHI E ALLA PANNA
Chicken with Cream and Mushrooms

Quick and easy, this dish is always a success.
There is little in it to go wrong, provided you buy
a good fresh chicken, which nowadays is not a tall
order, and follow my instructions.

SERVES 4 OR 5
a free-range chicken of about 1.5kg/3¼lb
1 lemon
20g/¾oz dried porcini
2 tbsp olive oil
salt and freshly ground black pepper
30g/1oz [US 2 tbsp] unsalted butter
1 small onion, finely chopped
200g/7oz brown mushrooms, coarsely chopped
300ml/10fl oz double cream [US heavy cream]

Ask the butcher to cut the chicken into 8 pieces.

When you are back home, skin the chicken pieces
and then wash and dry them. Cut the lemon in
half and rub each piece well with the cut lemon.

Put the dried porcini in a bowl and pour over
about 300ml/10fl oz of boiling water. Leave
them to reconstitute for about 1 hour (see page
13).

Heat the oil in a frying pan large enough to
hold all the chicken pieces in a single layer. When
very hot, add the chicken pieces and brown well
first on one side and then on the other. Now
season all the pieces with salt and pepper and
transfer them to a casserole.

Heat the oven to 180°C/350°F/Gas Mark 4.

Heat the butter in a smallish frying pan or
sauté pan and, when the butter foam starts to
diminish, add the onion. Season with 1 teaspoon
of salt and sauté until pale gold.

Meanwhile, fish the porcini out of the water
and rinse them in cold water, being careful to
remove any bits of soil embedded in their folds.
Pat them dry and cut them into small pieces.
Now go back to the liquid and filter it through a
sieve lined with muslin or cheesecloth.

Throw the porcini pieces into the onion pan
and, after 5 minutes, throw in the cultivated
mushrooms as well. Cook for 5 more minutes,
stirring frequently. Then add the cream, 4 or 5
tablespoons of the porcini liquid and salt and
pepper to taste. Simmer for a further minute,
then turn the whole thing over the chicken.

Place the casserole in the oven and cook until
the chicken is done, about 30 to 40 minutes.
Turn the chicken pieces over once or twice during
the cooking, and taste the sauce to correct seasoning.

If the sauce has dried up too much, transfer
the chicken to a serving dish and add a couple of
tablespoons of water to the sauce. Boil for 1
minute and then spoon over and around the
chicken.

PETTI DI POLLO ALL'EBRAICA
Chicken Breasts Jewish-Style

I was given this excellent recipe by a Jewish friend in Milan, whose family originally came from Piedmont. Recently I was looking through the best book on Piedmontese cooking, *La Cucina del Piemonte* by G. Goria, and there I found a very similar recipe, but the poultry used was a turkey breast. Goria writes that the dish originates from the Jewish community of Moncalvo, a lovely town in southern Piedmont. This community fitted happily into the local traditions, as did most Jewish communities in Italy up to the War. And many of their dishes had much in common with the local dishes. The Jewish community was dispersed during the persecutions of 1943 to 1945, but the dishes at least remain as witness to the Jewish culinary tradition.

Goria writes that the turkey was served with a sweet-and-sour relish, which is indeed very Middle Eastern. In my friend's recipe the chicken breasts were served by themselves. I cannot decide whether they are better with or without the relish. So I am giving you the recipe for the relish, and I leave it to you to decide. Maybe you prefer to serve it as an antipasto, as I do.

THE RECIPE
You can use the breast of a small turkey instead, although that is not too easy to find. The onions must be sweet, so use Spanish or red onions.

SERVES 4
4 chicken breasts [US breast halves]
salt and freshly ground pepper
1 tbsp chopped fresh sage
2 tbsp olive oil
900/2lb onions, very finely sliced

Heat the oven to 240°C/430°F/Gas Mark 8.

Rub the chicken breasts all over with salt and pepper and the sage. Grease a small roasting tin or shallow oven dish with half the oil. Lay the seasoned breasts in the dish and cover with the onion. Sprinkle with salt and pepper and pour over the remaining oil. Bake for half an hour or until the juices coming out of the thickest part of the breasts are pale and clear. The onion should be just tender – crisp on the top and juicy underneath. Serve immediately. A very easy dish indeed.

THE VEGETABLE RELISH
1 yellow sweet pepper of about 150g/5oz
125g/4oz aubergine [US eggplant]
100g/3½oz celery stalks
200ml/7fl oz red wine vinegar
salt and freshly ground pepper
4 tbsp extra virgin olive oil
1 tbsp concentrated tomato paste
3 tbsp sugar

Cut the vegetables into small pieces, about 1cm/½in. Put them in a saucepan with the vinegar and pour in 200ml/7fl oz of water. The liquid should be level with the vegetables. Add 1 teaspoon of salt and bring to the boil. Simmer for 10 minutes and then drain.

Heat the oil in a frying pan and stir in the tomato paste and the sugar. Cook for 5 minutes or so to caramelize the sugar a little, while stirring constantly. Now add the vegetables and turn them over and over to coat them in the caramelized oil. Turn the heat down and cook for a further 15 minutes. You must stir very frequently because there is very little liquid and you do not want the vegetables to catch. The vegetables should be just crisp at the end of the cooking. Season with plenty of pepper and check the salt.

Serve hot with the chicken; or warm or at room temperature as an antipasto.

PESCHE FARCITE ALLA PIEMONTESE

Stuffed Peaches

Piedmontese peaches are of the yellow kind, large and smooth, with beautiful gradations of colour from pale yellow to deep red. In this dish they are combined with two other ingredients loved by the Piedmontese, almonds and rum. The Piedmontese have a longstanding love affair with rum (see page 72). And the almond biscuits called amaretti were traditional in southern Piedmont long before Davide Lazzaroni started his very successful biscuit industry in Lombardy in the late 19th century, producing the best known amaretti – the amaretti di Saronno – a pair of crisp sugar-studded biscuits wrapped in the special paper.

Any respectable cookery book on northern Italian cooking must contain a recipe for pesche ripiene. My recipe is not really 'mine', but an adaptation of the recipe titled 'Pesche Farcite alla Borghese' which appears in the 19th-century book *Trattato di Cucina-Pasticceria Moderna* by Giovanni Vialardi. Vialardi was the chef-pâtissier to Carlo Alberto of Savoy, and to his son Victor Emanuel II, the first king of Italy. The book is a large collection of Italian and foreign recipes, but its value lies mainly in its recording of the many traditional Piedmontese recipes such as this one.

THE RECIPE

The peaches must be ripe yet firm, and of the freestone variety. Add a few drops of pure almond extract, not essence, which will give the stuffing a bitter almond flavour.

You are bound to have some filling left over. What I do is to pour it into 1 or 2 buttered ramekins and place these in the oven to bake alongside the peaches. It is my *bonne bouche* the next day when I eat it cold, with a drop of yogurt to counterbalance the unavoidable sweetness of the filling.

SERVES 6

6 yellow peaches
4 tbsp caster sugar [US granulated sugar]
100ml/3½fl oz white wine
30g/1oz [US 2 tbsp] unsalted butter
3 tbsp Marsala
125g/4oz amaretti
a few drops of pure almond extract
2 egg yolks plus 1 egg white
2 tbsp dark rum
2 pinches of ground cinnamon

Wash and dry the peaches. Cut them in half, and open them by twisting the two halves in opposite directions. Remove the stones.

Heat the oven to 170°C/325°F/Gas Mark 3.

Put 2 tablespoons of the sugar and the wine in a small saucepan and bring gently to the boil. When the sugar has dissolved pour the syrup into a shallow oven dish large enough to hold the peach halves.

Now with a sharp teaspoon, a small knife or, better still, a curved grapefruit knife, scoop some of the pulp out of each half peach, leaving about 1cm/½in of pulp all around. Set the pulp aside and place the peach halves in the dish, cut sides up. Place a tiny blob of butter in each half. Bake for 15 minutes – just enough to soften the fruit. Remove the peaches, then turn the oven up to 190°C/375°F/Gas Mark 5.

Put the rest of the butter and the remaining sugar in a small frying pan. Add the scooped-out peach pulp and sauté for a couple of minutes, then pour in the Marsala. Continue cooking gently for 10 minutes.

Now you can make the filling. Spoon the peach pulp and all the juices into a food processor. Add the amaretti and the almond extract and process until smooth. Transfer to a bowl and mix in the egg yolks, rum and cinnamon. Whisk the egg white until stiff and fold gently into the mixture.

Fill each peach half with some of the mixture and then bake for 20 minutes or thereabouts until the top is set to the touch. Serve hot.

PERE AL BAROLO
Pears Baked in Red Wine

The pears used in the traditional recipe are the Martin Sech, a fairly small, rust-coloured pear which grows in Valle d'Aosta. Nowadays this variety is practically unavailable outside this region. Conference pears have a similar grainy texture as Martin Sech, but I find English Conference unreliable because they are often picked too early, before the flavour has developed. William's, Bartlett or Rocha are good substitutes and, on the whole, are more reliable pears.

Barolo, the wine in which the pears are poached, is one of the great wines from Piedmont made from Nebbiolo grapes. It is full-bodied and rich, ideal to counterbalance the sweetness of the fruit.

SERVES 6

375ml/13fl oz (½ bottle) Barolo or other full-bodied red wine
the pared rind and juice of 1 unwaxed lemon
the pared rind and juice of ½ unwaxed orange
2 cloves
½ cinnamon stick
4 peppercorns
1 bay leaf
180g/6oz caster sugar [US ¾ cup + 2 tbsp granulated sugar]
6 pears, ripe but firm

Heat the oven to 150°C/300°F/Gas Mark 2.

Put all the ingredients except the pears in a saucepan. Add 150ml/5 fl oz of water and bring slowly to the boil, stirring constantly to dissolve the sugar. Boil for about 15 minutes, stirring occasionally.

Wash the pears, leaving the skin and the stalk on. Choose an oven dish into which the pears will fit snugly standing up. Pour the wine syrup around the pears in the dish and bake uncovered for about 1¼ to 1½ hours, until the pears can easily be pierced through by the point of a small knife.

Stand a pear on each plate and spoon the syrup around it. They look very pretty.

These pears can be served warm or cold, but not straight from the oven or chilled. If you like you can hand around a bowl of whipped cream or crème fraîche.

You could also hand around a mascarpone and cream mixture. For this you will need 200ml/7fl oz of whipping cream and the same quantity of mascarpone. Whip the cream until stiff and then add the mascarpone, first breaking it up with a fork and then folding it in thoroughly with a spoon. The cream and mascarpone mixture is tastier than plain whipping cream and sweeter than crème fraîche.

TORTA DI NOCI
Walnut Pie

I was in two minds about whether to place this pie in Emilia instead of here, in Piedmont. In Emilia there is a cake called La Bonissima which is very similar. But when I recently discovered this Piedmontese version, I found it more successful. The fresh breadcrumbs, which do not appear in La Bonissima, make a filling more substantial and yet more subtle. Also, because of the baking powder, the pastry is not genuine pastry; it is half way between a sponge and a pâte sucrée. Being bready rather than biscuity it makes the ideal container for the nutty filling.

Walnuts are one of my hobby horses. It is extremely difficult in this country to get shelled walnuts that are fresh. Walnuts, in fact, have a very short shelf-life. They might appear to be still all right, with their sell-by date as much as 6 months ahead, but good they are not. The wonderful flavour of the walnut has evaporated, to be replaced by the beginnings of rancidity. My advice is to buy a good supply of walnuts in their shells at Christmas. After you have had as many as you want just like that, put the rest in this pudding.

The honey used in Piedmont is the very scented and sweet acacia honey. You can serve the pie at tea-time, or any time. As a dessert it is excellent with pouring cream.

SERVES 6 TO 8

FOR THE PASTRY
150g/5oz [US 1¼ cups] flour, preferably Italian 00
1 tsp baking powder
a pinch of salt
75g/2½oz caster sugar [US 6 tbsp granulated sugar]
75g/2½oz [US 5 tbsp] unsalted butter, cut into small pieces
the grated rind of 1 unwaxed lemon
1 size-2 egg [US extra-large egg], lightly beaten
butter for the tin

FOR THE FILLING
150g/5oz [US 1 heaped cup] walnut kernels
60g/2oz good country-type white bread, crust removed
150g/5oz [US ½ cup] honey
2 tbsp dark rum
1 tbsp lemon juice
icing sugar [US confectioners' sugar], to finish

First make the pastry. Sift the flour, baking powder and salt on to a working surface. Mix in the sugar and then rub in the butter, using the tips of your fingers. Add the lemon rind and the egg. Work the mixture quickly together to form a ball. Wrap the dough in cling film and refrigerate for at least half an hour. (You can make the pastry in a food processor by simply putting all the ingredients in the bowl and processing until it forms a ball.)

While the pastry is chilling, put the walnuts, and the bread cut into 3 or 4 large pieces, into the food processor and process to coarse crumbs. If you do not have a food processor, chop the mixture by hand.

Heat the honey in a small saucepan, add the walnut and bread mixture and cook gently until it is all nicely coated. Draw the pan off the heat and add the rum and the lemon juice. Mix very well and leave to cool.

Heat the oven to 180°C/350°F/Gas Mark 4. Generously butter a 20cm/8in tart tin or a pie plate.

Bring the pastry back on to the work surface, and divide it in half. This pastry is quite difficult to roll out. I find it much easier to roll it out between two sheets of well-floured greaseproof or parchment paper. When you have rolled out half the dough, lift away the top piece of paper and turn the bottom paper over so that the dough falls into the tin. Press it down properly, and up the edge. Spoon the walnut mixture into the tin. Proceed to roll out the top in the same way and flip this over the filling. Seal the edges tightly, pressing them together.

Make a few holes in the top of the pie with the point of a knife and bake for about 30 to 40 minutes, until the pastry is golden brown. Let the pie cool in the tin before you turn it over on to a dish for bringing to the table.

Sprinkle a lot of sifted icing sugar over the top before serving.

BONET
Amaretti Pudding

A *bönet* is a soft cap in Piedmontese dialect, the word clearly coming from the French *bonnet*. The name describes the shape of this pudding, which is rather like a mob-cap.

Bönet is characteristic of Piedmontese cooking in its almondy flavour, laced with Marsala and rum. Rum appears in many Piedmontese dishes. Giovanni Goria, my mentor in these matters, gives an explanation of the love affair between Piedmont and rum. The Duke of Savoia, during the second half of the 16th century, established a Piedmontese navy based in the port of Villefranche, which was Savoyard territory. Its sailors were the first to bring this spirit, made from the Caribbean sugar cane, to Piedmont, and

it soon found favour with the locals.

Bönet is a very popular pudding, and the variations are endless. There is, for instance, a *bönet giallo* – a yellow bönet, in which the coffee and cocoa are eliminated and the flavouring is vanilla.

The original version is made with milk rather than cream, not much of which is used in Piedmontese cooking. But milk as it used to be, especially if it was country milk, was a different thing from our pasteurized milk. So I decided to replace some of the milk with cream, and it works well. The other 'liberty' taken is that I have replaced part of the amaretti with some Savoiardi because I find that the flavour of amaretti can be slightly overpowering. The Savoiardi bring a lighter touch and a softer texture, and they are totally in keeping with the origins of the bönet.

THE RECIPE

The flavour of light Muscovado sugar is perfect in a bönet; I use the delicious Billington sugar. Good Savoiardi and amaretti are now available in most large supermarkets and in Italian food shops. I use the espresso powder in sachets, which is perfect for this purpose, but not good enough for a proper cup of coffee.

For the traditional bönet shape you need a 1.5l/2½pt [US 1½qt] dome-shaped metal bowl. However, you can use a soufflé dish, little individual ramekins or popover moulds.

SERVES 6

450ml/15fl oz full fat milk
300ml/10fl oz double cream [US heavy cream]
4 size-2 eggs [US extra-large eggs]
50g/1¾oz [US ¼ cup] sugar, preferably light Muscovado
2½ tbsp unsweetened cocoa powder
1 sachet (2 tsp) instant espresso coffee
2 tbsp dark rum
1 tbsp Marsala
125g/4oz amaretti
50g/1¾oz Savoiardi

FOR THE CARAMEL
125g/4oz caster sugar [US ½ cup + 2 tbsp granulated sugar]
1 tsp lemon juice

First prepare the caramel. Start by heating the mould (see introduction) for the bönet in a low oven. I find that if the mould is cold, the caramel hardens before it can cover all the surface of the mould smoothly.

Put the sugar, 2 tablespoons of water and the lemon juice in a small heavy saucepan. Heat over very gentle heat, stirring until the sugar has completely dissolved. Now remove the spoon, turn the heat up and let the syrup caramelize. Do not stir any more, but stand there and be patient, ready to withdraw the pan. The syrup will become blond first, and then quickly turn into a beautiful dark colour. Swirl the saucepan occasionally while the syrup is becoming caramelized.

Take the mould out of the oven and pour the caramel into it. Swirl the caramel around to cover all the surface nicely. And now that the mould is ready, prepare the pudding.

Heat the oven to 180°C/350°F/Gas Mark 4.
Bring the milk and cream to a simmer. While this mixture is heating beat the eggs with the sugar. Add the milk mixture in a thin stream, letting it fall from a height so that the egg mixture will not be affected by too high a heat.

Add the cocoa powder, letting it fall into the egg and milk mixture through a sieve. Add also the espresso powder, rum and Marsala. Mix thoroughly.

Crumble the amaretti and Savoiardi with a rolling pin. You can also do this in a food processor, but do not over-process. Spoon the crumbled biscuits into the egg and milk mixture and fold everything together well.

Pour the mixture into the prepared mould. Put the mould in a roasting tin and pour boiling water into the tin to come three-quarters of the way up the side of the mould. Now place the roasting tin with the mould in the oven and cook

until the bönet is set – at least 1 hour. The time can differ depending on whether the mould is metal or ceramic, large or individual. When ready, the blade of a small knife inserted into the middle of the pudding should come out clean.

Unmould while still hot on to a round dish that is deep enough to hold the lovely caramel sauce as well. When cold, put in the refrigerator to chill.

In Piedmont, bönet is served on its own, but you can decorate it with some piped whipped cream and serve some more cream in a bowl on the side. It goes very well.

LE TAZZINE DI MADDALENA
Chocolate and Hazelnut Truffle Cups

Maddalena Bonino is the chef at the Bertorelli Restaurant in London. As a true Piedmontese she has developed quite a few interesting dishes based on the flavours of her native region. This recipe is one such; it comes from her lovely book *Fast and Fresh Entertaining.*

The flavour of the tazzine is strongly reminiscent of the delicious Gianduiotti, the Torinese chocolates, traditionally wrapped in gold paper, made with a mixture of hazelnuts and chocolate.

SERVES 4
180g/6oz dark chocolate
2–3 tbsp rum or brandy
125g/4oz [US ¾ cup] hazelnuts, toasted, skins removed and roughly chopped
2 egg whites
2 tbsp caster sugar [US granulated sugar]
300ml/10fl oz double cream [US heavy cream]

Melt the chocolate with the rum or brandy and the hazelnuts in a bowl over a pan of simmering water. When melted, remove from the heat and cool, stirring occasionally, until lukewarm.

Whisk the egg whites until they hold their shape, then add the sugar and whisk until stiff. Set aside.

Whip the cream until thick.

Fold the egg whites into the chocolate mixture, mixing evenly, then fold in the cream. Spoon into serving cups, chill for 10 minutes and serve.

PANNA COTTA AL CAFFÉ
Coffee-flavoured Cream Pudding

Some dishes catch people's imagination more than others. Panna cotta is one of them. This dessert, which has existed in Piedmont for centuries, has now become popular, first all over Italy and then abroad, in the space of just a few years. This new-found popularity is perhaps due to the fact that panna cotta has a clean taste and looks very attractive in the way it is served nowadays – brilliantly white, surrounded by a red fruit coulis. But in the past, panna cotta was always served by itself, so that one could appreciate the excellence of good cream.

Although I am a purist and a traditionalist, I too have succumbed to fashion in this case. I do not very much like panna cotta with fruit, but I find the coffee-flavoured version even better than the plain panna cotta of the old days.

THE RECIPE
The secret of a good panna cotta is to add the minimum of gelatine, just enough for the dish to be unmoulded. It should be wobbling and trembly, never firm. I always use gelatine leaves,

which dissolve much more evenly than powdered gelatine and have no flavour at all. They vary in size, so I give the weight of the gelatine needed, which can also apply to the powder.

SERVES 6

10g/⅓oz gelatine leaves or 2 tsp unflavoured gelatine powder
450ml/15fl oz double cream [US heavy cream]
150ml/5fl oz full fat milk
125g/4oz caster sugar [US ½ cup + 2 tbsp granulated sugar]
2 tsp instant espresso coffee powder
½ tsp pure vanilla extract
4 tbsp dark rum

FOR DECORATION
125g/4oz chocolate-coated coffee beans

If you are using gelatine leaves, put them in a bowl and fill the bowl with water. As soon as the leaves soften, bend them so that they are totally submerged in water. Leave to soak for 15 to 20 minutes. Squeeze the leaves out and put them in a saucepan with 4 tablespoons of water. Dissolve over very low heat while stirring constantly.

If you are using powdered gelatine, put 4 tablespoons of water in a small saucepan and sprinkle over the gelatine. Leave to sponge for 10 minutes or so and then heat the mixture gently until the gelatine has dissolved completely. Do not let the liquid come to the boil.

Mix the cream and milk together in a saucepan. Add the sugar and heat slowly to dissolve. Stir in the coffee powder and the vanilla and bring to the boil. Draw off the heat and add the rum and the gelatine. Mix very thoroughly.

Brush six 150ml/5fl oz ramekins with a little flavourless oil. Pour the panna cotta into the ramekins. Allow to cool, then cover with cling film and chill until set, at least 3 hours.

To unmould, place the ramekins in a sink of hot water for about 30 seconds. Run a thin knife around the sides of the ramekins, put a dessert plate over the top and turn the plate and the ramekin over. Give a knock or two to the base of the ramekin and then lift it away. It should come away easily, but if the pudding is still stuck, put the ramekin back in hot water for a few more seconds. Put the unmoulded puddings back into the fridge.

Before serving, sprinkle some of the chocolate-coated coffee beans here and there around the panna cotta. They look pretty and their flavour is an ideal match to the delicacy of the pudding.

BRUTTI MA BUONI

Knobbly Nutty Biscuits

The name of this recipe means 'ugly but good'. I certainly think they are good, but I don't find them ugly, perhaps because I like them so much. These hard, knobbly biscuits, or cookies, are a speciality of northern Piedmont. In Tuscany similar biscuits, called brutti *e* buoni, are made with almonds instead of hazelnuts. The recipe is more or less the same, so you can use either of the nuts, or a mixture of the two.

I specify the quantity of egg whites by weight because it is important to have just the right amount. Eggs differ in size, but the weight is constant and precise.

MAKES ABOUT 70

400g/14oz [US 3 cups] shelled hazelnuts
180g/6oz [US ⅔ cup] egg whites
350g/12oz caster sugar [US 1¾ cups superfine sugar]
a pinch of ground cinnamon
10 drops of vanilla extract
butter for the oven trays

Heat the oven to 180°C/350°F/Gas Mark 4.

Spread the hazelnuts out on baking trays and toast them in the oven for about 10 minutes, until the aroma rises and they begin to get brown. Now get rid of some of the skin by putting them in a Turkish or other rough towel and rubbing them against each other. There is no need to take all the skin off, which would be a difficult task in any case, as you need some of the skin still on. Put all the nuts in a food processor and process until the nuts are evenly ground.

Whisk the egg whites until stiff. This should be done by hand with a large balloon whisk because it incorporates more air than an electric mixer. When the whites are really stiff, gradually fold in the sugar. Mix well and then fold in the ground hazelnuts, cinnamon and vanilla. Mix very thoroughly, but lightly, and then transfer the mixture to a very heavy-based saucepan. Put the saucepan on a very low heat – I use a flame diffuser – and let the mixture cook very very slowly, so that it dries a little, for 20 minutes or so, while you stir very frequently with a metal spoon.

Heat the oven to 150°C/300°F/Gas Mark 2.

Prepare the oven trays by buttering them quite generously. When the hazelnut mixture has cooled a little, place small mounds of it on the trays. These meringues do not grow, so you can put them quite close. Bake them for about 30 minutes, until hard.

Brutti ma buoni are delicious with zabaglione, vanilla or chocolate ice-cream, or any other cream or custard-based pudding. They are also good just like that, on their own.

TRENTINO-ALTO ADIGE

A lthough considered as one region, I find Trentino and Alto Adige very different in most respects. When you are in Trentino you are still definitely in Italy: everyone speaks Italian, there are no road-signs in German and the food is predominantly Italian. Admittedly you do begin to detect some 'Mitteleuropean' influence, making a cuisine that is not easy to define. In Alto Adige, however, the cooking – and everything else – is Austrian, even if there is a slight Italian influence.

There is one element that sets Trentino apart and makes it the Mecca for gourmets: the fungi. In Trento there is an extraordinary open market for fungi where up to 250 different species can be found. The market takes place from May through to the autumn when it is in its full glory. As the famous chef Gualtiero Marchesi writes in his *La Cucina Regionale Italiana* (a very valid book): 'Fungi are not, thank goodness, a veg-etable, so they can be repeated within a menu.'

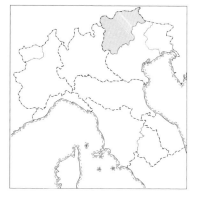

And that is what I chose to do at the trattoria Il Crucolo, high in the mountains above Trento. What a lunch that was! It was a cold, wet Sunday in June. My husband, in the typical English way, wanted to book a table. I, in typical Italian fashion, laughed the sugges-tion off. With such appalling weather who would drive up to 800 metres amongst the clouds for lunch? Up and up we drove – more rain, stronger wind, thicker clouds, until suddenly we were confronted by a sea of parked cars. All Italy and his wife had come to eat at Crucolo. Cars with a Modena number plate were parked next to the MI of Milan and the VE of Venezia. After one hour of waiting, which I spent happily with Signora Purini in the kitchen, where 200 meals were prepared that day, we sat down to an antipasto of tradi-tional *salumi*, mostly smoked, demonstrating the Austrian influence, and pre-served porcini, followed by a superb zupa de brise – mushroom soup (page 78), followed by *cotechino* with sauerkraut and funghi trifolati – sautéed porcini. The dessert was a torta saracena, made with buckwheat flour and again reminding me of our proximity to South Tyrol where buckwheat flour is very popular. This cake, incidentally, is the *pièce de resistance* of the elegant pasticceria König in Merano (page 86).

Another item of food that sets Trentino apart from any other region is the apple. Trentino is a luscious orchard full of every kind of apple. Whether juicy, dry, sweet, tart, red, green or yellow, they are eaten raw, poached, baked, fried, encased in pastry as in the strudel, decorating a tart or used in a budino (page 85).

Driving north towards the Dolomites the apple orchards give way to vineyards, salads disappear from traditional menus, cream is piled up next to puddings, and Italian becomes a foreign language. The gastronomic attractions are the smoked cured meats and the bread. Bread comes in endless shapes, flavours and colours, cheering the shop windows and scenting the nearby air. I saw more different kinds of bread in South Tyrol in a week than I would see in a year in the rest of Italy.

While I was staying in Merano I went to Lana to see Frau Heidi Schmidt (her real name!) whose bakery is well known thereabouts and whose knowledge of breadmaking is profound. She showed me rye bread, buckwheat bread, white bread and brown bread, dressed with cumin, aniseeds, linseeds, fennel seeds, coriander and even a special variety of clover that grows high in the mountains. These dressed breads are mostly eaten at breakfast with cheeses and cured meats as in Germany. *Speck*, the local speciality, is always on the breakfast table, and what a treat it is to start the day with the mild and subtle smoked flavour of a slice of speck. Speck is the flank of a pig, first cured in a spiced brine and then smoked gently and gradually for a few hours a day and aged for at least six months. That is the genuine speck; what passes for speck in some places is another matter. Speck is also added to *knödel*, or bread gnocchi, which by tradition are served with meat. But I like them, and serve them, by themselves, with plenty of cheese inside, dressed with butter and a green snow of snipped chives, in a rather Italian way, as I had them at an inn (and it was definitely an Austrian inn, not an Italian *osteria*) in Cortaccia near Lake Caldaro, with a bottle of *eccellente Marzemino*, like Don Giovanni at his last supper.

I can see why the Germans have chosen Alto Adige as their stamping ground, apart, that is, from the fact that everyone speaks their language. The food is good, the pâtisserie is delicious, the wines are superb, the prices at hotels and restaurants are low, and the scenery is breathtakingly beautiful.

Schwammersuppe Ⓥ
Mushroom Soup

I have recently discovered a book that is new to me, although it was first published in Germany in 1822, three years before the well-known *Physiology of Taste* by Brillat-Savarin. The book in question is *The Essence of Cooking* by Karl Freiherr von Rumohr, published by Prospect Books in an excellent translation. Comparing it to the Brillat-Savarin classic, Alan Davidson writes: 'In some ways it is a better book, meatier and less preten-tious.' I would go even further and say it is better in most ways. Rumohr's advice is more valid, sounder and more adaptable to modern cooking. Maybe I am biased towards Rumohr because of his great love and understanding of Italian cooking. However, I do recommend this book to anybody interested in food and cooking, and, par-ticularly, in food and cooking as an aspect of national characters and cultures. For instance: 'The art of cooking is closely linked to national character and to the intellectual development of separate races . . .' and, further on, 'The Italians wholeheartedly applied their love of art and their sense of beauty to the table.'

But to return to the Schwammersuppe and its connection to Rumohr, he writes at length about the browning of flour. Here are three extracts. 'The cook should be very careful when browning flour because, if this process is rushed, small parti-cles will become burnt and will then impart a bitter harsh flavour instead of the requisite full, roasted flavour.' 'It is not true that if flour is burnt its nutritional value is destroyed.' 'Moreover a well browned flour has a very benefi-cial effect on the stomach.'

THE RECIPE
Just as the name of this soup is not Italian, nor is the use of sour cream. Yet the soup shows a strong Italian influence, that of sautéing the mushrooms separately with garlic and parsley. As in many dishes from South Tyrol and Friuli, the butter and flour roux is cooked to a hazelnut colour before the stock is added. This gives the dish a characteristic and pleasant, slightly burnt taste.

In South Tyrol this soup is made with wild wood mushrooms, usually an assortment just as they are picked, as in this recipe. And, of course, these are the best mushrooms to use. But I find that you can successfully use cultivated mush-rooms, as long as you add a handful of dried porcini and their soaking liquid.

This soup is usually served with croûtons, sautéed in butter. Oil is not a cooking fat of the region.

SERVES 4
75g/2½oz [US 5 tbsp] unsalted butter
100g/3½oz [US ½ cup] onion, finely chopped
1 garlic clove, finely chopped
15g/½oz fresh flat-leaf parsley, chopped
225g/8oz selection of wild mushrooms: boletes, chanterelles, saffron milk caps, honey fungi etc.
4 tbsp milk
salt and freshly ground black pepper
grated nutmeg
1.2l [US 5 cups] vegetable stock (page 231) or chicken stock
40g/1½oz [US ¼ cup] flour
4 tbsp sour cream

Heat half the butter with the onion, garlic and parsley in a sauté pan and sauté for 5 minutes, stirring frequently.

Cut the fresh mushrooms into small dice and then throw them into the sauté pan. Sauté them for 5 minutes, until they have absorbed all the butter. Pour in the milk and season with salt and nutmeg. Cook for a further few minutes.

Heat the stock to simmering point.

In another saucepan melt the remaining butter until the foam begins to subside. Draw the pan off the heat and beat in the flour. Return the pan to the heat and cook over low heat until the mixture becomes first pale gold and then deeper in colour. Draw the pan off the heat once more and begin to add the stock gradually, by the ladle-ful. Stir constantly to avoid lumps forming. Return the pan to a low heat. When all the stock has been added, add the mushrooms and all their rich cooking juices. Bring the whole thing to the boil and simmer for 20 minutes. Add pepper, and taste to check the salt.

Ladle the soup into individual bowls and then spoon a tablespoon of sour cream into the middle of each bowl.

POLENTA PASTICCIATA Ⓥ
Baked Polenta with Mushrooms and Cheese

Pasticciata means 'messed about', but there is no messing about in this well-constructed and bal-anced dish. Polenta can be 'pasticciata' in many ways, according to local traditions, to the cook's preference and the ingredients available. The most common way to prepare the dish is by layer-ing the slices of polenta with a good meat ragù, such as you would do with lasagne. Another excellent polenta pasticciata is made with three or four different cheeses and béchamel. My recipe here adds mushrooms to the cheeses, typical of mountain regions.

If you can find wild cèpes and chanterelles, use these, omitting the dried porcini.

SERVES 6

polenta made with 300g/10oz maize (polenta)
flour [US 2½ cups coarse cornmeal]
20g/¾oz dried porcini
a béchamel sauce (page 228), made with 60g/2oz
[US 4 tbsp] unsalted butter, 40g/1½oz [US ¼ cup]
flour, 450ml/15fl oz full fat milk
30g/1oz [US 2 tbsp] unsalted butter
1 garlic clove, bruised
150g/5oz mixed cultivated mushrooms: brown
mushrooms, field mushrooms, oyster mushrooms,
sliced
salt and freshly ground pepper
5 tbsp milk
40g/1½oz fontina or gruyère
40g/1½oz young pecorino [US romano]
40g/1½oz taleggio
6 tbsp freshly grated Parmesan
grated nutmeg
butter for the dish

Make the polenta at least 3 hours in advance to give it time to cool completely. You can even make it 1 or 2 days in advance. The baked method on page 234 is ideal for this recipe. When you remove it from the oven, cover the top with a clean sheet of buttered foil to prevent a hard crust from forming.

An hour or so before you start cooking, put the dried porcini in a bowl and cover with boiling water. Leave to soak for about 1 hour (see page 13) and then lift them out of the liquid. Check that there is no grit trapped in the folds of the porcini. If you see any, rinse under a cold tap. Dry thoroughly and chop the porcini.

Filter the porcini liquid through a sieve lined with muslin or cheesecloth and set aside.

Now make the béchamel. While the béchamel is gently bubbling away, heat the butter with the garlic in a frying pan. When the aroma of the garlic begins to rise, fish the garlic out and discard it. Add the porcini and sauté for 5 minutes. Now add the fresh mushrooms and sauté for 2 or 3 minutes, turning them over frequently. Season with salt and pepper. When the mushrooms begin to release their liquid, turn the heat up to evaporate it, cooking for 2 or 3 minutes. Pour in the milk, stir well and continue cooking for a further 10 minutes. If the milk evaporates too quickly, add a couple of tablespoons of the mushroom liquid. Taste and check seasoning.

Cut the polenta into 1cm/½in slices. Slice the cheeses thinly.

Heat the oven to 180°C/350°F/Gas Mark 4.

Now you can assemble the dish. Choose an ovenproof dish in which you can make 3 layers of polenta. I use a 20 × 16cm/8 × 6in dish. Butter the dish generously and then spread a couple of tablespoons of béchamel over the bottom. Lay about one-third of the polenta slices over the sauce and cover with half the mushrooms, half the sliced cheeses, 2 tablespoons of the Parmesan and a couple of tablespoons of béchamel. Now place another layer of polenta slices in the dish and cover with the same layers of ingredients. The top layer is polenta, well covered with the remaining béchamel and sprinkled with the remaining 2 tablespoons of Parmesan.

Place the dish in the oven to bake for 30 minutes, until the polenta is hot through. To test it, push the blade of a small knife into the middle of the dish and then touch it gently against your lip. It should feel burning hot. If it doesn't, place the dish back in the oven for a few more minutes. Let the dish rest for about 6 to 7 minutes outside the oven for the flavours to blend and then bring it to the table.

FUNGHI IN UMIDO Ⓥ
Fungi Stew

This dish is at its best when made with a selection of wild fungi. This is easy to do in Trento where, between the months of May and November, there is a large fungi market. At the peak time 250 different species are on sale there, all checked by mycologist inspectors who look, smell, sniff and even taste all the specimens brought by the pickers in their baskets. As in other parts of Italy, porcini – *boletus edulis* – are the favourites, but the woods of the nearby Dolomites provide a host of other species.

For this recipe, if you cannot use wild fungi, use a selection of cultivated mushrooms plus 30g/1oz of dried porcini, which you must soak in hot water for about an hour (see page 13).

A note on health. Wild fungi are very difficult to digest because they contain toxic substances. I know that to be so from my own experience, and I always advise people to eat them sparingly.

SERVES 4 TO 6
700g/1½lb mixed wild fungi or cultivated mushrooms
a bunch of fresh flat-leaf parsley, chopped
2 garlic cloves, very finely chopped
2 tbsp olive oil
40g/1½oz [US 3 tbsp] unsalted butter
salt and freshly ground black pepper
8 tbsp full fat milk

Scrape off any grit from the stalks of the wild fungi and wipe them all over very carefully with dampened kitchen paper towel. Cut the caps into 5mm/¼in slices and the stalks lengthwise into similar slices. If you are using cultivated mushrooms, wipe them with kitchen paper towel and slice in a similar manner.

Put half the parsley, the garlic, oil and butter in a large sauté pan and cook until the fat sizzles and the aroma of the *soffritto* (frying mixture) rises.

If you are using dried porcini, add them to the pan 5 minutes before you add the fresh mushrooms. Now throw in the fungi or mushrooms, turn them over and over so that they all get a chance of absorbing some of the fat, and cook at a lively heat. Season with salt and pepper and continue cooking until the liquid that has at first come out of the fungi has evaporated. (Different species of mushrooms contain different amounts of water.) After that lower the heat and add the milk. Cook gently, stirring occasionally, for half an hour if you are using wild fungi, or for 15 minutes for the cultivated species. Taste and check seasoning.

These stewed fungi or mushrooms are a perfect accompaniment to the venison on page 84, to the shin of pork on page 83 or to a mountain of golden polenta for a vegetarian meal.

MANZO ALLA TRENTINA
Beef Braised in Vinegar and Cream

The best cut for this recipe is a piece of chuck steak, or brisket or silverside. The meat should not be too fresh and should have a little fat around. It should also be neatly rolled into a not-too-large piece, ideally of about 10cm/4in diameter.

I prefer to cook any braised or stewed meat a day in advance so that I can easily remove the solidified fat from the top.

I like to serve this beef with polenta made with a mixture of maize (polenta) flour and buckwheat flour because it has a nutty and 'dark' flavour that is a perfect foil to the oniony sauce. The recipe for this polenta is on page 233. Prepare the recipe without the addition of the butter and cheese.

SERVES 4

450g/1lb small white onions or pickling onions
75g/2½oz smoked pancetta
the needles from 2 fresh rosemary sprigs, each about 20cm/8in long
salt and freshly ground black pepper
a 1.5kg/3¼lb piece of boneless beef
60g/2oz [US 4 tbsp] unsalted butter
1 tbsp olive oil
150ml/5fl oz wine vinegar
300ml/10fl oz single cream [US light cream]

First peel the onions. If you want to do this the easy way, and without shedding too many tears, put them in a bowl and cover them with boiling water. When you peel them, leave the root on the onion so that it can keep the onion whole. If you are using small white sweet onions, you can now set them apart, ready to be added to the meat. But if you use pickling onions, put them back in the bowl and cover with boiling water again so that you get rid of some of their too strong oniony flavour. Leave them to soak for 15 minutes before draining.

Chop the pancetta and the rosemary needles together very finely. (I find that the quickest and best way to make this type of *battuto*, or pounded mixture, containing pancetta is to use a food processor. The mixture becomes a real *battuto* in a split second.) Season this mixture with salt and pepper.

Make deep incisions in the meat along the grain and push into it some of the *battuto*, pushing it well in with a chopstick. When you have done one end, turn the meat over and lard from the other end, so that the whole length of the piece will be larded. Pat the meat with salt and pepper all over and with any left-over *battuto*.

Heat the oven to 170°C/325°F/Gas Mark 3.

Heat the butter and oil in a flameproof casserole. When the butter foam begins to subside add the meat and brown on all sides. Add the onions

A D I G E

and sauté for 5 minutes, then pour over the vinegar and boil briskly for a further 3 or 4 minutes.

Meanwhile, heat the cream. When it is nearly boiling, add it to the casserole with some salt and pepper. Cover the casserole tightly and place it in the oven. Cook for 1 hour, then turn the heat down to 150°C/300°F/Gas Mark 2 and continue cooking for another 2½ to 3 hours, until the meat is very tender indeed.

Transfer the beef to a carving board and cut it into thickish slices with a very sharp knife. (I find an electric knife invaluable for slicing this type of meat.) Lay the slices, slightly overlapping, on a heated dish. Check the seasoning of the sauce before spooning 2 or 3 tablespoons over the meat. Ladle the rest of the sauce and the little onions into a terrine and serve with polenta, as they do in Trentino.

SPEZZATINO DI MAIALE ALLA BOLZANESE

Pork Stew with Paprika

I have been making this dish for as long as I can remember. It is an old favourite which I always thought was from Bolzano in Alto Adige. Recently, however, I saw an almost identical recipe in a book on the cooking of Venezia Giulia. The dish was called gulash alla triestina.

The two different sources of the same dish bear witness to the influence of the Austro-Hungarian empire on the cooking of all eastern Italy, an area that had been dominated by that empire for centuries. Almost the only difference is that whereas this, the Alto-Adige recipe, contains wine, the Triestina version has no wine but includes marjoram and rosemary. Still, this squares with the well-known fact that the people

of Trentino and Alto-Adige are among the heaviest consumers of wine in Italy.

This dish is usually accompanied by polenta (page 233).

SERVES 4 OR 5

800g/1¾lb pork steaks
30g/1oz [US 2 tbsp] butter
125g/4oz smoked pancetta, cut into cubes
225g/8oz sweet onions, sliced
salt
1 tbsp paprika, approximately – depending on its strength
1 tbsp flour
200ml/7fl oz dry white wine
300ml/10fl oz tomato passata
1 dozen fresh sage leaves, snipped
2 bay leaves

Remove the sinews and gristle from the pork but leave the fat. Cut the meat into neat chunks of about 2.5cm/1in.

Heat the butter with the pancetta in your stewing pan. Sauté for 5 minutes, until the fat of the pancetta has melted. Add the onion and 2 pinches of salt and cook for 20 minutes or so, stirring frequently.

Throw the meat into the pan and fry on all sides for 10 minutes, then mix in the paprika and the flour. Cook for 1 minute. Splash with the wine and bring to the boil. Cook for a couple of minutes, then add the passata, sage and bay leaves. Season with salt, stir well and cook gently uncovered for 1½ to 2 hours, adding a couple of tablespoons of boiling water whenever the sauce gets too dry.

Fish out the bay leaves and discard. Taste and check seasoning before bringing the dish to the table with a mound of smoking golden polenta.

Stinco di Maiale alla Tirolese
Pot-roasted Shin of Pork

The cooking of South Tyrol contains elements of Italian, Austrian and Middle European cooking. I find this dish, however, distinctly Italian both in the way it is prepared and in its flavour.

Any self-respecting butcher can supply you with pork shins (not trotters), which weigh about 700g/1½lb each. One shin is enough for 2 to 3 portions. Remember to take any meat out of the fridge about 2 hours before cooking, if you can.

Choose a casserole into which the shins will fit snugly, though not so tight that you cannot turn them over.

If you prefer a smoother sauce, purée the cooking juices into a small pan. Work together 15g/½oz [US 1 tbsp] of butter with 2 tsp of flour with a fork and drop this mixture (*beurre manié*) little by little into the simmering puréed cooking juices, adding a little more stock if necessary.

SERVES 4 TO 6
2 pork shins [US fresh ham hocks]
salt and freshly ground pepper
2 tbsp olive oil
1 celery stalk
½ onion, chopped
1 small carrot
1 garlic clove
5 fresh sage leaves
the needles from a rosemary sprig about 5cm/2in long
150ml/5fl oz dry white wine
3 tbsp Grappa or eau-de-vie
2 juniper berries, bruised
150ml/5fl oz meat stock (page 230)

Heat the oven to 200°C/400°F/Gas Mark 6.

Burn any stubborn hairs off the rind of the shins. Wash and dry them. Season with salt and pepper all over.

Put the oil in a flameproof casserole and brown the shins well on all sides. Lift them out and put them on a side dish.

While the meat is browning, chop the celery, onion, carrot, garlic, sage and rosemary very finely. When the meat is out of the pan, throw this mixture into the pan with ½ teaspoon of salt and sauté gently for 5 minutes. Place the shins on top of the mixture and turn the heat up. Pour over the wine and Grappa and let them bubble rapidly for a minute or so, turning the meat over once. After that throw in the juniper berries and add half the stock.

Cover the casserole and place it in the oven. Cook for about 1½ hours, turning the shins over twice and adding a little more stock if the cooking juices are too dry. The meat is ready when it is tender. Remove the rind, which is quite good, and cut into strips for the people who like it. Cut the meat into chunks and spoon the cooking juices over and around it, unless you prefer to make the smooth sauce described in the introduction.

CAPRIOLO ALLA ALTO ATESINA
Stewed Venison

In Alto Adige fur game is still eaten a lot during the shooting season, the most prized being chamois, a small deer with beautiful hooked horns, which live high up in the Alps and the Appennines. The chamois venison found on the market is often from farmed animals whose meat has less flavour, but needs to be hung for a shorter period. In this country I have made the dish with venison, which usually is the meat of red deer. Sour cream is used a lot in this region, whose cooking is redolent of the Austro-Hungarian empire.

SERVES 6

1.3kg/3lb boneless venison
4 tbsp olive oil
2 tbsp flour
60g/2oz smoked pancetta, diced
60g/2oz pure lard
1 Spanish onion, about 225g/8oz, very thinly sliced
salt and freshly ground pepper
¼ tsp ground cinnamon
¼ tsp ground cloves
300ml/10fl oz sour cream

FOR THE MARINADE
1 carrot, cut into pieces
1½ onions, coarsely sliced
1 celery stalk, cut into pieces
1 tbsp coarse sea salt
1 dozen juniper berries, crushed
8 peppercorns, bruised
3 cloves
1 fresh rosemary sprig
2–3 fresh thyme sprigs
1 fresh sage sprig
3 tbsp olive oil
3 bay leaves
3 garlic cloves
1 bottle good full-bodied red wine (750ml)

Heat all the ingredients for the marinade until just boiling.

Cut the venison into pieces about 5cm/2in thick. Put these in a bowl and add the marinade. Cover the bowl and leave for 2 days, preferably in a cool larder rather than in the fridge.

Lift the meat from the marinade and pat dry with kitchen paper towel. Drain the marinade, saving only the liquid.

Heat the oven to 170°C/325°F/Gas 3.

Heat 2 tablespoons of the oil in a large cast-iron frying pan. Add the meat and brown very thoroughly on each side. Fry in two batches rather than crowding the meat together, when it wouldn't brown properly. Transfer the meat to a side plate.

Add the flour to the frying pan and cook until brown, stirring and scraping the bottom of the pan with a metal spoon. Add about half the marinade liquid. Bring to the boil, stirring constantly and breaking down any lumps of flour with the back of the spoon.

Put the rest of the oil, the pancetta and lard in a flameproof casserole and cook for 5 minutes. Add the onion and a pinch of salt and continue cooking until the onion is really soft, about 15 minutes. Add a couple of tablespoons of hot water to prevent the onion from burning.

Now add the meat with all the juice that has leaked out, the roux from the frying pan and about 150ml/5fl oz of the remaining marinade liquid. Season with salt and pepper and with the spices and bring slowly to the boil. Cover the casserole and place in the oven. Cook for about 1 hour, or until the meat is very tender, adding a little more marinade liquid twice during the cooking.

Add the sour cream to the casserole. Return the pot to the oven and cook for a further half an hour or until the meat is very tender. It is difficult to say how long the cooking takes since it depends on the quality and age of the animal.

Serve with polenta and with a dish of stewed mushrooms.

BUDINO DI MELE
Apple Pudding

This recipe is like an apple charlotte, but it tastes different, the bread having been mixed into the apples in the form of dried breadcrumbs. It combines two popular local foods, apples and bread.

The breadcrumbs must be made from the best bread, which could be white or wholemeal, but it must be good. For the apples I have successfully used Bramleys and also windfalls, as long as they are tasty. What you must do is correct the sugar according to the acidity of the apples.

SERVES 4 TO 6

60g/2oz [US 7 tbsp] raisins
450g/1lb cooking apples
about 100ml/3½fl oz dry white wine
about 90g/3oz caster sugar [US ½ cup granulated sugar]
30g/1oz [US 2 tbsp] unsalted butter
the grated rind of ½ unwaxed lemon
¼ tsp ground cinnamon
5 tbsp fine dried breadcrumbs
2 egg yolks plus 3 egg whites
butter and breadcrumbs for the tin
300ml/10fl oz whipping cream, whipped, to serve

Puff up the raisins in hot water for about half an hour. When you are ready to start the pudding, drain and dry them.

Peel and core the apples and slice them finely. Pour enough wine into a fairly large sauté pan to cover the bottom. Add the apples and cook, covered, until the apples have become a soft purée. Beat them up, add nearly all the sugar and put the pan back on the heat to dry the purée. Do this on a lively heat, stirring constantly.

When the purée is nice and dry, draw the pan off the heat and add the butter, lemon rind, cinnamon, raisins and breadcrumbs. Mix very thoroughly and then drop in the egg yolks, incorporating one yolk at a time. Now taste the purée and check the sugar. You may want to add a little more; it all depends on your taste and the acidity of the apples.

Heat the oven to 180°C/350°F/Gas Mark 4. Whisk the egg whites until stiff and fold gently into the apple purée.

Butter very generously a metal tin of 1l/1¾pt [US 1qt] capacity. A charlotte tin is the traditional one to use, but you can use a cake tin or an oval bread tin. Fill the prepared tin with the apple mixture and bake the pudding for about 40 minutes, until it is spongy to the touch and has shrunk away from the side of the tin. Allow to cool a little in the tin and then unmould it. Serve hot with whipped cream.

TORTA DI GRANO SARACENO
Buckwheat Cake

Buckwheat, which will grow at altitudes as high as 800m/2600ft, is used in a few dishes from South Tyrol and various of the Alpine valleys. Buckwheat is not a *graminacea*, a cereal, but belongs to the family of the *poligonacee*. It is treated as a cereal because it presents the same nutritional properties as the cereals, being rich in proteins, vitamins, iron and mineral salts.

While buckwheat used to be the grain of the poor in these valleys, now it is the grain of the rich because only a few mills have the right machines to deal with it. Buckwheat flour is dark in colour and, once cooked, has a very pleasing bitter taste and a rather sticky consistency. It is more perishable than wheat flour and I advise you to keep it in the freezer.

THE RECIPE
The delightful town of Merano is brimming with elegant shops, and smart cafés where the locals and the tourists sit around to have a rest after their shopping spree. The oldest and best known café is the Pasticceria König, founded in 1893 and still the property of the fifth generation of the family.

Margherita König, who is in charge of this elegant meeting place, was kind enough to give me the König recipe for one of the traditional cakes of South Tyrol. La Torta di Grano Saraceno is a cake to be enjoyed at any time of the day, which is what everybody seems to do at the Pasticceria König. I have halved Signora König's quantities to make a cake more suitable for a family. An ideal cake for gluten-free diets.

SERVES 8

125g/4oz [US ¾ cup] shelled almonds
125g/4oz caster sugar [US ½ cup + 2 tbsp
granulated sugar]
125g/4oz [US 1 stick] butter, softened
3 size-3 eggs [US extra-large eggs], separated
125g/4oz [US 1¼ cups] fine buckwheat flour
2 tsp baking powder
a pinch of salt
1 tsp grated rind from an unwaxed lemon
2 pinches of ground cinnamon
butter for the tin
about 350g/12oz [US 1 cup] best blackcurrant jam
icing sugar [US confectioners' sugar], to finish

Heat the oven to 180°C/350°F/Gas Mark 4.

Blanch the almonds in boiling water for 30 seconds. Drain and skin them by squeezing out the almond between your thumb and index finger. The fresher the almonds, the easier it is to remove the skin. Spread them out on an oven tray and pop the tray in the oven to toast for 10 minutes. (Almonds release more flavour when toasted.) When cold, transfer them to a food processor and grind them finely.

Measure out 75g/2½oz [US 6 tbsp] of the sugar and put it in a bowl. Add the softened butter and beat together until creamy.

Incorporate the egg yolks thoroughly into the butter-cream and then add the buckwheat flour, baking powder, salt, lemon rind, almonds and ground cinnamon. Mix very thoroughly.

Whisk the egg whites until soft peaks form. Whisk in half the remaining sugar by the table-spoon and finally fold in the rest of the sugar. Now fold the meringue into the buckwheat mixture, using a large metal spoon and a gentle but deep movement.

Butter a 20cm/8in spring-clip tin and line the bottom with a disc of parchment paper. Lightly butter the paper too. Spoon the cake mixture into the tin and bake for about 30 to 40 minutes, until a wooden toothpick pushed into the middle of the cake comes out dry. Unmould the cake on to a wire rack. (Be very careful because this is a fragile cake.) Leave it to cool. Peel off the parchment paper.

Using a serrated knife, cut the cake in half horizontally to form two flat rounds. Spread the jam over the bottom half and place the other half on top. Sprinkle lavishly with icing sugar before serving.

VENETO

Whenever I think of Veneto, one place comes to my mind, obliterating all else. That unique place is, of course, Venezia, where I spent many blissful months, shopping at the Rialto market, gazing at palazzi and churches, and walking about in the leisurely way that is only possible in car-less Venice.

The food is as interesting as everything else connected with that magical city. Unfortunately very few of the local restaurants do justice to its cuisine, which stands slightly apart from that of all the rest of Italy. The Venetians have assimilated the flavours of their former dominions more than any other maritime republic. They assimilated and adapted them to their own cooking, ignoring, even in more recent years, the flavours of southern Italy that have conquered the North. Tomato rarely appears in Venetian cooking or, for that matter, in the cooking of all Veneto, while curry, for instance, used nowhere else in Italy, comes into a few Venetian dishes.

The most vivid example of this marriage of flavours from East and West is a dish of sfogi in saor. *Sfogi* is sole in Venetian dialect, and *saor* is sauce. The sole, a characteristic fish of the Adriatic, is first fried and then marinated in a vinegary sauce containing many spices, sultanas and pine nuts. It is the dish eaten for the Festa del Redentore, the third Sunday in July, when the whole of Venice and the surrounding *terraferma* (hinterland) gathers on and around the laguna and the Giudecca, where the splendid Palladian church of the Redentore stands, built as an 'ex voto' for the end of the plague in 1576. I have been in Venice for the Feast of the Redentore on three occasions, eating sfogi, anara rosta – roast duck – and then juicy iced watermelon, while sitting on the quay of the Giudecca and watching the display of fireworks which set the bacino di San Marco aglow. One of those memories that make life worth living.

Due to its topography, traditions die harder in Venice than in any other part of Italy and this applies also to gastronomic traditions. On St Mark's Day, 25th April, every Venetian man arrives home with a *bocolo* (a red rose bud) for his *innamorata*, ready to eat a voluptuous dish of risi e bisi (page 96) – rice with peas. The peas are the first to arrive at the Rialto market from the rich vegetable gardens on the islands of the lagoon. Even my English husband used to come home with the bocolo during the years we had a flat in Venice. But often, instead of risi e bisi at home, we used to go to the local *bacaro* – a Venetian snack bar – called La Vedova, for a *cicchetto* and an *ombra* – a snack and a glass of wine. The snacks were 'drowned' octopus, sardines 'in saor', Lamon beans, creamy garlicky stockfish or, best of all, seafood, simply boiled and dressed with a drizzle of the delicate oil from Lake Garda.

No meat here on the counter of a bacaro, just vegetables and fish. And from La Vedova, if you take the ferry at Santa Sofia, to be transported across the Canal Grande while doing a balancing act standing in the gondola, and arrive at the Rialto market, the first glance around will give you an idea of the abundance and variety of Venetian vegetables and fish. Shellfish of every kind, crustaceans and cephalopods of every size, blue fish, red fish, silver fish from the tiny whitebait to the beautiful sea bass, they all contend for the attention of the choosy and thrifty Venetian housewife.

There are two supreme seafood specialities in Venice, beloved also in the terraferma: *moleche* and *grancevole* – soft shell crab or shore crab, and spider crab. Moleche have been cultivated in the lagoon since the 18th century and they are now a large industry. The male crabs are kept in large baskets called *vieri*, immersed in the water, and, just at the moment of changing their shells in the spring and autumn, when the shells become soft, they are taken out and sold. I still remember the pleasure as a child, when we spent an Easter holiday at the Lido, of digging my young teeth into a tender fried moleca. I still wonder whether it was a plain moleca or a *moleca col pien* (stuffed). This dish is one of the great Venetian gourmandises. The live soft crabs are put in a bowl containing beaten egg yolks and Parmesan and are left there for two to three hours. The moleche fill up with the mixture and die happy. They are then floured and fried in olive oil.

This, and the grancevola (granceola in Venetian) are the only crabs I like – yet another instance that makes me wonder how much the like or dislike of a particular food derives from memories of previous experiences, and the surrounding atmosphere. Memories of Venice can make any dish taste a thousand times better!

Vegetables are another important element in the cooking of Veneto, creating a mellow and gentle cuisine, never aggressive yet always positive and well defined.

If you want to taste real Veneto cooking, a trattoria in one of the smaller towns – Padua, Treviso or Bassano – would be the ideal place. There you would eat traditional food prepared for the locals who, just like all other Italians, go to a restaurant in the expectation of eating a better edition of their favourite dish. They go to Treviso to have a *sopa coâda* – 'broody' soup – made with pigeon and lots of vegetables, a soup which was ennobled in Verona to become a zuppa alla scaligera, said to have been served at the court of the Della Scala, the lords of Verona. The original recipe has recently been rediscovered and published by the great Veronese gastronome, Giorgio Gioco, of the famous restaurant I Dodici Apostoli in Verona.

One of the best meals I ever had was at Alla Riviera in charming Bassano. The restaurant is next to the beautiful wooden bridge across the Brenta river, where the Bassanesi, and the tourists, take their *passeggiata* before going home, or to Alla Riviera, for lunch. I was there not long ago on a cold and wet Saturday, but my spirits were soon restored when I started my lunch with *nervetti caldi* – hot brawn. This was a surprise, since I always connected nervetti with Milan, where they are served cold with onions and other *sottaceti*. After the nervetti I had one of the best pasta e fagioli ever, and a perfect baccalà alla vicentina – stockfish, not salt cod, in Veneto – cooked in milk with anchovy fillets, parsley and a good deal of olive oil from Lake Garda. The fagioli were borlotti beans from Lamon. These are in a different class from normal borlotti: silky, velvety and large, they fill your mouth and exquisitely and slowly melt in it. The local asparagus, my favourite asparagus, were not, alas, in season. Large, white and incredibly tasty, they are served hot with a sauce of pounded hard-boiled eggs and olive oil.

Another vegetable I must mention is radicchio, of which there are three traditional varieties: Treviso, Verona and Castelfranco. Now there is also the modern radicchio di Chioggia, the one we see in shops outside Italy and, alas, the least interesting of them all, with its coarse cabbagey texture and flavour.

The risotto made in Treviso with the local radicchio is the one that best expresses the creativity of the Veneti for making the most delectable vegetable risotti. They combine rice with all the seasonal vegetables. Even I, a Milanese, have to grant the Veneti supremacy in this field. In Milan we might have created the best known risotto, that with saffron (page 27), but in Veneto they can boast an infinite variety of risotti, mostly with vegetables and fish. There are said to be 365 different risotti in Veneto, one for each day of the year. The rice for these risotti is Vialone Nano, a chubby semi-fino rice, a highly important produce of the province of Verona. Giovanni Capnist, vice-president of the Accademia della Cucina Italiana, writes in his erudite book *La Cucina Veronese* that contemporary documents confirm that in the 16th century, buildings, yards and stores were built for the handling and storage of rice, which was even then an important industry. Still now, rice is the first course of a meal in the Veneto, not only in the form of a risotto but also in one of an infinite variety of rice soups.

These rice dishes are mainly based on a *soffritto* made with olive oil. The oil is the local oil of Lake Garda, which is sweet and has nothing of the pepperiness of the *fruttato* oils. It is similar to the Ligurian oil, though even sweeter. This rare oil is made from olive trees that grow at this most northern latitude, thanks to the very temperate climate that exists around the lake.

The other popular first course is potato gnocchi (page 64), which here are usually made with eggs and dressed with a lovely tomato sauce (page 228), or with the juices of a roast.

With this wealth of first courses, who wants pasta? After all, there is only one local pasta, *bigoli*, a thick spaghetti made with a blend of wholewheat flour and white flour and traditionally dressed with a piquant anchovy sauce or with the juices of the roast duck that follows, accompanied by salsa peverada (page 104).

There are plenty of dolci. In Venice some show an oriental influence, while in other parts there is an Austrian flavour, as in tortion (page 110) which is very similar to strudel. Finally, I must mention that tiramisù comes originally from Treviso. It is a relatively modern dish that, like all dishes that achieve universal success, has been subjected to endless variations. I have not included a recipe in this book because I think tiramisù has been done to death, and should be left to rest in peace.

LINGUINE E CAPESANTE ALLA VENEZIANA

Linguine and Scallops Venetian Style

The scallops from the Adriatic are amongst the tastiest in the world, and the Venetians know how to make the best of them. The texture of the breadcrumbs is in sharp contrast to the softness of the pasta and the seafood, while their flavours are in complete harmony.

The sauce takes less time to prepare than the pasta takes to cook. The secret of this sauce lies in correct timing, both for the scallops and for the pasta; neither should be overcooked.

The use of curry powder in Italy is found only in the Venetian cuisine. The reason is simple – Venice, in the past, always looked towards the sea, and her main trade was with the East. Just think of Marco Polo, a Venetian after all.

SERVES 4

350g/12oz linguine or spaghetti
120ml/4fl oz extra virgin olive oil
60g/2oz [US heaping ½ cup] dried white breadcrumbs
2 tbsp chopped fresh parsley, preferably flat-leaf
4 garlic cloves, bruised
2 tsp best curry powder
350g/12oz shelled scallops [US sea scallops]
salt and freshly ground pepper

Put a large pot of water on the heat and cook the linguine in the usual way.

Meanwhile, put half the oil in a small frying pan. When the oil is hot add the breadcrumbs and stir-fry until golden. Set aside.

Clean the scallops and rinse them quickly under cold water. Pat dry with kitchen paper

towel. Detach the little coral tongues and set aside. Cut the white part into very small pieces.

Choose a large frying pan and heat the remaining oil with the parsley, garlic and curry powder. When you can smell the garlic aroma, fish the garlic out of the oil and discard it.

When the linguine are very nearly cooked, add the white part of the scallops to the frying pan containing the parsley. Stir-fry for no longer than 30 seconds, until the scallops begin to become opaque.

Drain the pasta and turn it immediately into the frying pan. Add the coral tongues and stir rapidly, lifting the linguine up high so that each strand is coated with the oil. Do this for a minute or so, then transfer to a heated bowl and top with the fried breadcrumbs. Serve immediately.

PASTICCIO DI TAGLIATELLE E PESCE

Fish and Tagliatelle Pie

There are many versions of this dish from Venice and the islands of the lagoon. One of the best versions comes from San Pietro in Volta on the island of Pellestrina, south of Venice, and the other from Burano, an island to the north of Venice, close to Torcello.

I have chosen the Burano recipe simply because I find Burano so enchanting that I like anything remotely connected with it, from the *tombolo* (local lace) to the little houses gaily painted in ice-cream colours all along the wide canals. I like, too, the *panetterie* (bakers' shops), brimming with *zaleti*, polenta biscuits, and *baicoli*, which are crisp biscuits [US cookies] to be dunked in wine from Cyprus or in large cups of steaming hot chocolate, sitting at a café on the laguna.

Back to my pie. It is a rather elaborate dish that calls for first class ingredients and care. I would advise you to make your own tagliatelle. Short of that, buy good fresh pasta. Some supermarkets make good fresh pasta with imported Italian flour and eggs, while others import dried egg pasta from Italy such as that made by Spinosi or Cipriani, two of the best producers.

SERVES 6

tagliatelle made with 3 eggs and 300g/10oz [US 2½ cups] Italian 00 flour; or 500g/1lb 2oz fresh tagliatelle; or 300g/10oz best dried tagliatelle

200ml/7fl oz dry white wine

½ small onion

2 bay leaves

salt and freshly ground pepper, preferably white

450g/1lb sole fillets, skinned

225g/8oz raw king or tiger prawns in shell [US large raw shrimp]

600ml/1pt [US 2½ cups] full fat milk

125g/4oz [US 1 stick] unsalted butter

3 tbsp flour

4 tbsp chopped fresh flat-leaf parsley

60g/2oz [US ½ cup] freshly grated Parmesan

If you are making your own pasta, start by doing this, following the instructions on page 232.

Put the wine in a large sauté pan. Add the onion, bay leaves and salt and bring to the boil. Add the fish and the prawns. When the wine has come back to the boil turn the heat down and simmer for 5 minutes. Strain the liquid into another pan and add the milk. Put the pan on the heat and bring to simmering point.

Peel the prawns and cut into pieces. Cut the sole into strips. Set aside.

Melt half the butter in a heavy-based saucepan. Mix in the flour and cook for half a minute, stirring constantly. Remove from the heat and gradually add the milk and fish liquid, whisking the whole time. (If you do this off the heat you are less likely to finish with a lumpy white sauce. But

if this should happen, don't worry – just turn the whole thing into a food processor and give it a whizz. This is easier than trying to remove the lumps by squashing them one by one against the side of the pan.) Return the pan to a low heat and bring to the boil. To make a velvety sauce you should cook it for about 15 to 20 minutes, either in a bain-marie (setting the pan in a larger pan half full of simmering water) or using a flame diffuser – an invaluable tool easily available in most kitchen shops. Mix in the parsley, salt and pepper to taste, and the Parmesan.

Cook the pasta in plenty of boiling salted water. Drain, but be careful not to overdrain, and return the pasta to the saucepan. Dress it with one-third of the sauce.

Heat the oven to 190°C/375°F/Gas Mark 5.

Butter a shallow oven dish with a little of the remaining butter. Cover with half the pasta. Spoon the fish over it and pour over a couple of tablespoons of the sauce. Cover with the rest of the pasta and spread the remaining sauce all over the top. Melt the remaining butter and pour over the surface.

Bake for 20 minutes. Do not serve straight away after taking the pasticcio out of the oven. Let it rest and cool down for 5 minutes or so for the flavours to blend.

PANCOTTO VENEZIANO
Venetian Bread Soup

It always surprises me that, in this country, the best-known Italian dishes are from Tuscany. I quite see that a lot of British people spend their holidays there, but I am sure it's not only that. I feel it is the ability of the Tuscans who, unlike the rest of the Italians, are good at selling their region and its products.

Look at olive oil, for instance. There are excellent estate oils from most other regions – totally unknown – but the Tuscan oil reigns supreme. Or bread soups, which are made in most regions. Why has only pappa col pomodoro from Tuscany (see page 180) become famous? It certainly is good, but so are others. It all depends on the recipe and what you put in the dish.

So I give here another bread soup, which is from Veneto and totally different from pappa col pomodoro. No tomatoes here, as with many Veneto dishes, but a touch of the Orient instead in the form of the spices and pine nuts, the characteristic Venetian flavours. This is a warming and nourishing soup.

THE RECIPE
I do not recommend using the normal sandwich loaf; when soaked its texture becomes gluey and quite horrid. You can of course make your own bread, with unbleached stone-ground flour, or you can buy a Pugliese loaf or a French country bread. Try to use only good home-made meat stock.

SERVES 6

150g/5oz country-type white bread
1.35l/2¼pt [US 5½ cups] meat stock (page 230)
60g/2oz [US 4 tbsp] unsalted butter
1 garlic clove, very finely sliced
1 bay leaf
2 tbsp pine nuts
salt and freshly ground black pepper
3 eggs
6 tbsp freshly grated Parmesan
½ tsp grated nutmeg
a pinch of ground cinnamon

Heat the oven to 150°C/300°F/Gas Mark 2.

Break the bread into pieces and spread it on a baking tray. Bake for about 30 minutes, until toasted. Now put it into a saucepan.

Keep aside 200ml/7fl oz of the stock and pour the rest over the bread. Leave to soak for about 15 minutes. When the bread has absorbed the stock, add the butter, garlic and bay leaf and put the pan on a low heat.

Chop the pine nuts by hand or in a food processor and mix into the bread mixture. Stir in the reserved stock and season to taste. (Be careful with the salt because at the end you will be adding a fair amount of Parmesan, which is salty.) Bring the mixture slowly to the boil, stirring constantly, and then let it simmer gently for half an hour while you beat it with a wire whisk as often as you can. It should be beaten constantly, but I find that I can do a few other things around the kitchen in between one good whisking and the next.

Lightly beat the eggs with the cheese and the spices in a small bowl.

When the soup is done, remove from the heat. Let it rest for 5 minutes, then whisk in the egg mixture. Ladle the soup into individual bowls and serve.

RISOTTO NERO
Cuttlefish Risotto

This recipe from Venice uses cuttlefish, a favourite seafood of the Venetians. The cuttlefish ink is used too, not just to give a black 'designer' look to the risotto, but also – and most importantly – for the stronger fish flavour.

Cuttlefish are sometimes available in good fishmongers in this country. They are often caught in British waters, mainly during the early spring. Local cuttlefish are usually large, about 450g/1lb each, and they are more suitable for slow cooking, as in this recipe, than for grilling and frying.

You can use squid, which are more easily available, instead of cuttlefish. They cook more quickly, and the flavour is similar to cuttlefish although less strong.

Ask your fishmonger to clean your cuttlefish and to give you the little ink sac or sacs intact. You might find it easier to buy cuttlefish ink already prepared in little sachets. These come from France or Spain, and are good. For this recipe you would need 2 sachets of ink. Squeeze them into a cupful of hot water and pour a little water into the sachet to rinse out all the ink.

The rice used in Venice is Vialone Nano, a *semifino* variety available in good Italian food shops. However, the more common Arborio will do perfectly well.

You can cook the cuttlefish in advance, even the day before, and keep it refrigerated. Heat before you add it to the rice.

SERVES 4 TO 5 AS A MAIN COURSE

900g/2lb cuttlefish, or 600g/1¼lb cleaned weight
1 onion, finely chopped
2 garlic cloves, very finely chopped
3 tbsp olive oil
salt and freshly ground black pepper
300ml/10fl oz dry white wine
1.5l/2½pt [US 1½qt] vegetable stock (page 231) or light fish stock (page 231)
75g/2½oz [US 5 tbsp] butter
450g/1lb [US 2¼ cups] Italian rice, preferably Vialone Nano
2 tbsp brandy
2 tbsp freshly grated Parmesan

Wash the cuttlefish, and slice the body into thin short strips and the tentacles into morsels. If you are using them, keep the ink sacs separate and do not lose them!

Put the onion, garlic, oil and 1 teaspoon of salt in a heavy-based saucepan and cook gently until the onion is soft and translucent.

Throw in the cuttlefish and sauté gently for 10 minutes or so, stirring frequently. Add half the wine and cover the pan. Now the cuttlefish must cook until tender on the lowest heat, which will take at least 45 minutes. Keep a watch on the pan. Stir every now and then and check that the cuttlefish is always cooking in some liquid. If necessary, add a little boiling water.

Heat the stock and keep it gently simmering all through the preparation of the risotto. In another large, heavy-based saucepan heat half the butter until just sizzling and add the rice. 'Toast' the rice (as we say in Italian) over a lively heat for about 1 to 1½ minutes and then pour over the rest of the wine. Stir and cook for 1 minute to reduce the alcohol content of the wine.

Now you begin to make the risotto proper by adding the simmering stock by the ladleful. Halfway through the cooking – Vialone Nano takes about 15 minutes to cook, Arborio a couple of minutes longer – scoop in the cuttlefish and all the juices. Squeeze in the ink from the sacs, or add the water with the ink sachets dissolved in it (see introduction). Mix well and continue the cooking of the risotto until the rice is done.

A few minutes before you think the rice is ready, stir in the brandy. Draw the pan from the heat and add the remaining butter, plenty of pepper and the Parmesan. Leave covered for a minute or two, then give the risotto a good stir and transfer it to your warm serving dish. Risotto does not like waiting: serve it immediately.

RISI E BISI Ⓥ
Rice and Peas

This dish is a good example of the excellence of Venetian home cooking. Homely and even humble it may be, but it is one of very few dishes that can boast the patronage of the Doges.

Risi e bisi was served to the Doge on St Mark's Day, the 25th April, when the first peas arrive at the Rialto market. The Doge had first claim on the *primizie* – early crops – from the islands on the lagoon, and particularly the peas from the island of Sant' Erasmo. As Dino Boscorato, owner of the well-known Trattoria Dall' Amelia, put it, the Doge had '*ius primi bisi*' – the right, not of the first night, but of the first peas. When I went to his restaurant in Mestre not long ago I had a remarkable meal as well as an interesting talk. He was very dismissive of some new versions of risi e bisi which add cream at the end of the cooking or where, instead of the stock being made with the pea pods to accentuate its sweet flavour, it is made with meat, chicken or vegetable stock.

THE RECIPE

This recipe derives from the risi e bisi I ate at Dall' Amelia. It is like a very thick soup – half-way between a risotto and a soup – and should be eaten with a spoon. The Venetian peas are just like small petits pois, not easy to find in this country. But nowadays you can buy sugar snap peas, which are often large but can still be eaten whole, pod and all. I find them suitable for this recipe because the pods, which go in the soup, are sweet and fleshy, and not stringy. If the sugar snap peas are very fresh and small, you can liquidize and process the cooked pods and add the purée directly to the stock. If they are older and bigger, I advise you first to process the pods and then push them through a food mill to rid them of the strings.

An old Venetian recipe adds a few fennel seeds, a very imaginative and successful addition.

SERVES 4

900g/2lb young fresh petits pois or sugar snap peas
salt and freshly ground black pepper
30g/1oz [US 2 tbsp] unsalted butter
2 tbsp extra virgin olive oil of a delicate flavour, e.g.
an oil from Liguria or Lake Garda
1 small onion, very finely chopped
3 tbsp chopped fresh flat-leaf parsley
225g/8oz [US 1 cup + 2 tbsp] Italian rice,
preferably Vialone Nano
½-1 tbsp fennel seeds, according to taste, crushed
45g/1¾oz [US ¼ cup] freshly ground Parmesan

Top and tail and pod the peas, keeping the pods and peas separate. Discard any blemished pods and wash the others. Put them in a pan and add 1.5l/2½pt [US 1½qt] of water and 2 teaspoons of salt. Boil until the pods are very tender. Drain, reserving the liquid, and process the pods. If stringy, and I find that they usually are, work them through the small hole disc of a food mill or through a metal sieve. Measure 1l/1¾pt [US 1qt] of the liquid and add to the purée. Put the mixture in a saucepan and bring slowly to the boil.

Meanwhile, put the butter, oil, onion and 1 tablespoon of the parsley in a stockpot. Sauté very gently for 5 minutes or so and then throw in the podded peas. Cook, stirring them constantly, for 2 minutes.

Add the rice and stir to coat the grains in the butter and oil. Pour over the simmering pod stock containing the pod purée. Mix well and bring to the boil. Now add the fennel seeds and some freshly ground pepper and boil, covered, until the rice is cooked – about 15 to 20 minutes depending on the quality of the rice. Turn off the heat and mix in the Parmesan and the remaining parsley. Ladle the soup into individual soup bowls and serve immediately. Alternatively, transfer the soup to a soup terrine and bring the terrine to the table, this being the way it is done in Venetian homes.

ASPARAGI IN SALSINA D'UOVO E LIMONE Ⓥ

Asparagus with Egg and Lemon Sauce

Asparagus should be properly cooked, which means that they should be not crunchy but just resistant to the bite, and bend graciously when you pick them up to lower them into your mouth. I shall long remember the horror in the eyes of an Italian friend, eating in a very well-known restaurant, when she picked up an asparagus spear that stayed as rigid as a stick. '*Ma questi sono crudi!*' (but these are raw) she exclaimed, and left them without even trying one. It is difficult to specify the time it takes to cook asparagus. When thin and fresh they can take as little as 5 minutes, but when thick and not so fresh I find that 15 minutes is the minimum.

The accompanying sauce is similar to mayonnaise, but much lighter and kinder on the stomach. It is a sauce from Veneto, where some of the best asparagus – those of Bassano – grow.

SERVES 4 TO 5

1.3kg/3lb asparagus

3 eggs

the juice of 1 lemon, or more or less according to taste

salt and freshly ground black pepper

6 tbsp olive oil

First slice off about 2.5cm/1in of the end of each asparagus spear. Next pare, if necessary, or just scrape the stalks. Wash the asparagus thoroughly in plenty of cold water.

If you haven't got an asparagus boiler, use a large sauté or frying pan in which the asparagus can lie flat. Fill with water, bring to the boil and add salt in the proportion of 1 tablespoon per 450g/1lb of asparagus. When the water boils, slide in the asparagus, cover the pan so as to bring the water back to the boil as quickly as possible, and then cook, uncovered, until they are done.

When the asparagus are cooked lift them out of the water and place them on kitchen paper towel to drain properly before you transfer them on to an oval dish.

To make the sauce put the eggs, lemon juice, salt and a generous grinding of pepper in a heat-proof bowl and whisk until pale. Slowly add the oil while beating with a small balloon whisk to emulsify the sauce. Set the bowl over a saucepan of just simmering water and cook, whisking constantly, until the sauce begins to thicken. Do not let the water in the pan boil or the eggs will curdle. Serve warm.

Asparagus should always be served warm or at room temperature, never piping hot, nor chilled.

Verze Sofegae
Stewed Savoy Cabbage

Vegetables are one of the main ingredients of the cuisine of Veneto, and slow cooking is a typical way of preparing them. The literal translation of this recipe's Venetian name is 'smothered Savoy cabbage'. By the end of the cooking this humble vegetable is transformed into a dish that can be enjoyed on its own, just with some lovely bread.

I use an earthenware pot of the sort you can put directly on the heat, this being the ideal for long, slow cooking. I have also cooked a Primo cabbage in this way. Primo cabbage has a less strong flavour but it works quite well too.

SERVES 4

1 medium Savoy cabbage
125g/4oz unsmoked pancetta or unsmoked streaky bacon
1 onion
1 tbsp fresh rosemary needles
1 garlic clove, peeled
2 tbsp olive oil
salt and freshly ground pepper
180ml/6fl oz dry white wine

Remove and discard the outer dark green leaves of the cabbage. Cut into quarters, cut off and discard the hard core and cut the cabbage into 1cm/½in strips. Put in a sink of cold water to wash and then drain in a colander.

Finely chop together the pancetta, onion, rosemary and garlic (you can do this very well and very quickly in a food processor). Heat with the oil in a heavy saucepan. Cook slowly for 10 minutes and then add the cabbage. The cabbage will wilt as it begins to cook. Turn it over and over to coat in the *soffritto* (the fried mixture). Season with salt and pepper and add the wine. Bring to the boil, cover the saucepan and cook very gently for 1½ hours.

ZUCCA E ZUCCHINE IN SAOR Ⓥ
Squash and Courgettes in a Sweet and Sour Sauce

I never use what I call Hallowe'en pumpkin for cooking. It tastes of nothing and it is so watery that it creates problems. But butternut squash or onion squash are good, and there are plenty of them in the shops between October and February.

This recipe is a classic of old Venetian cooking, where many ingredients are prepared *in saor* – a Venetian contraction of the word *sapore*. Sapore means flavour, and in the old days the word was used for a sauce, such as this one, that was particularly rich in flavour.

The balsamic vinegar (not a Venetian ingredient) is my addition because I find that it rounds out the flavours of the wine vinegar and the wine. Use good – in other words, expensive – vinegars, since they are the only ones made from good wine and free from chemical additives.

SERVES 6

450g/1lb butternut or onion squash
350g/12oz courgettes [US zucchini]
salt and freshly ground black pepper
30g/1oz [US 3 tbsp] raisins
oil for frying
3 tbsp extra virgin olive oil
1 large Spanish onion, or 2 red onions, about 225g/8oz, very finely sliced
15g/½oz [US 2½ tbsp] pine nuts
2 cloves
a pinch of ground cinnamon
1 tsp grated rind from an unwaxed lemon
100ml/3½fl oz good red wine vinegar
4 tbsp balsamic vinegar
150ml/5fl oz dry white wine

Cut the squash in half, skin it and scoop out any seeds and filaments. Cut each half into 5mm/¼in slices.

Wash and dry the courgettes and cut them into slices of the same thickness. Put the courgette and squash slices in two bowls and sprinkle with salt. Leave for 1 hour to disgorge some of the water, then drain and pat dry.

Soak the raisins in some boiling water for about 15 minutes to plump them up, then drain them.

Heat a wok or a frying pan. Add your frying oil and when it is very hot slide in about half of the squash. Fry until the slices begin to turn gold at the edge. Turn them over and fry for a further 2 or 3 minutes. Retrieve the slices with a fish slice or a slotted spoon. Let the oil drip back into the pan and then transfer the squash slices to a dish lined with kitchen paper towel to absorb the excess oil.

Next, do the same with the rest of the squash and then with the courgettes. Remember to put plenty of kitchen paper towel between each batch of fried vegetables.

Now prepare the *saor*. Put the olive oil and the onion in a frying or sauté pan and sauté until soft. Do this on a low heat, turning the onion very often and mixing in small additions of hot water, so that the onion stews rather than fries. After about 20 minutes add the drained raisins, the pine nuts and cloves and season with cinnamon, lemon rind, salt and pepper. Cook, stirring, for 2 minutes.

Add the two vinegars and the wine and boil for 5 minutes. Do not boil too fast or too much will evaporate. Pour this hot marinade over the vegetables. (Do not forget to remove the layers of kitchen paper towel from the vegetable dish before you pour over the wine mixture!)

Leave to cool, then cover with cling film and keep in the fridge for 48 hours before eating – you can actually keep it for up to 4 days. Do not serve the dish chilled: let it come back to room temperature, which takes about 2 to 3 hours.

Radicchio con la Puré di Borlotti Ⓥ
Red Radicchio with Borlotti Bean Purée

Red radicchio and borlotti are a classic combination in the Veneto cuisine. The mealy nuttiness of the borlotti is the perfect foil to the bitterness of the radicchio, which ideally should be the real radicchio of Treviso. One of the typical regional dishes is a superb soup of borlotti finished off with radicchio. Here is another classic.

In the spring, the radicchio is the wild species just picked from the fields, at the same time as the borlotti are fresh on the market. For obvious reasons I have had to adapt the traditional recipe to the radicchio and the dried borlotti available here. And I decided to purée half the beans instead of leaving them whole, because this gives a total combination of the two flavours with each spoonful. It works very well, and is a most attractive dish in its subtle hues of red.

After many trials I have come to the conclusion that I prefer to cook pulses in the oven. If you want to do them on top of the stove you must cook them over the lowest possible heat, so that the surface of the liquid is just broken by the occasional bubble. You might also have to add a little boiling water. That is why I find the oven method safer and more reliable.

SERVES 4
180g/6oz [US 1 cup] dried borlotti beans
6 garlic cloves
1 bay leaf
salt and freshly ground black pepper
vegetable stock (page 231)
250g/9oz red radicchio
6 tbsp extra virgin olive oil
1 tbsp wine vinegar

The day before you want to serve this salad, put the borlotti in a bowl and cover with cold water. If you live in an area where the water is very hard, you should use filtered water. Leave to soak overnight.

Heat the oven to 150°C/300°F/ Gas Mark 2.

Drain and rinse the beans and transfer to a heavy-based saucepan with an ovenproof handle and lid, or to an earthenware pot that you can put directly on the heat. Cover with water by about 4cm/1½in and add the garlic, bay leaf and 1 teaspoon of salt. Bring to the boil, then put the lid on the pan and place it in the oven. Let the beans cook gently until very soft, which will take at least 1½ hours.

When the beans are very tender fish out and discard the bay leaf. Then scoop out half of the beans and the garlic cloves, and transfer to a food processor, a blender or a food mill. Add some of the cooking liquid and process to a purée, adding a little more liquid to help with the operation.

Transfer the purée to a bowl and add enough of the beans' cooking liquid to make a runny purée. If you do not have enough cooking liquid, you must add some vegetable stock. Please do not ask how much. It is impossible for me to say without seeing, but the purée must be half-way between a vegetable cream soup and puréed potatoes. Season with plenty of pepper and then taste and adjust the salt.

Wash and dry the radicchio. Cut it into very thin strips and dress it with half the oil, the vinegar, salt and pepper. Toss well and transfer to the middle of a round dish.

Mix the whole beans into the purée and spoon the lot around the radicchio. Drizzle the remaining oil all over.

Serve at room temperature, taking care that the radicchio is also at room temperature and not straight from the fridge.

SOGLIOLE RIPIENE
Stuffed Sole in Saffron Sauce

Saffron was used a lot in old Venetian cooking, as a sign of wealth and to give food the coveted colour of real gold, instead of using gold leaf. Buy good saffron – it is very expensive – and use it in moderation. Saffron adds a deliciously complex and exotic flavour to a dish, but it can also ruin it if used with too generous a hand.

The addition of pine nuts and sultanas is characteristic of Venetian cooking, which has been strongly influenced by the cooking of the Middle East. After all, Venice dominated part of the Near and Middle East for centuries, and there was a considerable exchange of cultures.

SERVES 6

2 tbsp sultanas [US golden raisins]

3 Dover soles, filleted

salt and freshly ground pepper

125g/4oz young spinach

2 tbsp pine nuts

about 25 saffron strands

½ tsp sugar

120ml/4fl oz Prosecco wine

40g/1½ oz [US 3 tbsp] unsalted butter, cut into small pieces

FOR THE FISH FUMET

the heads and bones of the soles

1 onion, unpeeled, stuck with 1 clove

1 carrot

1 celery stalk

1 bay leaf

6 peppercorns

1 tsp salt

250ml/9fl oz dry white wine

First make the fumet. Put all the ingredients in a pot. Add 1l/1¾pt [US 1 qt] of water and bring to the boil. Boil fast for 30 minutes, until reduced and tasty, then strain the liquid into a large sauté pan. You should have about 600ml/1pt [US 2½ cups] of liquid.

Cover the sultanas with hot water and leave them to plump up. Then drain them and pat dry with kitchen paper towel.

Season the sole fillets lightly with salt and pepper on both sides. Lay some spinach leaves over the fillets and place a few sultanas and a few pine nuts on each fillet. Roll up the fillets and tie them with string, or pin with a wooden toothpick.

Bring the fumet to the boil. Turn the heat down, then add the fish bundles and poach gently, covered, for 6 minutes.

Meanwhile, put the saffron strands with the sugar in a small mortar and pound until crushed. Add a tablespoon or two of the hot fish liquid to dissolve the mixture.

Take the sole bundles out of the liquid and keep hot.

Pour the saffron mixture and the Prosecco into the liquid and boil to reduce by half over high heat, until full of flavour. Mix in the cold butter bit by bit. When all the butter has been absorbed, taste and check seasoning. Spoon the sauce around the fish bundles and serve.

Baccalà Mantecato
Creamed Salt Cod with Garlic and Parsley

Dried cod, whether in the form of salt cod or stockfish (air-dried, not salted) is the most popular type of fish all over Italy. I find it quite fascinating that a foreign food should have so entirely conquered Italian kitchens because Italians are very suspicious of foreign food. Up to the Second World War they used, more or less, to eat only the food they actually saw growing or being produced. Pasta was ignored in the North as rice was in the South. And here is a food coming from Norway (there is no cod in the Mediterranean), which has become part of the cooking repertoire of nearly every region, such an intrinsic part that in any regional cookery book there are more recipes for salt cod or stockfish than for any other sort of fish!

Perhaps salt cod and stockfish have been in Italy for so long that they have by now been totally assimilated into the national cuisine. After all, dried cod arrived in Italy centuries ago, brought there by the Normans. The Italians, ever appreciative of good food, made it their own and developed innumerable recipes for it. They even wrote poems, such as this one in Venetian dialect: '*Chi xe che ga inventà/polenta e baccalà?/Disèmelo creature/sto nome'sto portento che toga le misure/per farghe un monumento.*' (Tell me who invented polenta and baccalà, and I will take his name and measurements so that I can make a monument to him.)

In this recipe from Venice the fish used is stockfish, which the Veneti call *baccalà*. In proper Italian, of course, stockfish is – as you would expect – *stoccafisso*, and salt cod is *baccalà*. To confuse matters further, I have to admit that I am suggesting the use of salt cod in a recipe that calls

for stockfish. This is simply because stockfish is virtually unavailable in Britain, and even if you found a supplier the chances are that the stockfish would be woody, and woolly, no matter how long you cooked it.

THE RECIPE
There is plenty of salt cod in Portuguese, Spanish and Italian food shops and in the best fishmongers, such as my supplier, Jarvis in Kingston. So I suggest you buy a good piece of salt cod, at least 3cm/1¼in thick.

Because I love this dish so much I have made it with Finnan smoked haddock when I could not find salt cod. It is not the same, and it is not quite as good, but Finnan haddock is available in most fishmongers and this is a new and healthy way to prepare it.

Baccalà mantecato makes a lovely antipasto, or a supper dish served with grilled polenta or boiled potatoes. You must remember to buy the fish at least 2 days before you want to cook it. Once soaked, baccalà must be cooked straight away. If possible use a sweet olive oil, such as a Ligurian one.

SERVES 3 TO 4
450g/1lb salt cod
½ dozen black peppercorns
1 bay leaf
2 cloves
600ml/1pt semi-skimmed milk [US 2½ cups low-fat milk]
4 garlic cloves
120ml/4fl oz extra virgin olive oil
freshly ground black pepper
2 tbsp chopped fresh flat-leaf parsley

Ask the fishmonger to cut the salt cod into chunks. When you arrive home, put the salt cod in a bowl and leave it under running water for 48 hours, or leave it to soak for the same length of time, changing the water at least four times a day.

Do not cut down on the 2 days' soaking, as some recipes suggest; you'd have a tough, dried and unpleasantly salty piece of fish.

Put the soaked baccalà, skin side up, in a sauté pan with the peppercorns, bay leaf and cloves. Cover with the milk and bring slowly to the boil. Simmer for 15 minutes, until soft through the thickest part, then lift the fish out on to a board to cool enough for you to handle it.

Meanwhile, pour about 120ml/4fl oz of the cooking milk into a small saucepan. Add the garlic and simmer for 15 minutes.

Remove the skin and any bones from the fish pieces and transfer them to a large mortar or a heavy bowl. Add the cooked garlic, and the milk in which it has cooked, to the fish and pound with a pestle to break the fibres of the fish. Beat and pound until the baccalà is broken up, if necessary adding a couple of tablespoons more of the cooking milk. Now gradually add the oil in a thin stream, as you would for a mayonnaise. Season with pepper and mix in the parsley. The mixture should be quite thick, like mashed – rather than puréed – potatoes. Taste and check the seasoning, and serve. It is very good.

I have tried to do this pounding of the fish in a food processor, but I'm afraid the result is different and less satisfactory, because the fish is cut and puréed, not broken and beaten. Still . . . it is a far easier and quicker way!

SARDE RIPIENE
Stuffed Sardines

Sardines are stuffed in many different ways all up and down the Italian coast. In Veneto rosemary is added, and I think rosemary combines perfectly with baked blue fish.

Unfortunately sardines in Britain are often not as fresh as they should be. In that case I prefer to buy frozen sardines, or fresh herrings or sprats, less strong in flavour, maybe, but usually much fresher. Both herrings and sprats belong to the same family, *culpidae*, as sardines.

SERVES 4

800g/1¾lb fresh sardines
4 tbsp dried breadcrumbs
4 tbsp freshly grated Parmesan
1 tbsp chopped fresh rosemary
1 tbsp chopped fresh flat-leaf parsley
2 garlic cloves, finely chopped
salt and freshly ground black pepper
6 tbsp extra virgin olive oil
the juice of 1 lemon

Ask your fishmonger to fillet your sardines, keeping them in one piece at the back. If you buy frozen sardines you will have to do this yourself once they have thawed. And this is how you should do it. Give a good pull to the head and remove it. Using your fingers, open up the belly all the way down to the tail. Now place the sardine, open-side down, on a board and press down along the spine. The fish will flatten out and you can then easily remove the backbone.

Wash all the fish and dry them thoroughly.

Heat the oven to 200°C/400°F/ Gas Mark 6.

For the stuffing, put the breadcrumbs, Parmesan, rosemary, parsley, garlic, salt and pepper in a bowl and mix them all up with a fork. Pour in 4 tablespoons of the oil and blend everything together. Place a little stuffing on each open sardine and close it up so that it resumes its original shape, although headless. Choose a roasting tin in which the sardines will fit very tightly but in a single layer and brush it with oil. Arrange the sardines in the tin and sprinkle with salt and pepper. Drizzle with the remaining oil and with the lemon juice.

Bake for 10 to 15 minutes, until the flesh is white, opaque and compact. Serve warm, or at room temperature, as a delicious but simple first course.

Salsa Peverada per gli Arrosti da Penne
Peppery Sauce for Roast Fowl

The Veneti are very fond of fowl of any sort and, as so often happens in such a case, they have created the best recipes for these birds. They have them stuffed, roasted, boiled, braised . . . in lots of ways, all of them good.

When they serve roast guinea fowl, roast pheasant or even roast chicken they like to put this sauce on the table. It is a strong, rich sauce with a touch of acidity, and I have tasted, and tested, many versions of it. This is my favourite one and it comes from a book, *Antica Cucina Veneziana*, written by two people I admire a lot – the food historian Massimo Alberini and the teacher and writer Romana Bosco. Alberini wrote the fascinating introduction and chose the recipes; Romana wrote and tested them. The ideal combination of talents.

Romana's peverada contains vinegar instead of the more usual wine, and the result is more of a sweet-and-sour type of sauce. I like it very much and hope you will too.

SERVES 4

2 tbsp olive oil
1 garlic clove, finely chopped
1 small onion, finely chopped
salt and freshly ground black pepper
100g/3½oz luganega or other mild, coarse-ground, pure pork sausage, skinned and crumbled
1 fresh sage leaf, chopped
1 tbsp chopped fresh flat-leaf parsley
100g/3½oz chicken livers, cleaned and chopped
a small pinch of ground cinnamon
4 tbsp red wine vinegar
1 tbsp sugar

Heat the oil in a sauté pan with the garlic, onion, 1 teaspoon of salt and a couple of tablespoons of hot water. Let the mixture stew gently for 15 minutes or so and then add the luganega, sage and half the parsley. Sauté for a couple of minutes, then add the chicken livers and season with the cinnamon and plenty of pepper. Let the sauce cook for 10 to 15 minutes while giving it an occasional stir.

Meanwhile, put the vinegar in a small pan. Add the sugar and simmer over gentle heat until the sugar has dissolved. Mix the vinegar into the chicken liver mixture together with the remaining parsley. Taste and adjust seasoning before spooning the sauce into a bowl and bringing it to the table with the roast bird.

Il Brasato della Nonna Caterina
My Grandmother's Braised Beef

Although many of my colleagues say they were taught to cook by their grandmothers, this is a claim I cannot make. One of my grandmothers died when I was a baby and the other when I was seven. But I do remember this second one, Nonna Caterina, and two things about her cooking. One is that she made the only *caffè e latte* (coffee and milk) that I would drink for my *merenda*; the other being the most delicious cooking smell that I loved to sniff along the long corridor leading to the kitchen of her flat in Milan. Later on I learnt that the heavenly smell came from her brasato. My mother, of course, made it too, with the identical recipe, but to me it wasn't the same.

I have always found smells the most evocative of all senses. It may be that I loved her brasato because I loved her and her house. Nonna Caterina came from Venice, and her brasato might have been a Venetian version, although it contains what are known as 'the four Lombard spices': pepper, cinnamon, nutmeg and cloves. Brasati or stufati are in fact made everywhere from Valle d'Aosta to Trieste. It is a typical northern Italian dish, always prepared with one piece of beef, which should be from a young animal. Served with polenta, it is the Italian answer to the English roast beef and Yorkshire pudding, to be prepared on Sundays or for important feasts.

THE RECIPE
A piece of chuck, of top rump or round, or the eye of the silverside are all suitable cuts. But make sure that the beef is not too fresh or it will be tough however long you cook it.

SERVES 6 TO 8
a 1.6kg/3½lb boneless piece of beef, tied up in a neat roll
1 large onion, cut into chunks
2 carrots, cut into chunks
1 or 2 celery stalks, depending on size, cut into pieces
2 bay leaves
75g/2½oz [US 5 tbsp] unsalted butter
2 tbsp olive oil
grated nutmeg
2 pinches of ground cloves
½ tsp ground cinnamon
salt and freshly ground pepper
150ml/5fl oz dry Marsala
about 150ml/5fl oz meat stock (page 230)

FOR THE MARINADE
300ml/10fl oz red wine
½ onion, cut into pieces
1 celery stalk, cut into pieces
1 carrot, cut into pieces
6 peppercorns, bruised
1 tbsp sea salt

Put the meat in a bowl and add all the ingredients for the marinade. Leave it, covered, for 6 to 8 hours out of the fridge. (All marinating should be done out of the fridge unless the weather is very hot.) Turn the meat over as often as you can remember. When the meat is ready for cooking, take it out of the marinade and dry it thoroughly. Discard the marinade.

Heat the oven to 170°C/325°F/Gas Mark 3.

Put the onion, carrots, celery, bay leaves, half the butter and the oil in an oval flameproof casserole just large enough for the meat to fit snugly. Now set the meat on the vegetables and cook the whole thing for about 10 minutes, turning the meat over a few times. Season with the spices and salt and add the Marsala. Raise the heat and boil briskly for a couple of minutes to evaporate the alcohol. Now add half the stock, cover the casserole and place in the oven to cook for 3 to 3½ hours. Turn the meat over and baste every 20 to 30 minutes.

If your meat is good and does not contain water, all the liquid in the casserole might have evaporated before the meat is done. If this should happen, add the remaining stock and some water if necessary. If, however, there is more than about 200ml/7fl oz of liquid when the meat is ready (it should be very tender when prodded with a fork) take the meat out of the pot, keep it warm covered with foil, turn the heat up to high and boil the liquid briskly to reduce. Remove and discard the bay leaves.

Now you must pour the contents of the pot – but not the meat! – into a food processor to be puréed. Or, better still for a smoother sauce, you should purée it through a food mill. Pour the sauce into a small saucepan and add the rest of the butter. Cook gently until the butter has melted, then have a last tasting of the sauce to check the salt.

Place the beef on a carving board and slice it rather thickly. Arrange the slices on a heated dish, pour over the sauce and bring to the table.

TORTA CAROTINA

Carrot Cake

When my 93-year-old mother was in a home near Pavia, in southern Lombardy, I used to go and see her as often as I could. Sitting there with my knitting I got to know a lot of local people and, of course, all the nurses, the cook and the various helpers. They were fascinated with my profession of cookery writer, all giving me tips, recipes, asking about food in England, the English and, of course, 'Diana e Carlo', about whom they knew far more than I did!

In the course of my visits I learned a lot about the locality and, more importantly, about its cooking. The food at the old peoples' home was very good, always prepared with the utmost care. The lovely cook, Giovanna, helped by her sister, used to say, 'The poor old things, they have nothing to look forward to except what I bring up from the kitchen.' And those poor old things were very fussy indeed! A favourite dish of theirs, and mine too, was a veal stew cooked on a bed of onions and covered with bay leaves.

One of the helpers, Wilma Magagnato, had a pasta shop in the village, run by her daughter. Wilma prepared the pasta and cakes in the morning before starting work in the home. Her cakes were quite delicious; they had the sophisti-cated simplicity of home-made cakes, made, of course, to perfection. One of her jewels, and she was very proud of it, is this carrot cake. I was amazed, never having come across a carrot cake in Italy. I thought it must be yet another American import, like hamburgers and Coke. 'Ma no, signora,' Wilma replied, 'my father used to make it for us when we were little. And as we didn't have an oven at home, he used to take it to the baker to be baked in the bread oven.' Wilma's father came from near Belluno in Veneto. Apparently carrot cake is popular in that area, although this is something I haven't yet had a chance to verify.

THE RECIPE

This is a very good cake, the fragrant freshness of the almond acquiring a deeper side through the darker flavour of the carrot and the rum. It is also an ideal cake for people who are allergic to dairy products and/or gluten, since it contains neither.

Buy almonds in their skin. They are usually fresher than the skinned ones. Potato flour is available in speciality food shops and good supermarkets. When making this cake I have used Billington's golden granulated sugar, which is so good, and ideal in this recipe. It is available in most good grocers and supermarkets. As with most country cakes, the finishing touch is simply a thick layer of icing sugar.

150g/5oz [US 1 cup] almonds

3 eggs, separated

125g/4oz [US ½ cup + 2 tbsp] sugar

60g/2oz [US ½ cup] potato flour

salt

1½ tsp baking powder

150g/5oz [US 1⅓ cups] carrots, grated

2 tbsp rum

butter and dried breadcrumbs for the tin

icing sugar [US confectioners' sugar], to finish

Heat the oven to 180°C/350°F/Gas Mark 4.

Slide the almonds into a saucepan of boiling water. Boil for 20 seconds, then drain and skin them. The fresher they are, the easier it is to skin them by squeezing them between thumb and forefinger. Put the skinned almonds on a baking tray and dry them in the oven for 7 to 10 minutes. (Keep the oven on for baking the cake.) After that, chop them finely in a food processor or by hand. They should be chopped very fine, but not as fine as ground almonds.

Beat the egg yolks with the sugar until they have doubled their volume.

Sift the potato flour with the salt and baking powder and add with a large metal spoon to the egg and sugar mixture. Fold well and then add the almonds, carrots and the rum. Mix thoroughly.

Whisk the egg whites until standing in firm peaks. Fold them into the carrot mixture by the spoonful, gradually and carefully.

Butter an 18cm/7in spring-clip tin. Line the bottom with a disc of parchment paper and butter the paper. Sprinkle about 2 tablespoons of dried breadcrumbs over the bottom and side of the tin and then shake out any excess crumbs.

Spoon the cake mixture into the prepared tin and bake for 40 to 45 minutes, until the cake is lovely and golden brown. It will have shrunk from the side of the tin, and a wooden toothpick inserted into the middle of the cake should come out dry.

Remove the cake from the tin and turn it over on to a wire rack. Peel off the paper and let the cake cool. Serve covered with icing sugar.

A Venetian Sorbet

Sgropin is a chilled drink which, as its name in dialect indicates, is drunk at the end of a good meal to clean the palate and stomach. I have transformed the drink into a sorbet, first because I like it better this way, and secondly because I shall never forget a glass of sgropin cascading down the chest of the man sitting next to me at a dinner I organized for Venice in Peril. The sgropin was solid at the top but liquid underneath, and when the top broke the rest came out in a flood.

SERVES 4 OR 5

4 unwaxed lemons
1 unwaxed orange
200g/7oz caster sugar [US 1 cup granulated sugar]
100ml/3½fl oz Grappa

Thinly peel the rind from the lemons and the orange, leaving the white pith on the fruit. Put the rind in a frying pan. Add the sugar and 300ml/10fl oz of water. Bring slowly to the boil to dissolve the sugar, then turn the heat up and boil for 5 minutes. Add the Grappa and set aside to cool.

Squeeze the fruit. Mix the juice with the cold syrup, then strain the whole mixture. Pour into an ice-cream maker and freeze according to the manufacturer's instructions.

Because of the high alcohol content the mixture does not freeze hard. Spoon it into chilled flute glasses for serving.

Polenta Cake

I was amazed when, a few years ago, I first set eyes on the name of this cake in bakers' shops in Venice. It was obviously the old-fashioned polenta cake, but it had been baked in a new shape of tin, cylindrical and wavy. Why 'Amor Polenta'? The name is catchy, I agree, but does a good old-fashioned cake need a new name?

The excellence of this simple cake depends totally on the almonds. Buy the best almonds you can find, or bring back a supply from Italy or France and keep them in the freezer. They must have a fresh, plump appearance, without any wrinkles.

Serve your polenta cake for tea or with a glass of wine. A white Albana from Romagna or the more easily available Vinsanto would be the best.

100g/3½oz [US ⅔ cup] shelled almonds
75g/2½oz [US ½ cup+2 tbsp] Italian 00 flour
2 tsp baking powder
a pinch of salt
125g/4oz [US 1 stick] unsalted butter, softened
125g/4oz caster sugar [US ½ cup + 2 tbsp granulated sugar]
2 size-2 eggs plus 2 egg yolks [US extra-large eggs]
100g/3½oz maize (polenta) flour [US ¾ cup + 2 tbsp coarse cornmeal]
butter and fine dried breadcrumbs for the tin

Heat the oven to 180°C/350°F/Gas Mark 4.

Blanch the almonds for 20 seconds in boiling water. Drain and squeeze the almonds out of their skins – an easy job, especially if they are fresh, as indeed they should be. Put the skinned almonds on a baking tray and toast them in the oven for 10 minutes or so, until they begin to get brown. Remove from the oven, but leave the oven on.

Sift the white flour with the baking powder and the salt.

Put the butter and sugar in a bowl and beat well until smooth. (I cream them together first with a fork or, better still, with my hands, which being warm amalgamate the butter faster. Then I use a hand-held electric mixer at low speed, to prevent splattering the mixture everywhere.)

Lightly beat the eggs and egg yolks together and add to the butter-cream by the spoonful alternately with spoonfuls of the sifted flour mixture.

Grind the almonds in a food processor together with a couple of tablespoons of the maize flour, which will absorb the almond oil. Grind into grains, not to a coarse powder, and then add to the cake mixture together with the remaining maize flour. Mix thoroughly.

Butter a loaf tin that measures 17 × 5cm/ 7 × 2in. Sprinkle in a couple of tablespoons of breadcrumbs to coat all over and then shake out the excess. Spoon the cake mixture into the tin and bake for about 45 minutes, until the cake is cooked. Test by inserting a wooden toothpick in the middle – it should come out dry. The cake will be springy and have shrunk from the sides of the tin.

Loosen the cake all around the tin with a thin knife and turn it on to a wire rack to cool. Wrap it in foil if you do not want to eat it straight away; it keeps well for 3 or 4 days. It is pretty covered with sifted icing sugar [US confectioners' sugar].

Gnocchi Dolci di Latte
Sweet Milk Gnocchi

I had forgotten all about this pudding until the other day, when I saw it on the menu at Riva, our local Italian restaurant in Barnes. As soon as I tasted it I was taken back many many years to our cousins' villa on Lake Como, where their nanny made the best gnocchi di latte ever. Later on, I used to make them for my children when they were young, but I never succeeded in recapturing the flavour of Balia Teresa's gnocchi. Then here I was in Barnes, of all places, eating the gnocchi of my childhood. I wonder whether it is that Francesco, the talented young chef at Riva, comes from Pordenone in Veneto, as Balia Teresa did.

At Riva, of course, they are served in a grown-up honeyed rum sauce, while ours were either plain or with a blob of jam or honey on each gnocco. The shape is also different; our gnocchi were just rounds, while Francesco makes very pretty crescents which he surrounds with a few crescents of apple in a very attractive presentation.

THE RECIPE

Gnocchi di latte are made in Lombardy, Veneto and Emilia-Romagna, the regions famous for their dairy products. And then they are found again in Marche, a region further south which prides itself on an excellent breed of cow, where traditionally 2 tablespoons of Parmesan are added to the mixture. There are, however, some variations from one place to another. This is the gnocchi di latte served at Riva.

SERVES 4

4 size-2 egg yolks [US extra-large egg yolks]
200g/7oz [US 1 cup] sugar
60g/2oz cornflour [US ½ cup cornstarch]
½ tsp pure vanilla extract
a pinch of salt
500ml/16fl oz full fat milk

FOR THE SAUCE AND GARNISH
1 apple, unpeeled, sliced into very thin segments
100g/3½oz [US ⅓ cup] honey
200ml/7fl oz dark rum
45g/1¾oz [US 3½ tbsp] unsalted butter, cut into small cubes

In a bowl beat the egg yolks and sugar until creamy. Add the cornflour gradually, while beating constantly, until it has all been incorporated. Add the vanilla extract and the pinch of salt.

Slowly pour in the milk, mixing the whole time. Transfer the mixture to a saucepan and cook on medium heat, stirring constantly with a wooden spoon. When the mixture has thickened whisk it briefly to eliminate any possible lumps. Cook for a further couple of minutes, stirring constantly.

Moisten a baking tray or a large shallow dish with cold water and then pour the egg mixture into it. Spread it out to a thickness of about 1cm/½in. Cool it a little and then cover the tray or dish and put it in the fridge.

When cold, cut into shapes with a crescent-shaped biscuit cutter and place in an ovenproof dish.

Arrange the slices of apple around the gnocchi.

In a bowl blend together the honey and rum. Pour the mixture into the dish and add the butter here and there. Place in a hot oven, or under a preheated grill [US broiler], for about 10 minutes or until golden, and serve hot.

Francesco rightly suggests that these gnocchi can be prepared a day in advance and heated up just before serving them.

TORTION
A Venetian Strudel

In these Eastern regions there are many different kinds of strudel, going under different names and existing in different versions, although all have their origins in the Austrian or Slav cuisines. The tortion is the Venetian version, its name meaning 'curved' in Venetian dialect. And curved it is, since it is in the shape of a ring, sometimes totally closed, sometimes with the two ends not quite meeting.

I use filo pastry because the pastry for a strudel such as this should be rolled out very thin, which calls for considerable expertise. Filo pastry is there in the shop, all ready for you. But remember to be quite generous in brushing each layer with plenty of melted butter.

Buy the candied peel in segments; the kind that is already chopped is not good enough.

SERVES 6 TO 8

2 tbsp sultanas [US golden raisins]
2 tbsp dark rum
2 tart dessert apples
1 tbsp candied citron and/or lemon, cut into tiny cubes
1 tbsp pine nuts
2 pinches of ground cinnamon
4 Savoiardi, crushed into fine crumbs
100g/3½oz [US 7 tbsp] unsalted butter
225g/8oz filo pastry, approximate weight, defrosted if frozen

Soak the sultanas in the rum for 15 to 20 minutes.

Peel, core and quarter the apples and then cut them across into thin slices. Put them in a bowl and add the candied peel, sultanas and rum, pine nuts, cinnamon and Savoiardi.

Melt the butter in a small saucepan and add 2 tablespoons to the fruit mixture. Mix thoroughly.

Heat the oven to 180°C/350°F/Gas Mark 4.
Line an oven tray with a piece of foil and brush
the foil with a little melted butter. Unwrap the
filo pastry and lay a sheet of about 30 × 20cm/
12 × 8in on the foil. If the filo sheets are not big
enough, patch them up, overlapping a little, to
form a rectangle of more or less this size. Brush
the sheet with plenty of butter and then place
another sheet over it. If you are patching it, make
sure the joins come in different places for each
sheet. Lay 4 sheets in all in this manner, remembering the melted butter.

Spread the filling evenly over the pastry and
then roll up the pastry to form a large sausage.
Curve it around to form a fat ring. As mentioned
in the introduction, the ring should have a gap
between the two extremities.

Brush with all the remaining butter and bake
for 20 minutes.

Serve hot or warm.

MOSTARDA DI VENEZIA
Quince and Mustard Preserve

While I have never been successful in producing
good mostarda di Cremona, I have made excellent mostarda di Venezia.

There is another reason why I have never per-
severed with mostarda di Cremona, while I have
with the Venetian counterpart. Mostarda di
Cremona is on sale in most Italian food shops and
it is excellent. I have never met anyone in Italy
who makes their own. Mostarda di Venezia,
however, is very difficult to find in shops but is
very easy to make. This recipe is based on the one
published in *The Compleat Mustard*, a book by
Robin Weir and Rosamond Man, and on a recipe
given to me by my good and generous friend
Maria Deana. Maria is the daughter of the famous

Arturo Deana, the original owner of the
Ristorante La Colomba in Venice. The late
Arturo Deana used to serve traditional Venetian
food to the international élite before Harry's Bar
came on the scene. Good food was not Deana's
only passion, as he also loved good paintings,
some of which used to hang in his restaurant. His
collection started with the inevitable gift of a
painter who couldn't pay his bill; by the end of
his life Deana's collection included a number of
paintings by De Chirico, Chagall and Kokoschka.

At La Colomba, the mostarda di Venezia was
served with a sweetened mascarpone cream laced
with a small glass of rum. The little pastry biscuits
to accompany this delightful ensemble were
shaped like a *colomba* (dove). Maria said to me,
'In this way, cheese, pudding and fruit were all
supplied in a single dish.' Try it, it's a winner.

THE RECIPE
Buy proper candied peel sold in large segments
and not the chopped up kind.

1.8kg/4lb quinces
1 bottle of dry white wine (750ml)
the grated rind and juice of 1 unwaxed lemon
sugar
5 tablespoons mustard powder
salt
150g/5oz candied peel, cut into small cubes

Peel and core the quinces and cut into pieces. Put
them in a pan and cover them with the wine. Add
the lemon rind and juice. Cook until soft, about
40 minutes.

Purée the mixture and then add the same
weight in sugar. Return to the pan. Dissolve the
mustard powder in a little hot water and add to the
purée with 1 teaspoon of salt and the candied peel.
Cook gently until the liquid is reduced and the
mostarda becomes dense, about 20–30 minutes.

Sterilize some jars and fill with the mostarda.
When it is cool, cover, seal and store away. Keep
for about 1 month before you use it.

FRIULI-VENEZIA GIULIA

My love for this small region tucked away in the north-eastern corner of northern Italy began with my fondness for particular Friulani. First I must mention our cook Maria, to whom I was devoted, and two other maids who stayed in the family for years ('All the best servants come from Friuli' was a dictum I heard in Milan ages ago and which has always stuck in my mind.) But Friulani do not only make the best servants, they also make the best friends, thanks to their generosity, their cheerfulness and their warmth of character. Unfortunately my visits to that least touristy part of Italy have been far too sporadic and always too brief. There are plenty of good hotels and even better restaurants and *osterie* in the rolling hills covered with vines . . . and no tourists. I feel I really should not be broadcasting this secret!

Friuli – the name is a contraction of *Forum Juli* – has been occupied by many different tribes and peoples, from the Celts to the Austrians. All of them have left their mark. But the people whom the modern Friulani consider their ancestors are the Longobards – meaning long-bearded – a Germanic tribe that descended upon Italy in the 6th century and went as far as Pavia and Milan. Hence the name Lombardy. Maybe it is our shared ancestry that makes me feel so close to the Friulani.

As in Lombardy, the cooking excels in winter dishes: soups of every kind, vegetable stews (page 119), rich sausages and, of course, prosciutti and prosciutti and yet more prosciutti. This speciality of prosciutto-making benefits from a balance between the warm breezes coming from the Adriatic and the cold air from the mountains to the North, the right degree of humidity and, of course, the ability of the locals, who are excellent craftsmen in everything they touch. San Daniele is the prosciutto that springs to mind, but there are others. I also love the prosciutto of Sauris, with its very porky flavour and a touch of smoke. But the outstanding treat I had was a prosciutto made by a man called Gigi d'Osvaldo, who apparently hangs them up in his bedroom! He lives near Cormons, actually in Venezia Giulia, where there is one of the best restaurants in Italy, called La Subida.

You can spend a few blissful days at La Subida – it has rooms – while tasting such local specialities as potato ravioli (page 117), roast shin of veal and perfect venison with blueberry sauce – shades of Austria here – to finish with a rich *gubana*, a sort of strudel filled with dried fruit and nuts moistened with the superb Piccolit wine and then shaped round and round like a snail's shell. Very pretty, but I must confess I have never managed to achieve that lovely snail effect.

The region's cooking is fundamentally cucina very *povera*, with a glorious choice of soups, gnocchi, game (plenty of roebucks, deer and chamois in the mountains), sausages and cheeses. There is one cheese that I particularly like, and I loved the way it was served at the trattoria Blasut in Lavariano. Blasut is the sort of place that very cleverly manages to be elegant and rustic at the same time. A half cheese, *montasio* being the cheese in question, was brought to the table, a half of about 30cm/12in in diameter. The cheese was scooped out and cut into little cubes that you just picked up and popped into your mouth with great ease. Montasio is a DOC cheese (i.e. carries the stamp of origin) made with semi-skimmed cow's milk. It has a delicate milky flavour when young and used as a table cheese, getting sapid and deliciously tangy when mature, being then used mostly for making *frico*. This is a dish you would never have any-where else, even though it could be done with other semi-soft mountain cheeses. To make frico the montasio is very thinly sliced and fried in butter, oil or lard, with a little onion. The cheese will melt at first and then solidify, at which point it is time to turn it over like a pancake. Frico can accompany fried eggs or prosciutto, but I liked it best with very soft scrambled eggs made with red wine vinegar, a recipe by Gianna Modotti.

Gianna, who has a cookery school in the elegant town of Udine, has a deep knowledge of the cooking of the region. She told me that there is just one tra-ditional pasta dish, cialzons, which is first mentioned in a 14th-century docu-ment. There are endless variations of this type of ravioli, but there are only two basic types: the cialzons made in the low land around Udine and the cialzons of the mountain regions. The former contain meat and are served *in brodo* – in a meat stock, as a soup. There is a recipe for these meat cialzons, written by the Mother Superior of the Convento delle Dimesse in Udine, which contains roast chicken, brain and other delicacies, demonstrating yet again the culinary exper-tise of the nuns and their great appreciation of good food. The cialzons made in the mountains 'never contain meat, ricotta being the base', Gianna Modotti explained. Ricotta plus dried fruits, fresh fruits such as pears, quinces, apples, plums, and then cocoa, potatoes, cinnamon and similar ingredients. The filling is always flavoured with marjoram, and the cialzons are dressed with brown butter which is a trademark of this cuisine.

This same brown butter, plus a sprinkling of sugar, was the dressing of the lasagne al papavero – with poppy seeds, which I had in Trieste at the Hostaria Voliga, up near the splendid church of San Giusto. Lasagne with poppy seeds is the most successful marriage between Italian and Hungarian ingredients. Hungarian influences are also noticeable in the abundance of different gulasch, always less fierce in Venezia Giulia than the original Hungarian one.

In Venezia Giulia we have left behind the cooking of the mountains to embrace the cooking of the sea, with its superb seafood risotti, fish soups, *capelonghe* (razor clams) which are cooked in Trieste in a delicate *soffritto* of parsley and garlic and served hot, and *grancevole* (spider crabs), which remind you of the proximity to Venice. But Trieste is proud of a very personal type of cooking based on Austrian, Hungarian and Slav traditions, intermingled with oriental and Jewish influences. The Jewish settlement in Trieste was very strong.

A modern dish I recently came across in that part of Italy is orzotto, which is risotto made with *orzo* (pearl barley) instead of rice. Pearl barley appears quite often in Friulano cooking. The first time I had orzotto was at a very smart wedding in the country near Udine. The head caterer told me that they prefer to do this instead of risotto for parties, because pearl barley does not become *scotto* (overcooked) like rice does. The orzotto at the wedding was the porcini and truffle edition of the similar risotto, but I had an orzotto a few days later at a friend's house made with wonderful beans from Carnia, which are a highly prized variety of borlotti.

Finally, a view of Friuli from outside. In the small town of Crema in Lombardy, the patronne of the restaurant Cral, who gave me her recipe for her superb and unusual ravioli (page 28), was Friulana. When I pressed her about recipes of her own Friuli, she said, 'Eh no, it is too difficult, the cooking of Friuli does not export well. You must eat it in one of those large, dark country kitchens dominated by the *fogolar*.' And she is quite right. You need a fogolar, the raised open fireplace, to properly enjoy bean and barley soup (opposite), polenta and frico, *musetto* (a pork sausage made with the snout of the pig) and *brovada* – turnip fermented with the dregs of pressed grapes; an acquired taste, I dare say. All this would be washed down by the *tajut*, the glass of white wine which is a part of a ritual gregarious drinking. To finish you off you will be offered a *resentin*, a coffee *corretto* with an ample shot of Grappa.

MINESTRA DI FAGIOLI E ORZO

Bean and Barley Soup

Barley is only eaten in the Alpine regions of Italy, and most of the dishes it appears in are of foreign origin.

The recipe for this soup was given to me by Gianna Modotti of Udine, a most generous friend and an accomplished cook.

In some supermarkets you can find pancetta already cut into small cubes, which is ideal for this recipe.

SERVES 6

150g/5oz [US ¾ cup] dried borlotti beans
1 medium potato
1 medium onion
1 celery stalk
1 small carrot
1 fresh bay leaf
2 fresh sage leaves
1 fresh rosemary sprig
3 or 4 fresh flat-leaf parsley sprigs
1 garlic clove
salt and freshly ground black pepper
125g/4oz [US heaping ½ cup] pearl barley
125g/4oz smoked pancetta, chopped
2–3 tbsp extra virgin olive oil

Soak the beans in water for at least 8 hours. If you live in an area where the water is hard, use filtered water.

Drain and rinse the beans and put them in your stockpot or in an earthenware soup pot, earthenware being the best material for slow cooking. Add all the vegetables, cut into chunks, all the herbs and the garlic. Cover with 1l/1¾pt [US 1qt] of water and season with 1 teaspoon of salt. Bring to the boil and cook, covered, for at least 2 hours at the lowest simmer. 'The lowest simmer' are the crucial words here: the surface of the water should just be broken by the occasional

bubble. I have left the beans cooking away (because I forgot them) for 3 or 4 hours and they were better than ever – whole and soft, and they had time to develop all their sweet chestnutty flavour. The amount of water is enough if you boil the beans really slowly; otherwise you might have to add some boiling water during the cooking.

Rinse the barley under cold water, throw it into a large pan and add the pancetta, 1 teaspoon of salt and plenty of pepper. Cover with 1l/1¾pt [US 1qt] of water and cook until the barley is very tender, about 1 hour.

Now discard the bay leaf and rosemary stalk, then purée half the beans and all the cooking vegetables through a food mill. If you do not have this invaluable tool, purée in a food processor, although the result will not be as perfect because the skin of the beans, even though minutely cut up, will be in the soup.

Add the bean purée and the whole beans with all the liquid to the barley and mix well. Taste and adjust seasoning, then bring the whole thing to the boil. Simmer for 10 minutes. Although this is a thick soup, you may have to add a little hot water or stock because of the evaporation during the lengthy boiling.

Ladle the soup into individual bowls and drizzle a little olive oil into each bowl. Alternatively, put a bottle of your best olive oil on the table for everyone to add their own.

RISOTTO DI GAMBERI

Risotto with Prawns

Rice is fashionable, prawns are fashionable, hence risotto with prawns is one of the most fashionable of all risotti. But along the coast from Trieste to Venice this risotto is no new fad; it has been popular there for centuries.

This recipe is my interpretation of one of the best fish risotti I have ever had. It comes from Harry's Grill at the Hotel Duchi d'Aosta in Trieste. While I had this, my husband had an excellent risotto al nero – with squid ink. A delicious start to a good dinner, spoiled only by the local *bora*, the wind blowing down on Trieste from the north-east, which prevented us having our meal outside on that very elegant piazza.

SERVES 3 TO 4

450g/1lb raw king or tiger prawns in shell [US large raw shrimp]

2 tbsp extra virgin olive oil

60g/2oz [US 4 tbsp] unsalted butter

1 small onion, finely chopped

a bunch of fresh flat-leaf parsley

1 garlic clove

1.2l/2pt [US 5 cups] fish stock, preferably home-made (page 231)

2 ripe plum tomatoes

350g/12oz [US 1¾ cups] Italian rice, preferably Vialone Nano

2 pinches of chilli powder

150ml/5fl oz Prosecco wine, or other good sparkling wine

2 tbsp brandy

4–5 tbsp freshly grated Parmesan

salt

Peel the prawns and remove the dark veins. Wash them and dry them thoroughly with kitchen paper towel. Cut them into 1cm/½in pieces.

Heat the oil, 40g/1½oz [US 3 tbsp] of the butter and the onion in a heavy saucepan and sauté for 10 minutes or so.

Meanwhile, discard the stalks of the parsley. Chop the leaves with the garlic and then add to the onion. Continue cooking for 2 minutes.

Bring the fish stock to the simmer and keep it simmering gently, close to where you are cooking the risotto.

Peel the tomatoes, either by plunging them into boiling water for 30 seconds or, a quicker method, by holding them, speared on the prongs of a fork, over a gas flame until the skin cracks. When they are peeled, chop them coarsely and throw them into the pan. Let them cook briskly for 5 minutes, then mix in the rice.

Cook to 'toast' the rice for half a minute, while stirring it quickly. Sprinkle with the chilli powder and splash with the wine. Let it bubble away for a minute, then begin to add the fish stock, one ladleful at a time, while you stir the rice constantly. When all the liquid has been absorbed, add another ladleful, stirring and making sure to scrape the bottom and sides of the pan. Continue in this way for about 15 minutes. Now taste the rice; it is done when it is tender but still firm to the bite. Near the end of the cooking reduce the quantity of stock you add each time or you may have too much liquid when the rice is ready. By the end of the cooking the risotto should be moist but not runny.

When the rice is nearly ready, mix in the prawns and the brandy and cook, stirring, for the last 2 or 3 minutes.

Now draw the pan from the heat, and add the rest of the butter and the cheese. Leave to rest for a minute and then stir thoroughly. Taste and correct salt.

Ravioli di Patate
Potato Ravioli

In the eastern corner of Friuli, practically in Slovenia, there is a town called Cormòns, where there is a restaurant called La Subida, where there is a chef called Stefano. Recently Stefano flew to London to promote the food and the wines of that unknown pocket of Italy, and the lucky Londoners enjoyed a week of Friulano cooking at Sandrini in Knightsbridge. Now although Knightsbridge and Friuli are many miles apart, the dinners I had in Knightsbridge were more representative of traditional Friulano cooking than any meal I have had in Friuli. There, many restaurateurs are only too willing to defer to the tastes of their clients and serve fashionably healthy – yet so boring – *grigliate* (grills) of meat or fish.

Stefano's dinner in London consisted of seven courses. I cannot, here, describe them all, so after much heart-searching I chose these ravioli because they are so characteristic of the ability of the Friulani to produce interesting dishes out of everyday food.

These potato ravioli are a very unusual shape, unlike any stuffed pasta I have ever eaten, a sort of square parcel with pinched ends, like a wrapped toffee. I went down to the kitchen to see how they were made, but when I asked Stefano how I could possibly describe how to make that shape, his only answer was, 'That's your problem'! So I decided to forget the toffee shape and give you the instructions for lovely large, ravioli-shaped ravioli.

THE RECIPE
Traditionally, the potato ravioli are dressed in a juice of roast veal. If you happen to have this in the fridge, or if you are cooking a roast as a second course, well and good. If not, melted butter and a touch of cinnamon or poppy seeds is perfect. The butter must be more than melted, it must begin to colour, as they like it in Friuli. The use of cinnamon and poppy seeds in savoury dishes is typical of the region.

This is Stefano's recipe, which was absolutely perfect in the exactness of the quantities.

SERVES 6
700g/1½lb floury potatoes
30g/1oz onion
60g/2oz smoked pancetta
4 tbsp olive oil
salt and freshly ground black pepper
1 egg yolk
1 tbsp chopped fresh chives
2 tbsp chopped fresh marjoram
1 tbsp freshly grated Parmesan

FOR THE PASTA
300g/10oz [US 2½ cups] Italian 00 flour
3 eggs

FOR THE DRESSING
60g/2oz [US 4 tbsp] unsalted butter
1 tsp ground cinnamon or 2 tbsp poppy seeds
30g/1oz Parmesan shavings

First make the dough for the pasta, following the instructions on page 232. Wrap it in cling film and put aside to rest while you prepare the stuffing.

Boil the potatoes in their skins. When cooked, peel them (if you wear rubber gloves you can do this when they are still hot, which is quicker) and purée them through a food mill, or potato ricer, into a bowl.

Chop the onion and the pancetta very thoroughly. (When there is pancetta or prosciutto in a mixture to be chopped I find that the food processor does a very good job. It takes only a minute and the result is very much like a well-made *battuto*, which would take much longer.) Heat the oil in a large frying pan, add the battuto and sauté for 5 minutes. Mix in the potato purée and add salt to taste and a good grinding of pepper. Transfer the mixture back into the bowl and mix in the egg yolk, chives, marjoram and grated Parmesan. Mix very well and set aside to cool.

Unwrap the dough and place on a floured work surface. Roll out the dough, which should not be stretched too thin – about 1mm/1⁄25in is the ideal thickness. Work one sheet of dough at a time, keeping the rest covered to stop it drying up. Cut the rolled-out sheets into 8cm/just over 3in squares. Place a mound of stuffing the size of a walnut on one square and cover with another square. Seal the dough all around with dampened fingers, making sure that no air has been trapped in the dough. Place each raviolo on clean linen towels.

When all the ravioli are made, bring a large saucepan of water to the boil. Add 1½ tablespoons of salt and then gently slide in half the ravioli. Cook until done, from 3 to 8 minutes depending on whether the dough was still fresh, and then retrieve the ravioli with a slotted spoon and transfer, well drained, to a heated large and shallow dish. Cook the second batch and keep warm.

Melt the butter and cook until it begins to become brown. Pour over the ravioli, mix gently around and cover with a gentle spray of one or other of the spices.

To make Parmesan shavings, use a swivel-blade vegetable peeler, shaving a piece of Parmesan until you have prepared a nice little mound. Sprinkle the shavings over the ravioli and serve immediately.

FRITE DI ORT Ⓥ
A Dish of Mixed Garden Vegetables

'To make *Frite di Ort* you go into the vegetable garden (*ort* in local dialect) and pick what is ready. Just as three or four months earlier you would go into the fields and pick what was growing. And with whatever you picked you would be able to make the *Frite di Camp* (field).' These were the words of Gianna Modotti, who runs a cookery school in Udine and is the expert on the cooking of Friuli. She was explaining this recipe to me, and pointing out how it is typical of Friuli cooking, combining simplicity with quality. 'Simple ingredients, cooked so as to produce a good dish.'

I thought of myself, and most of my readers, going into the garden in Britain, and I realized that we could find nearly all the vegetables she was mentioning: spinach, Swiss chard, broccoli, leeks, celery; they all grow or could grow in this northern climate. And how nice to mix them together in a sort of northern ratatouille well suited to an autumnal supper in a cold climate. Sweet peppers, tomato and aubergine or eggplant can strike a discordant note in a northern setting. Food, after all, like clothes, has a time and a place.

THE RECIPE
Use a mild oil from Liguria or Lake Garda. A plain, good olive oil, rather than an extra virgin, is also suitable, since you do not want the flavour of a strong oil to come through.

SERVES 6
900g/2lb mixed vegetables: spinach, Swiss chard, broccoli, leek, celery, greens
60g/2oz [US 4 tbsp] unsalted butter
1 tbsp olive oil
2 garlic cloves, sliced
1 tbsp flour
salt and freshly ground black pepper

Wash the vegetables and cut them into large pieces. Keep them separate. Now blanch them separately. I heat 3 saucepans of salted water to the boil, and I blanch the vegetables in turn in these 3 pans. Blanch the vegetables briefly to keep them crunchy.

Lift the vegetables out of the pans with a slotted spoon or metal sieve and put them all together in a bowl; keep some of the liquid in one of the pans. Now take them out of the bowl, leaving the liquid behind, and place them on a board. Chop them coarsely and return them to the bowl.

Heat the butter, oil and garlic in a large sauté pan and sauté until the garlic begins to release its aroma. Mix in the flour and cook it for about 2 minutes, stirring constantly. The flour should begin to colour. Mix in a couple of tablespoons of the vegetable liquid and then spoon all the vegetables and the liquid in the bowl into the pan. Add salt and pepper to taste and cook, stirring frequently, for about 10 minutes, until the vegetables are tender. You might have to add a couple more tablespoons of the reserved liquid during the cooking. The vegetables, when ready to be brought to the table, should be just wet, but the dish should not be a soup.

Transfer to a heated dish. Use an earthenware dish if you have one as this keeps the vegetables hotter than any other type of dish. Frite is one of the few Italian dishes that is traditionally eaten 'piping hot'.

AGNELLO AL CREN
Lamb in Horseradish Sauce

Horseradish is hardly known in Italy except in some pockets of the north-eastern regions, whose cooking has been influenced either by Central Europe or by the Slav countries, or both.

This recipe comes originally from Venezia Giulia, which lies on the border with ex-Yugoslavia. But it has been in my repertoire for so many years that I cannot remember how it came there in the first place. The only thing I know is that it is a very good recipe.

SERVES 4 TO 6

a 1.8kg/4lb shoulder of lamb (weight with bone)
60g/2oz [US 4 tbsp] unsalted butter
2 tbsp olive oil
1 onion, sliced
1 fresh thyme sprig
3 bay leaves
6 tbsp good wine vinegar
180ml/6fl oz meat stock (page 230)
salt and freshly ground pepper
3 tbsp horseradish sauce (not the creamed kind)
4 tbsp chopped fresh flat-leaf parsley

Ask your butcher to bone the meat for you. Then, at home, remove and discard most of the fat and all the gristle and cut the meat into 2.5cm/1in cubes.

Put half the butter, the oil, onion, thyme, bay leaves, vinegar, stock, salt and pepper into a heavy flameproof casserole (ideally an earthenware pot that you can put directly on the heat) and bring slowly to the boil. Add the meat and cook, covered, for about 1 hour. By this time the meat should be very tender; if not, let it cook away for a further 20 minutes or so.

When the meat is ready there should be very little liquid in the pan. If there is a lot of liquid, fish out the meat with a slotted spoon, keep it warm and boil the liquid to reduce over high heat. Return the meat to the pot.

Melt the remaining butter in a small saucepan and mix in the horseradish and the parsley. Cook, stirring constantly, for 1 minute. Pour the horse-radish sauce over the meat and mix thoroughly to coat the meat with the sauce. Taste and check seasoning before you bring the pot to the table.

PANDOLOS CUL FENOLI Ⓥ
Biscuits with Fennel

Pandolo is the biscuit [US cookie] of Friuli. In local dialect the word means a tall person, good for nothing. (What the connection is between the two, nobody could explain!) Pandoli are oval, about 6 × 3cm/2½ × 1¼in. They are eaten at the end of a meal, or at other times of day, with the Verduzzo di Ramandolo, a wine made from the Friuli verduzzo grape. Ramandolo has a honeyed, fruity bouquet, very distinctive and interesting, and a lovely straw colour with gold flashes.

MAKES ABOUT 40

150g/5oz [US 1¼ cups] white flour, preferably Italian 00

1 size-2 egg [US extra-large egg]

30g/1oz [US 2 tbsp] unsalted butter, cut into small pieces, at room temperature

75g/2½oz caster sugar [US 6½ tbsp granulated sugar]

a pinch of salt

1½ tsp baking powder

½ tsp fennel seeds

butter for the tray

Put the flour on the work top, make a well and break the egg into it. Mix with a little flour and then add the butter, sugar, salt and baking powder to the well.

Pound the fennel seeds in a mortar or under the blade of a large knife and add to the mixture. Mix and knead quickly to form a ball of dough. (The dough can also be made in a food processor.) Wrap the dough in cling film and refrigerate for at least half an hour.

Heat the oven to 180°C/350°F/Gas Mark 4.

Dust the work top with flour and roll out the dough to a thickness of about 3mm/⅛in. Stamp out the biscuits with an oval cutter. Butter an oven tray, lay the biscuits on it and bake for 10–15 minutes, until golden.

LIGURIA

I f I were to be told that I could eat dishes from only one of Italy's 20 regions, I would unhesitatingly choose Liguria. I would find in them the kind of food that most appeals to me: aromatic, delicate, with few spices but with many herbs. The dishes are complex, with different flavours that always combine well and never clash. The cooking is usually slow, to bring the best out of the ingredients, which are humble, and such as can be found everywhere – but always of the best quality.

Liguria is a boomerang-shaped strip of land, only about 10 kilometres deep, stretching from the French frontier to the Gulf of Spezia, some 270 kilometres. This strip is very mountainous, with many narrow and precipitous valleys running down to the sea – no flat meadows or gentle hills. *Un terreno da capra* (a land for goats), which makes the growing of any crop difficult and laborious. The sides of the mountains are so steep that they have to be terraced. Olive trees, fruit trees, vines, vegetable gardens are all crammed on to these small terraces, kept up by dry stone walls, now, as since time immemorial. No machine here to pick grapes, olives or tomatoes – a great advantage this, for the quality of the produce. And in every garden, patio and window box herbs are grown, mingled with geraniums, nasturtiums and marigolds.

The cooking of Liguria has been totally conditioned by these geographical factors. Yet, although making anything grow is a hard task, the Ligurians have created in this narrow strip of land one of the most luscious vegetable gardens in Europe. In this they have been helped by a temperate climate and the beneficial effect of the sea air. The result is to be seen in the abundance of wild salads and aromatic herbs carpeting the Ligurian mountains. This produce of the land goes to provide the favourite ingredients of the local cooks, but they are used differently, and differently combined, according to whether you are in the western or eastern part of the region.

I was recently in Bordighera, a delightful town only 6 kilometres from the French border, where the smart English set used to winter in the 19th century before they moved westwards to Nice and the Côte d'Azur. Bordighera has a very mild microclimate that allows date palms to grow to impressive heights. A curiosity I came across there is that it is the privilege of Bordighera to supply the young palm shoots – *i palmorelli* – to the Vatican on Palm Sunday. But I was more interested in the food than in the palm trees. And I noticed that nearly all the restaurants that were recommended were away from the coast. That was because the coast and its food was given over to the tourists and what they want to eat, and the truly Ligurian fare receded to the hinterland.

The 'truly Ligurian' cooking of the western Riviera, especially in places near the French border, is more similar to the cooking of Provence than to that of any other part of Italy. Then, when you drive towards Genoa and past, the cooking changes, being influenced first by Piedmont and then, at the tip of the opposite corner of the boomerang, by Tuscany and Emilia-Romagna. The dish that exemplifies these changes most is a torta di verdura – vegetable pie or tourte. These *torte* are one of the hallmarks of all Ligurian cooking, though with endless variations. However, in the western end of the western Riviera, close to France, they are made without ricotta or other soft cheeses, much in the manner of French tourtes.

All dishes are liberally doused with the local olive oil. I found that the same oil is used all over Liguria. Even close to Tuscany, in the province of La Spezia, the oil used to douse their *mesciua* – the poorest yet most delicious soup made with beans, lentils and wheat germ – is the Ligurian oil, a delicate sweet oil with very little peppery aftertaste, produced in the western Riviera, in the province of Imperia.

I went to see two producers of excellent extra virgin olive oil, Roy in Valle Argentina and Crespi in Valle Armea. I was with a business colleague who pointedly commented that I seemed to do my research only in the most beautiful spots. There is a great difference between these two valleys: the Argentina precipitous and narrow with dramatic gorges, the Val Armea wide and serene, almost arcadian. Both are surrounded by hills carpeted with silver olive trees, small vines and beautifully kept vegetable gardens, all fighting for room on the narrow terraces.

The olive trees grown there are one of the most highly prized species. It is the Taggiasca which produces very small olives, similar to those of Provence, with a high concentration of oil in the small amount of pulp. The olives themselves are the favourite of most connoisseurs. The locals use these olives in their cooking, for example to flavour pot-roasted rabbit, or to add to pasta sauces such as I had at the Ristorante del Ponte in Badalucco, where the rubicund Bastianina serves a magnificent dish of crêpes cut into ribbons, dressed with pesto, tomatoes and olives.

This Ligurian oil is the only oil that should be used for pesto, its fruitiness being delicate enough not to interfere with the flavour of the basil, another great product of Liguria. It is interesting that almost the only Ligurian dish that has travelled beyond the borders of Liguria is pesto, when in fact it is the one that most needs the local oil and basil. Of course you can buy Genoese basil everywhere – and at the time of writing it is growing on my window sill in London – but alas you cannot buy the two essentials for an aromatic yet sweet basil, the Ligurian sun and the Mediterranean breezes.

Another herb used a lot in the local cooking is marjoram, which is often mixed with parsley in basic sauces or vegetable dishes. The other trademark of Ligurian cooking is the use of mushrooms, and especially porcini, whether eaten by themselves or as a flavouring for most things from vegetables to fish and especially for chicken and rabbit.

Herbs and vegetables in abundance, therefore, but beef, lamb and even pork – the meat of peasants – seldom appear on Ligurian tables. Rabbit is a favourite local meat; being a delicate meat it goes well with the various herbs. But the other meats, when they do appear, are masquerading in elaborate stuffings, for no better reason than that meat was scarce and expensive. A little meat is made to go a long way by adding cheese, egg, bread, offal and mushrooms.

Oddly enough, the cooking of a region with such a long coastline contains few recipes for fish. The Ligurian sea yields a poor harvest, and the Ligurian people, thrifty and hard working as they are, have to make the best of what there is. They have created delicious, simple dishes from humble fish, such as mackerel with peas, or seppie in zimino (page 142). Their ciuppin and brodino (pages 128 and 129) again use everyday fish. But fish of higher quality, such as sea bass, turbot and daurade, are treated simply, out of respect for their intrinsic flavour. They are roasted, poached or boiled, and served with no sauce but with a generous dribbling of golden olive oil.

The fish, however, that – as in most other regions – brings the creativity of the locals to the fore is stockfish or salt cod. (This used to be the fish of the poor people, but now costs so much as to have become the fish of the rich.) I can demonstrate its importance by reference to the best book on Ligurian cooking, *Cuciniera Genovese* by G B & Giovanni Ratto. Out of 37 recipes for fish, the book has 12 recipes for stockfish or salt cod, all cooked in the most inventive ways such as salt cod stuffed with porcini, pine nuts, whitebait and Parmesan.

The scarcity of recipes for fresh fish makes sense when one looks at the region's history. Genoa was one of the great maritime republics. Her sailors were at sea for months at a time, and the food they had was all preserved. The endless proximity to the sea and its smell must have made anything to do with it pall on their senses. The ship reeked of the sea and of the spices that were being brought back, spices that never touched the sailors' food. When eventually they arrived home all they wanted was fresh food, especially the lovely vegetables and herbs of their beloved hills. The meal to welcome the sailors home was remarkably elaborate, with pansôti – ravioli stuffed with wild herbs and dressed with walnut sauce – stuffed breast of veal, many vegetable pies, and triumphantly in the middle of the table, in all its glory, a beautiful cappon magro (page 138). These dishes, all of which are still strong in the Ligurian repertoire, must all have cost the women hours of labour. There can surely be few greater proofs of love and devotion than such an array of time-consuming dishes.

I have been unable to discover what sweets were prepared for the welcoming party. There would probably have been masses of fresh and candied fruit, together with bowls of confectionery.

Genoa is the motherland of the best candied fruit. The Genoese, and of course the Venetians, were the first to import cane sugar from Egypt, and they discovered how much better a sweetener it was than honey. They soon learned from Arabian traders how to preserve fruit and flower petals by coating them with sugar. They became great experts, and the candied fruit industry was the first industry established in Genoa at the end of the 18th century. European royal houses, the Mountbattens included (or Battenburgs, as they were called then), were clients of the famous Confetteria Romanengo, founded in the 1780s and still flourishing. Even Giuseppe Verdi, not known as a gourmet, dropped into Romanengo's whenever he went to Genoa. In 1881 he wrote to the Maestro Arrivabene: '. . . I had never noticed that at Romanengo they are able to candy any kind of fruit in such an exquisite manner.'

The few Ligurian cakes are typical of northern Italy – more like sweet bread than cakes – and, of these, the *pandolce* is the best known. It is similar to the Milanese panettone but has a more compact texture, is richer in candied and dried fruit, and is flavoured with fennel seeds and orange water, a flavouring reminiscent of the aromas of Arabia. The biscuits [US cookies] too, are dry and simple. Like most of the region's cooking, its sweets reflect the complex character of its inhabitants: brusque yet gentle, thrifty but never mean, honest and direct, and always surprising you with hidden wit.

Focaccia ⓥ

Focaccia is a popular dish everywhere now. Its motherland is Liguria, where the version made with cheese is probably the most popular. Here is the basic recipe for plain focaccia. You can add chopped fresh rosemary (or sage) and garlic to the dough, or olives. Alternatively you can top the focaccia with chopped peeled tomatoes, or very finely sliced sweet onion. The important thing is to be able to make a good basic focaccia, soft and tasty.

I prefer to use easy-blend dried yeast, first because it does blend more easily than fresh or ordinary dried yeast, and secondly because I can always have some to hand when I want to make focaccia or bread.

MAKES 1 LARGE SHAPE

500g/1lb 2oz [US 4½ cups] Italian 00 flour
1½ tsp easy-blend dried yeast [US rapid-rise dry yeast]
1 heaped tsp fine salt
6 tbsp extra virgin olive oil
1 tsp coarse sea salt

Put the flour in a bowl. Sprinkle with the yeast and the fine salt and pour in about 4 tablespoons of the oil. Mix very quickly and then gradually add about 300–350ml/10–12fl oz of water. Mix again quickly and stop as soon as the dough is blended. Put the dough on the floured work surface and knead quickly for 1 to 2 minutes. This dough is very damp. Wash the bowl and dry it, then oil it lightly. Return the dough and cover the bowl with a damp cloth, folded over. Leave in a warm corner of the kitchen until doubled in size, about 2 hours.

Punch the dough down. Turn it over and over, punching it all over. Put it into a 30 × 23cm/ 12 × 9in baking tray and press out in an even layer. Cover and leave in a warm place for a further hour or so, until the dough is soft and light.

Heat the oven to 240°C/475°F/Gas Mark 9.

Mix the remaining oil with a little water. Dip your fingers into this mixture and press down into the focaccia to form hollows. Sprinkle with the coarse sea salt and brush the top with the remaining oil and water mixture. (The water, mixed with the oil, keeps the surface soft during the baking.)

Turn the heat down to 220°C/425°F/Gas Mark 7 and bake the focaccia until golden, about 20 minutes. Turn the focaccia out on to a wire rack and eat while still warm. Otherwise, reheat it in a low oven before eating.

FARINATA ⓥ

Chick-pea Flour Pancake

Farinata is made from Ventimiglia (where it is also called *soca*, as in Nice) to Livorno, all around the boomerang coast of Liguria and down the straight Tuscan coast. In Versiglia, the coastal strip that stretches from the border of Liguria to Livorno, farinata changes its name and becomes *calda-calda* – hot-hot.

Farinata is mainly eaten there and then, in the street outside the shop, or near the stall, where it is made in a huge round copper pan.

You can use chick-pea flour or gram flour, which is the flour of a variety of chick-pea called chana dahl. This is available in Indian and oriental shops. Doves Farm produces an excellent gram flour, perfect for farinata. I like to serve farinata with pre-prandial drinks – with plenty of paper napkins for wiping oily fingers!

SERVES ABOUT 6 AS AN APPETIZER
150g/5oz [US 1¼ cups] chick-pea flour
400ml/14fl oz lukewarm water
½ tsp salt
the needles of a fresh rosemary sprig about 25cm/10in long
4 tbsp extra virgin olive oil
freshly ground pepper

Put the chick-pea flour in a large bowl. Add the water gradually while beating hard. (I use a hand-held electric mixer.) Season with salt and continue beating for a further minute. Set aside for 4 to 6 hours.

Heat the oven to 240°C/475°F/Gas Mark 9.

Skim off the froth from the surface of the chick-pea mixture using a slotted spoon. Whisk again briefly and then add the rosemary. Pour the oil into a 30cm/12in shallow tin or a 22 × 32cm/ 8½ × 13in oven tray. Stir the chick-pea mixture and then pour into the tin.

Place the tin in the oven. Turn the heat down to 220°C/425°C/Gas Mark 7 and bake for about 20 minutes, until the mixture has set. Grind a lot of pepper all over the top of the farinata. Leave out of the oven for 10 minutes before serving. Farinata is best served hot, but it is also good at room temperature.

IL CIUPPIN DI SESTRI LEVANTE E IL BRODINO DI LERICI
Two Ligurian Fish Soups

Although based on the same ingredients and
similar cooking methods, these two soups are sur-
prisingly dissimilar, being finished off differently.

I had Il Ciuppin at the Ristorante Angiolina in
Sestri Levante, an old-fashioned resort half-way
down the eastern Riviera. There it is a speciality
of the house, as it certainly deserves to be. The
fish was in neat chunks, only the head being
removed, but the chunks of fish were complete
with their bones and other bits and pieces, something that the southern Europeans, like the
Orientals, do not mind, but that annoys the
British. Here the diners have to do the work at
the table, while in the other soup – the Brodino
di Lerici – it is the cook who does the work.

For both soups you must use only white fish,
no oily blue fish or salmon.

IL CIUPPIN
Chunky Fish Soup

SERVES 8

*900g/2lb assorted fish, such as hake, grouper,
dogfish, whiting, John Dory, haddock*
1 large onion, chopped
1 celery stalk, chopped
1 carrot, chopped
*1 garlic clove, chopped, plus a few peeled garlic
cloves*
120ml/4fl oz olive oil
150ml/5fl oz dry white wine
*225g/8oz [US 1 cup] canned plum tomatoes, with
their juice, chopped*
salt and freshly ground black pepper
slices of country-type white bread, such as Pugliese
3 tbsp chopped fresh parsley

Clean and wash the fish and cut into large
chunks. Discard the head and tail.

In a large saucepan, fry all the vegetables and
the chopped garlic gently in 90ml/3fl oz of the
oil for 10 minutes, stirring frequently. Add the
fish, mix thoroughly and fry gently for 5 minutes,
turning it over frequently. Pour over the wine and
boil rapidly to reduce by half.

Pour over 2l/3½pt [US 2qt] of boiling water
and add the tomatoes and seasoning. Return the
soup to the boil and simmer for 20 minutes.
Taste and check seasoning.

Toast the bread for 10 minutes in a hot oven.
Rub with peeled garlic cloves split in half and
then place a piece or two of bread in individual
soup bowls. Ladle the soup over the bread.
Drizzle with the remaining oil, sprinkle over the
parsley and serve.

FLORENTINE ROAST PORK (PAGE 194);
CANNELLINI BEANS WITH GARLIC,
SAGE AND OIL (PAGE 184)

FENNEL AND PRAWNS
IN A WINEY SAUCE, LEFT (PAGE 218);
RED RADICCHIO WITH BORLOTTI BEAN
PURÉE (PAGE 100)

GENOESE FISH AND VEGETABLE SALAD
(PAGE 138)

CLOCKWISE FROM TOP:
MELON WITH BALSAMIC VINEGAR
(PAGE 169); COFFEE-FLAVOURED CREAM
PUDDING (PAGE 74); STRAWBERRIES WITH
BALSAMIC VINEGAR (PAGE 169)

CUTTLEFISH RISOTTO
(PAGE 95)

IL BRODINO
Smooth Fish Soup

Lerici is a delightful little town in the so-called Golfo dei Poeti – the Gulf of La Spezia – at the southernmost end of the Ligurian arc. It is here that Byron showed his mettle by swimming across the Gulf from Lerici to Portovenere, some 5 kilometres, and it is from here that Shelley embarked on his last, and fatal, sea journey.

Somehow Lerici has managed to keep some of the atmosphere that must have captivated these men. A kind of gentle and genteel adagio breathes through the palm trees along the promenade, while pensioners and young mothers with their babies enjoy the sun, sitting on the benches in the municipal *giardinetti*, cheered by the ubiquitous snap-dragons, tagetis and petunias in their clashing colours.

The fish market suitably reflects this atmosphere. It is a small, family affair: three fishwives with their stalls and the most beautiful greystriped cat, who struck me as the happiest-looking cat I had ever seen. I soon discovered why. When I offered him a sardine, he turned and walked slowly away in dignified disgust. '*Ah, ma lui mangia solo le triglie*' (he only eats red mullet), explained one of the women, and they had to be *di scoglio* (rock red mullet) she added, laughing. I had forgotten that in Italy even the animals have discerning palates.

The three women are the wives of the fishermen who, weather permitting, go out every day at 4 a.m., and come back at about 9 a.m. with their catch. For all the hard work they do, the catch is poor. The Ligurian sea has been depleted by pollution and overfishing. Now the situation is a little better, because of the cleaning of the sea and the ban on fishing during one or two months of the year. But I saw with my own eyes during the week I recently spent there that the fishermen bring home very little. Only once did I see a splended sea bass of about 4kg/8¾lb, such a difference from the omnipresent sea bass offered in restaurants, each weighing precisely 250g/9oz, all coming from the nearby fish farms.

The rest of the catch while I was there was cuttlefish, a few silvery anchovies, red mullet, slim mackerel, one or two turbot and a handful of sole. There were a few other fish that I did not know, so different were they from those here in England or those caught in the Adriatic with which I am more familiar.

One of these odd species were the Sparli, a fish of the large Sparidae family which includes all the breams. I asked one of the women how she cooked them. And, as always in Italy, the recipe came out with all the vague 'two fingers of this' and 'a little of that', plus the comments and corrections of the other fishwives and of the few shoppers standing around.

THE RECIPE

This is my interpretation of the recipe given to me by Caterina Padulo and Giovanna Simeone of the Lerici market. Brodino means little stock, but it is hardly that, since it consists of a fairly thick liquid with pasta floating in it. The addition of the pasta gives the soup a different texture and tones down the fishiness of the liquid. The fact that it is puréed makes the soup very easy to eat at the table.

In Lerici they use only fish of one kind when they make Il Brodino.

Ideally this soup should be made in an earthenware pot of the kind that you can put straight on the heat. If you don't have one, use a heavybased saucepan.

SERVES 6
6 tbsp olive oil
125g/4oz onion, cut into chunks
100g/3½oz celery, cut into chunks
60g/2oz carrot, cut into chunks
2 garlic cloves, chopped
15g/½oz fresh flat-leaf parsley, chopped
½ dried hot chilli pepper, crumbled
salt and freshly ground pepper
150g/5oz potato, cubed
2 tomatoes, peeled and chopped
700g/1½lb sea bream, hake, gurnard or whiting
90g/3oz small pasta, such as ditalini or
conchigliette

Heat the oil in the pot with the onion, celery, carrot, garlic, parsley, chilli and 1 teaspoon of salt and cook very gently for 10 minutes, stirring occasionally. Now add the potato and the tomatoes and cook for a further 15 minutes or so.

While this is going on, wash the cleaned fish and cut it into chunks. Throw it into the pot – heads, tails, the lot – and sauté in the *soffritto* for 5 minutes, turning the pieces over and over. (The head is cooked in the soup because it has a delicious strong flavour.) Pour over 1.8l/3pt [US 7½ cups] of boiling water and simmer for 20 minutes, uncovered.

Lift the chunks of fish out on to a plate and leave aside to cool a little, then remove and discard the head, backbones and fins. Strain the liquid into a clean saucepan. Pick out the pieces of vegetable and any pieces of fish left in the strainer. Remove any bone you can see and discard. Add the vegetables and the rest to the cleaned fish. Look again and feel with your hands (the best tool) for any bones you might have missed.

Spoon this lot into a food processor, add a ladleful or two of the liquid and process to a coarse purée. Pour this purée into the rest of the liquid in the saucepan and bring to the boil.

Before you add the pasta, add a little boiling water if the soup is too thick. Check salt and pepper. Cook the pasta gently, not at a roaring boil, as you would when making *pasta asciutta* (pasta cooked the normal way).

Pesto Ⓥ

And what is this scent of Alpine herbs that mixes so strangely with the smell of the rocks, pervading the air of all the Riviera from Lerici to Turbia? All the region is enveloped by it as from the surf of the sea. It is a lively and exciting scent. . . It is the scent of pesto, the condiment made with basil, pecorino, garlic, pine nuts, beaten in a mortar and diluted with olive oil. Is that all? Yes, that is all, and a unique thing is created. There are condiments that appear in many regions, but this is solely Ligurian; it speaks the Ligurian dialect.

Thus wrote Paolo Monelli in his best seller *Il Ghiottone Errante*, a gastronomic tour of Italy published in 1935.

I was in Liguria in July 1994 to visit an artisanal factory, Crespi in Cernaia, which produces what I rate as the best bottled pesto. As soon as I got out of the car the pungent scent of basil reminded me of that piece by Monelli. It was an unpleasantly hot day, but the scent revived me and reminded me of endless meals under a canopy of vines in the silvery-green hills of Liguria. There, pesto would be dressing a dish of *trenette* – Ligurian tagliatelle, *picagge* – narrow local lasagne, or deliciously thick *trofiette*, which look like tiny spinning tops and which, as children, we tried to spin. All home-made Ligurian pasta is 'poor man's' pasta, i.e. containing a higher proportion of water to egg. But for me, the best use of pesto is on a dish of feather-light potato gnocchi.

THE RECIPE

There are two things that I ask people to observe when making pesto. One is the use of the right oil, the other the use of fresh pine nuts. By 'fresh' I mean pine nuts that have been shelled within the year. You may well ask how you can tell the age of a pine nut. In fact, if you look carefully at the nuts they will tell you. They must be large

and smooth, of a creamy ivory colour, and without any darker patches. Although Chinese pine nuts are more easily available than Italian ones, the Italian pine nuts have a better flavour.

The right oil is a Ligurian oil, i.e. a *dolce* (sweet oil) and not a *fruttato* (peppery oil), such as a Tuscan oil. There are some good Ligurian oils on the market that you can keep for your pesto, for salsa verde or for dressing steamed fish or vegetables when a fruttato would be too aggressive.

The purists make pesto by hand, pounding the basil leaves in the mortar with a pestle. They point out that making pesto in a food processor or a blender is risky because the oil might 'cook' the basil as a result of the heat produced by the machine. If you want to use the food processor or the blender, switch the machine on and off very often so that the blade does not heat up.

Old-fashioned pesto consisted only of basil leaves, garlic and olive oil. This is the pesto that is mixed into a minestrone alla genovese (page 132), when the cheese is added at the table.

FOR 4 PORTIONS OF PASTA OR GNOCCHI

PESTO MADE IN THE MORTAR
20g/³⁄₄oz [US 3½ tbsp] pine nuts
60g/2oz fresh basil leaves
1 garlic clove
a pinch of coarse sea salt
4 tbsp freshly grated Parmesan
2 tbsp freshly grated aged pecorino [US romano] (If you cannot get pecorino, replace the pecorino with additional Parmesan)
120ml/4fl oz extra virgin olive oil, preferably Ligurian

Heat the oven to 180°C/350°F/Gas Mark 4. Spread the pine nuts on a baking tray and put the tray in the oven for 3 to 4 minutes. I do this because toasting releases the aroma in nuts.

Put the basil leaves, the garlic, pine nuts and

salt in a mortar and grind against the sides of the mortar with the pestle, crushing all the ingredients, until the mixture has become a paste.

Mix in the grated cheeses and pour over the oil very gradually, beating with a wooden spoon.

PESTO MADE IN A FOOD PROCESSOR OR A BLENDER

Heat the oven to 180°C/350°F/Gas Mark 4. Spread the pine nuts on a baking tray and put the tray in the oven for 3 to 4 minutes.

Put all the ingredients, except the cheeses, in the bowl of the food processor or blender. Process at high speed, and when evenly blended transfer to a bowl.

Mix in the cheeses.

Pesto freezes very well. Omit the garlic and the cheeses, and add them just before you are going to use the sauce.

PASTA WITH PESTO

Put the pesto in the serving bowl and place this in a very low oven to heat up a little. Now cook the pasta.

The suitable shapes of pasta are: tagliatelle, fettuccine, linguine and spaghetti. In western Liguria a potato cut into cubes and a handful of French or other fine green beans, cut into small pieces, are thrown into the pasta water. When they are nearly cooked, and by this I mean soft and not crunchy, is the time to slide in the pasta. When the pasta is ready, retrieve a mugful of the pasta water and stir 2 or 3 tablespoons of it into the pesto. This is absolutely necessary to give the pasta the right fluidity. Drain the pasta (plus the potato and beans) and transfer to the bowl with the pesto. Here I do something that is not accepted by the purists – I add a piece of unsalted butter to sweeten the pesto and to make the pasta more creamy. Toss well and serve at once.

MINESTRONE COL PESTO Ⓥ
Minestrone with Pesto

Of all the different minestroni, the Genoese, when properly made, has the cleanest and the freshest flavour. G B & Giovanni Ratto write as follows in their cookery book, which is considered to be the best on Ligurian cooking: 'This soup, very characteristic of the Genoese, has the most exquisite taste when well made. It is usually made during the season in which there are more and better vegetables on the market. . . It can be eaten hot or cold.'

This is Ratto's recipe with very slight alterations. The best green beans to use are the large flat ones.

SERVES 6

150g/5oz aubergine [US eggplant], cut into 1cm/½in cubes
150g/5oz green beans, topped and tailed and broken into short pieces
400g/14oz cooked or canned borlotti beans
200g/7oz potatoes, cut into 1cm/½in cubes
200g/7oz cabbage, very coarsely shredded
250g/9oz sweet onion, thickly sliced
150g/5oz courgette [US zucchini], cut into 1cm/½in cubes
2 celery stalks, cut into small pieces
100g/3½oz flat mushrooms, cut into small pieces
4 ripe tomatoes, peeled and coarsely chopped
salt and freshly ground pepper
150g/5oz small tubular pasta, such as ditalini
4 tbsp pesto (page 131)
freshly grated Parmesan for the table

Fill your stockpot with 2l/3½pt [US 2qt] of water. Add 1 tablespoon of salt, and bring to the boil. Add all the vegetables and simmer very gently, covered, for about 2½ to 3 hours. The longer you cook a minestrone, the better it will be. The vegetables do not break or become a mush during the cooking; they keep their shape perfectly.

The last thing is to throw in the pasta, but before you do that, check that there is enough liquid. If not, add a ladleful or two of boiling water. Remember, however, that this is a very thick soup. The pasta should cook gently, contrary to the way of cooking pasta when served *asciutta* (drained).

When the pasta is ready, taste and check salt and then add a good grinding of pepper and the pesto. Mix well and serve with plenty of cheese on the side. In the summer, when you can get the best vegetables, I recommend serving the minestrone at room temperature. It is excellent this way.

Two Vegetable Tourtes

In Liguria, and only there, polpettone means a baked dish of vegetables. Anywhere else in Italy it means a meat loaf.

There are several vegetable polpettoni, but these two are the most popular. The polpettone di fagiolini comes from the province of Genoa, while the Swiss chard polpettone is a traditional dish from the valley of the river Magra, the border between Liguria and Tuscany. Tarragon, a herb used mainly in Tuscany, begins here to make its appearance.

Polpettoni used to be the dish that people took for a *scampagnata* (a picnic), when 'going for a picnic' meant to walk just outside the walls of the town and sit there on the field admiring the view. I bet that each polpettone at each picnic would have been different, albeit based on the two main ingredients, vegetables and eggs. My two following recipes exemplify just this.

POLPETTONE DI FAGIOLINI Ⓥ
Green Bean Tourte

The cheese traditionally used in many vegetable polpettoni is *quagliata*, which is known only in Liguria. It is a very soft creamy cheese, half-way between cream cheese and sour cream. After some trial and error I decided that a mixture of sour cream and ricotta makes a good substitute.

SERVES 6
20g/¾oz dried porcini
450g/1lb green beans
salt and freshly ground pepper
60g/2oz crustless white country-type bread
100ml/3½fl oz milk
5 tbsp extra virgin olive oil
2 garlic cloves, very finely chopped
1 tbsp chopped fresh marjoram
3 eggs
30g/1oz [US 2 tbsp] ricotta
4 tbsp sour cream
60g/2oz [US ½ cup] freshly grated Parmesan
40g/1½oz [US ½ cup] dried white breadcrumbs plus more for the tin

Soak the dried porcini in hot water for about an hour (see page 13). If they are still gritty when you lift them out of the water, rinse them under cold water. Dry them with kitchen paper towel and chop them coarsely.

Top and tail the beans and wash them. Plunge them into plenty of boiling salted water and cook them for just over 5 minutes. (Remember that the water in which beans are cooked needs more salt than is needed for any other vegetable.) Drain, refresh them under cold water and drain thoroughly. Now you have to chop them up coarsely, either by hand or in the food processor, being careful to stop the machine before the beans become a purée.

While the beans are cooking put the bread in a bowl, add the milk and leave it to soak.

Heat the oven to 180°C/350°F/Gas Mark 4.

Heat half the oil, the garlic and the marjoram in a frying pan. Throw in the dried porcini and the chopped beans and sauté gently for 2 or 3 minutes.

Squeeze the excess milk out of the bread and add the bread to the bean mixture, crumbling it through your fingers. Continue to fry for a further 5 minutes, turning the whole thing over and over to take up the flavours.

Beat the eggs together lightly in a large bowl. Crumble the ricotta and add to the eggs together with the sour cream, Parmesan, dried breadcrumbs and a generous grinding of pepper. Mix well and then scoop in all the contents of the frying pan. Mix thoroughly. Taste and check seasoning.

Grease a 20cm/8in spring-clip tin with a little of the remaining oil. Sprinkle with enough breadcrumbs to cover all the surface, but be sure to tip out any excess crumbs.

Spoon the bean mixture into the prepared tin and pour over the remaining oil in a thin stream. Bake for about 40 minutes, until a thin skewer or a wooden toothpick pushed into the middle of the tourte comes out dry. Let the tourte cool in the tin for 5 minutes and then unmould it on to a round dish.

Serve hot or warm, or even at room temperature as when part of a picnic.

POLPETTONE DI BIETOLE
Swiss Chard Tourte

Swiss chard polpettoni can be plain or can contain sausage, wild mushrooms or tuna. I think the tuna version is the most successful, as long, of course, as you buy proper tuna canned under olive oil and not skipjack tuna.

SERVES 4 TO 5
300g/10oz potatoes
salt and freshly ground black pepper
7 tbsp extra virgin olive oil
1kg/2¼lb Swiss chard
1 small onion, very finely chopped
1 garlic clove, very finely chopped
½ tbsp chopped fresh tarragon
2 tbsp chopped fresh parsley
2 eggs plus 1 egg yolk
4 tbsp freshly grated Parmesan
125g/4oz best Spanish or Italian canned tuna, drained
2 anchovy fillets, chopped
dried breadcrumbs for the tin

Cook the potatoes in their skins in boiling salted water until soft. Drain and peel them. Purée them into a large bowl through the small hole disc of a food mill or a potato ricer. Dress the purée with 2 tablespoons of the oil.

Remove the green leaf part from the white stalks of the Swiss chard. Set the white stalks aside for another dish, as for instance that on page 34. Wash the green leaves and put them in a pot with only the water that clings to them and 1 teaspoon of salt. Cook over a lively heat until tender. Drain and, as soon as it is cool enough, squeeze out all the moisture with your hands. Chop coarsely.

Sweat the onion in 3 tablespoons of the oil for 7 minutes or so. Add the garlic, tarragon and parsley. Sauté for 5 minutes and then mix in the Swiss chard. Sauté for 5 to 7 minutes, turning it

over frequently. Transfer the whole contents of the pan to the bowl containing the potatoes.

Heat the oven to 190°C/375°F/Gas Mark 5.

Add the eggs and egg yolk, Parmesan and pepper to the vegetable mixture and mix very thoroughly. Flake the tuna into small shreds and add that too, together with the anchovy fillets. Mix very thoroughly – hands are best. Taste and check seasoning.

Brush an 18cm/7in spring-clip tin with some of the remaining oil. Line with greaseproof paper [US wax paper] and brush with a little more oil. Sprinkle with the dried breadcrumbs and then shake out excess crumbs.

Spoon the Swiss chard mixture into the prepared tin and dribble the remaining oil over the top. Bake for 40 to 50 minutes, until set.

Allow to cool a little in the tin and then turn it over on to a round dish. Serve warm or at room temperature.

Torta di Zucchine ⓥ
Courgette Tourte

One of the glories of Ligurian cooking is its wealth of vegetable dishes. Vegetables are served stuffed, braised or fried, but the best to my mind are the vegetable tourtes.

The eggless pastry made there, and the way it is stretched, is very similar to filo, and I wonder whether the Genoese sailors did not bring the know-how back from their journeys to the eastern Mediterranean where they must have encountered filo pastry.

This pastry is used here to envelope a filling made with courgettes and rice. The rice is used raw, but it then sits in the rest of the filling for 2 hours, thus becoming soft. An interesting way to treat rice.

SERVES 4

325g/11oz courgettes [US zucchini]
1 white onion or ½ small Spanish onion
125g/4oz [US ½ cup + 2 tbsp] Italian rice, preferably Arborio
8 tbsp extra virgin olive oil
3 tbsp freshly grated Parmesan
1 tbsp finely chopped fresh marjoram, or 1 tsp dried marjoram or oregano
salt and freshly ground black pepper
2 size-2 eggs [US extra-large eggs]
125–150g/4–5oz filo pastry, defrosted if frozen

Put the courgettes in a sink full of cold water and scrub them gently, then rinse and dry them. Cut off and discard the ends of the courgettes, then slice them very finely indeed. (I use the fine disc slicer of the food processor.) Put the courgettes in a bowl.

Peel the onion and slice it paper-thin. Add to the courgettes together with the rice, 5 tablespoons of the oil, the Parmesan, marjoram, salt and a good grinding of pepper.

Beat the eggs lightly and add to the bowl. Mix the whole thing very thoroughly. (I find the best tool for this is a pair of clean hands.) Cover the bowl and set aside for a couple of hours. Mix again and again whenever you remember during this time, because the liquid sinks to the bottom and you want the rice and the courgette to sit in it equally.

Heat the oven to 180°C/350°F/Gas Mark 4.

Pour the remaining oil into a small bowl. Use a little of it to oil a 20cm/8in spring-clip tin.

Unfold the filo pastry leaves carefully, one at a time. Keep the rest covered while you work on each leaf because filo pastry dries out and cracks very quickly. Lay one leaf of pastry over the bottom and up the sides of the tin, allowing the ends to hang over the outside of the tin. Using a pastry brush, brush the pastry with a little of the oil, then lay another leaf of filo across the previous one so as to cover the sides of the tin completely. Brush with oil, and cover with 2 more leaves, brushing each leaf as before. You will then have 4 layers of filo pastry.

Stir the courgette mixture thoroughly and spoon it into the prepared case. Fold the overhanging pieces of pastry over the top, one at a time, brushing with oil in between each leaf. If necessary, patch up with pieces of filo so that the filling is totally covered. Trim the edges and fold them down into the sides of the tin.

Place the tin in the oven and bake for about 30 minutes. Turn the heat up to 200°C/400°F/Gas Mark 6 to crisp the top until it becomes a lovely golden brown colour.

Let the tourte cool slightly in the tin, then unmould and transfer to a round serving dish and serve warm or at room temperature. To cut, use a very sharp knife or the pastry will crumble.

TORTINO DI POMODORI Ⓥ
Tomato Crumble

I have two 19th-century cookery books on Genoese cooking. One, *Cuciniera Genovese* by G B & Giovanni Ratto, is the definitive book on the subject, and in the recipe for this dish the tomatoes are baked between two layers of breadcrumb mixture. The other book, *L'Antica Cuciniera Genovese*, has a similar recipe called Pomodori all'Inferno (why 'in hell'?) where the ingredients are the same, but the tomato halves are placed directly on the tin and the breadcrumb mixture is spread over the top. I prefer the first version; it makes a delicious thick tomato crumble.

As is often the case with old, and very simple, recipes, no quantities are given. So the quantities are mine, as also is the addition of a little vegetable stock which I find necessary to keep the crumb mixture moist during the baking. The stock replaces the delicious juices that the Ligurian tomatoes would produce.

THE RECIPE

Buy seasonal tomatoes, ripe but firm, and all of the same size. I find that the best way to deal with the new species of hard-skinned tomato is to keep them for 4 or 5 days on a sunny windowsill before using them. The skin gets softer and they manage to develop a little more flavour. The breadcrumbs must be made from good-quality white bread, but not olive or tomato bread or any other dressed bread.

SERVES 4

8 tomatoes
60g/2oz [US ⅔ cup] dried breadcrumbs
4 tbsp freshly grated Parmesan
4 tbsp chopped fresh flat-leaf parsley
3 tbsp chopped fresh oregano
2 tbsp capers, rinsed and dried (optional)
2 garlic cloves, finely chopped
salt and freshly ground black pepper
4 or 5 tbsp vegetable stock (page 231)
120ml/4fl oz extra virgin olive oil

Wash and dry the tomatoes. Cut them in half across the 'equator', and not across the two 'poles'. This is because you can discard many more seeds when you cut the tomatoes in this way. Squeeze out some of the seeds.

Mix the breadcrumbs, cheese, herbs, optional capers, garlic, salt and a generous grinding of pepper. Moisten with the stock and with half the olive oil.

Heat the oven to 180°C/350°F/Gas Mark 4. Grease a large oven tin with 1 tablespoon of the remaining oil. Spread about half the crumb mixture over the bottom and place the tomatoes, cut side up, on it. Sprinkle with the rest of the crumb mixture and pour over the remaining oil. Bake for about 40 minutes, until the tomatoes are soft and the crumbs at the top are toasted.

Serve warm or at room temperature, but neither straight from the oven nor straight from the fridge. In fact, this dish should never see the inside of the fridge. You can certainly make it a day in advance, but you must keep it outside the fridge.

CAPPON MAGRO
Genoese Fish and Vegetable Salad

The name of this dish means 'capon for a meatless day'. This seems a nonsense until one realizes that since capon was considered the most delicious of all meats, this dish, made with fish and vegetables, is comparable to capon because it is equally delicious. It is the elaborate dish originally made for Genoese sailors, to celebrate their homecoming after months at sea. There are many versions of the recipe even in Genoa, and successful variations can be created by using whichever are the best fish and vegetables available. All the ingredients are piled up in layers to make a cupola.

In the 19th-century book *Cuciniera Genovese*, which is considered the bible of Ligurian cooking, the authors G B and Giovanni Ratto write: 'As ravioli are the queen of all first courses, so Cappon Magro, when properly made, is the best of all known salads.'

THE RECIPE

I used to make this dish with crackers until I read Philippa Davenport, in the *Financial Times*, suggesting the use of baked bread. As usual, she was absolutely right. The bread baked at length becomes similar to the ships' biscuits used by the Genoese.

You can enrich cappon magro by placing oysters around the dish, or a small lobster on the top. Alternatively, you can cut out the Dublin Bay prawns and increase the quantity of cheaper prawns. But this would be a pity as cappon magro is a festive dish and needs a certain flourish. It is a lovely party piece.

SERVES 6 TO 8

1 large (round) Pugliese loaf or French country-type loaf
salt
½ onion
1 bay leaf
6 peppercorns
2 tbsp wine vinegar
700g/1½lb hake, haddock, bream or any good-quality firm white fish, filleted
150g/5oz French or other green beans, topped and tailed
225g/8oz new potatoes
125g/4oz carrots
150g/5oz cauliflower florets
120ml/4fl oz extra virgin olive oil, preferably Ligurian
the juice of ½ lemon
5 raw Dublin Bay prawns in shell
1 garlic clove
225g/8oz cooked peeled prawns [US cooked peeled small shrimp]

FOR THE SAUCE

30g/1oz crustless country-type bread
4 or 5 tbsp wine vinegar, depending on strength
30g/1oz fresh flat-leaf parsley, leaves only
1 garlic clove
2 tbsp capers
30g/1oz canned anchovy fillets, drained, or salted anchovies, cleaned and rinsed
4 tbsp pine nuts
the yolks of 2 hard-boiled eggs
6 green olives, pitted
150ml/5fl oz extra virgin olive oil
salt and freshly ground black pepper

FOR DECORATION

2 hard-boiled eggs
1 dozen black olives

Heat the oven to 150°C/300°F/Gas Mark 2.

Remove the crust from the base of the round loaf and then cut a 1cm/½in thick slice across the loaf. If your loaf is not a large one, i.e. about 20cm/8in, cut 2 slices. Remove the crust all around this disc, or discs, and then put the disc(s) in the oven. Bake for about ¾ to 1 hour, until very crisp.

Meanwhile, heat a pan of salted water with the onion half, bay leaf, peppercorns and 1 tablespoon of the vinegar to boiling. Add the fish and poach for about 2 to 5 minutes, depending on the thickness of the fillets. Remove from the heat, leaving the fish in the liquid.

Cook the French beans, unpeeled potatoes, carrots and cauliflower separately in boiling salted water until done. Drain thoroughly. Peel the potatoes and slice them and the carrots; cut the beans into short pieces. Keeping them separate, dress each vegetable with 1 tablespoon of the oil. Mix gently but thoroughly and set aside in separate bowls.

Remove the fish fillets from the cooking liquid and break into morsels, discarding any bones and skin. Dress with the lemon juice and 2 tablespoons of the oil. Mix and set aside.

Boil the Dublin Bay prawns for about 2 minutes in the fish liquid. Drain and set aside 3 prawns; peel and devein the other 2 prawns, cut them into pieces and mix into the fish.

Now make the sauce. Break the crustless bread into small pieces. Place these in the bowl of a food processor and pour over 4 tablespoons of the vinegar. Leave for 5 minutes to soak and then add the parsley, garlic, capers, anchovies, pine nuts, egg yolks and the olives. Whizz, while adding the oil through the funnel, until dense and creamy. Scoop the sauce out into a bowl, taste and add plenty of pepper and salt, if necessary. Also check the vinegar and add a little more to taste. The sauce should be very piquant.

Now everything is ready to assemble the dish. Rub the toasted disc or discs of bread on both sides with the garlic and place on a round dish. If you have 2 discs, cut off a small piece from each one, lay the slices one next to the other and then add the cut-off pieces at the top and bottom of the adjoining slices, so as to make a larger circle, however imperfect.

Mix the remaining 1 tablespoon of vinegar and 2 tablespoons of oil together and pour evenly over the bread. This is the base of the cappon magro. Spread a thin layer of sauce over the bread and then cover with a layer of beans, a couple of tablespoons of fish and prawn morsels, a layer of potatoes and then again some fish and prawn morsels, a layer of cauliflower and so on, and on, until you have piled everything up, making a sort of dome shape.

Spread the rest of the sauce all over the mound and scatter with the peeled cooked prawns. Place the three unshelled Dublin Bay prawns on top. Garnish the base of the cappon magro with the hard-boiled eggs, cut into wedges, and the black olives. Cover with cling film and chill until needed, but remove from the fridge at least 1 hour before serving.

PATATE ALL'ALBINA Ⓥ
Braised Potatoes

SERVES 4
800g/1¾lb waxy potatoes
3 tbsp extra virgin olive oil, preferably Ligurian
4 garlic cloves, peeled
salt and freshly ground pepper

A friend of mine in Santa Margherita has a lovely cook by the name of Albina, and it was Albina who gave me this recipe. Albina lives up the hill, behind Paraggi, in a small house surrounded by olive trees and vines, as well as mandarin, apricot and plum trees. Scrabbling chickens and munching rabbits complete the pastoral scene. The house overlooks the Golfo del Tigullio, the large bay that lies between Portofino and Sestri Levante. Albina was born in that house, and I sometimes wonder how much she takes the splendour of her surroundings for granted. It is one of the most beautiful spots I have seen, and it is still totally unspoilt. That part of the Portofino peninsula belongs to landowners who have been wise and sensitive enough to limit the building explosion, even during the prodigal spending of the '60s and '70s.

THE RECIPE
Use waxy potatoes of a kind that do not break while cooking. To the potatoes you can add some herbs, in keeping with the rest of the meal. Parsley is always suitable, while dried oregano or marjoram are better where the potatoes are accompanying a more robust kind of meat. If you serve the potatoes with fish, a teaspoon or two of crushed fennel seeds are ideal. Alternatively, you can forget the herbs, in which case the accent will be on the good olive oil and the lovely potatoes flavoured only with garlic.

Peel and wash the potatoes. Cut them into wedges and throw them into a sauté pan in which they will fit in roughly 2 layers. Add the oil and garlic and enough boiling water to come level with the potatoes, not to submerge them. Season with salt and bring back to the boil. Put the lid on the pan, lower the heat and cook until the potatoes are tender, about 20 to 25 minutes.

Shake the pan and turn the potatoes over occasionally during the cooking. Use a fork to turn them over, not a spoon which would be more likely to break them. Check that they do not cook dry; if they do, add a little boiling water.

When the potatoes are tender, all the liquid should have been absorbed. If not, transfer the potatoes to a serving bowl with a slotted spoon and reduce the liquid over high heat until only a couple of tablespoons are left. Pour over the potatoes. Taste to check the salt, and add pepper, if wanted.

LACERTI COI PISELLI
Mackerel with Peas

A characteristic trait of Ligurian cooking is to make dishes worthy of grand tables out of the poorest of fish. This is one such dish. It achieves its success through the way the sweetness of the peas relieves the oiliness of the fish. The dish should be made in the spring, when the young peas have just arrived and the mackerel are still plentiful: mackerel are less common in the summer months.

Mackerel must be fresh, i.e. their eyes should be bright, the gills red and the flesh firm. Mackerel that are past their 'sell-by date', as they are far too often in British fishmongers, have an unpleasant flavour and are highly indigestible.

This recipe can, of course, be made with frozen peas, but frozen peas do not have the mealy flavour that is necessary to counterbalance the fish oil. 'The frozen pea caricatures the real thing, but so closely that it spoils it,' wrote Jane Grigson in her admirable *Vegetable Book*. How well she puts it and how right she is! Of course it all depends on how much time you can spare to pod fresh peas. I only hope that, like me, you will find the operation 'restful and relaxing, like saying a rosary', as the food historian Massimo Alberini wrote.

SERVES 4

900g/2lb fresh garden peas
4 tbsp extra virgin olive oil
4 tbsp chopped fresh flat-leaf parsley
1 tbsp chopped fresh marjoram
1 garlic clove, finely chopped
salt and freshly ground pepper
4 small mackerel, about 200g/7oz each, or 2 larger ones
4 tbsp tomato passata

Pod the peas. Choose a large sauté pan that can later contain the fish and add the oil, half the parsley, the marjoram and garlic. Let them sauté for about 1 minute and then add the peas and 4 or 5 tablespoons of hot water. Season with salt and pepper. Cover the pan and cook gently for 5 to 10 minutes, depending on the size of the peas.

Meanwhile, wash and dry the fish and sprinkle some salt and pepper inside them.

Stir the passata into the peas and then lay the fish on top. Cover the pan firmly and cook for about 10 to 13 minutes or until, by lifting one side of the fish with a flat knife, you can see that the flesh is white and opaque next to the bone from which it comes easily away. Then, and only then, the fish is ready. You might have to add a couple more tablespoons of hot water during the cooking. Just keep a watch on the pan, but remember that there should be the minimum of liquid, so as to concentrate the flavour.

Transfer the fish to an oval dish and surround them with the peas. Scatter the remaining parsley all over and serve.

TONNO IN PADELLA
Tuna Fish with Dried Porcini and Anchovies

This delicious dish brings together the various flavours I most associate with Ligurian fish dishes.

The cooking of a steak of fresh tuna is critical as to its timing; undercooked and it is unpleasantly bloody, overcooked and it becomes dry and stringy. It is difficult to say how long the cooking time should be, since it depends on the thickness of the steak and the heat under the pan. I prefer my tuna steaks no thicker than 1.5cm/⅝in, and I cook them for about 2 minutes each side.

SERVES 4

15g/½oz dried porcini
2 garlic cloves
a lovely bunch of fresh flat-leaf parsley
a few fresh marjoram sprigs
3 salted anchovies, rinsed and cleaned, or 6 canned anchovy fillets, drained
1 tbsp capers, rinsed
6 tbsp extra virgin olive oil
1 tbsp flour
150ml/5fl oz dry white wine
salt and freshly ground black pepper
4 fresh tuna steaks, about 600g/1¼lb in total
the juice of ½ lemon

Soak the dried porcini in hot water for about an hour (see page 13). If gritty, rinse them under cold water. Dry them with kitchen paper towel and put them on a board. Add the garlic, parsley, marjoram, anchovies and capers and chop the whole lot together. (To save time this can be done in the food processor, but be careful not to grind the mixture too fine.)

Heat the oil and the parsley mixture in a large sauté or frying pan and sauté for 2 minutes, stirring frequently. Blend in the flour, cook for about

1 minute and then pour in the wine. Boil for 3 or 4 minutes, stirring the whole time. If the sauce seems too thick, pour in 4 or 5 tablespoons of boiling water. Add salt and plenty of pepper.

If still on, remove the skin from the tuna steaks. Rinse and dry them with kitchen paper towel and lay them in the pan in a single layer. Cook for 2 or 3 minutes, depending on their thickness, and then turn the steaks over and continue to cook until no blood comes to the surface. Push a small pointed knife into the middle of one of the steaks to see if it is cooked; if there is still some blood, cook a little longer.

Taste the sauce and adjust seasoning. Transfer the steaks to a heated serving dish or individual plates and spoon the sauce around them. Drizzle with the lemon juice and serve at once.

SEPPIE IN ZIMINO
Cuttlefish with Spinach

Cuttlefish is the traditional seafood for this dish from Liguria and Versilia, the Tuscan coast north of Livorno. But cuttlefish is difficult to find in this country. This is in spite of its being fairly common off the south coast of England, as Alan Davidson writes in his *Mediterranean Seafood* (my bible on the subject). I wonder where cuttlefish go after they are caught.

I have often used squid, which are easy to find on the market and good. I buy squid caught in British waters because they are fresh and full of flavour. They are also large, which is what you need for this dish that needs a long slow cooking.

I have given here the quantity of cooked spinach you need, because the waste varies according to the kind of spinach. If you buy young, pre-packed supermarket spinach there is much less waste than with large bunchy spinach.

To give an idea, you need from 700g to 900g/ 1½lb to 2lb of fresh spinach to get 450g/1lb of cooked spinach.

Nowadays most fishmongers will clean the cuttlefish or squid for you. If yours does not, find a more obliging fishmonger, or follow my instructions below.

If you have a good-looking pot, such as an earthenware one that you can put directly on the heat, use it for cooking this dish, and you can bring it straight to the table. Seppie in zimino is a peasant dish and should be treated as such.

SERVES 6 TO 8
1.8kg/4lb cuttlefish or squid
150g/5oz onion
150g/5oz celery
2 garlic cloves
1 dried hot chilli pepper
30g/1oz fresh flat-leaf parsley
75ml/2½fl oz olive oil
150g/5oz [US ¾ cup] chopped tomato
6 tbsp red wine
salt and freshly ground pepper
enough spinach to yield 450g/1lb when cooked

To clean the squid or the cuttlefish, hold the body in one hand and pull off the tentacles, which will come away with the inside. Cut the tentacles across above the eyes and discard everything from the eyes down. Squeeze off the small beak at the base of the tentacles. Remove the bone from the body and peel off the outer translucent skin. Wash the bodies and tentacles thoroughly. Drain and pat dry. Cut open the bodies and then slice them into 1cm/½in strips. Cut the tentacles into small pieces.

Chop together the onion, celery, garlic, chilli and parsley and put this *battuto* (beaten mixture) in a heavy-based saucepan together with the oil. Sauté gently for about 10 minutes, stirring frequently, and then mix in the tomato and cook for a further 5 minutes or so.

Now that the base is ready, you can slide in the fish. Turn them over and over for the first 2 or 3 minutes for them to take up the flavour. When the squid or cuttlefish turn opaque, splash with the wine and let it bubble away for a couple of minutes. Season with salt and pepper. Cover the pan and leave to cook very gently for about 45 minutes.

Meanwhile, wash the spinach thoroughly and put it in a large saucepan with no water – the water clinging to the leaves is enough. Add 2 teaspoons of salt and cook until just tender. Drain and, when cool, squeeze out any remaining liquid with your hands. Cut the spinach into strips more or less the same size as the squid bodies.

Add the spinach to the fish, mix well and continue to stew gently for 15 to 20 minutes, until the squid are tender. (Squid and cuttlefish must either cook very quickly in boiling oil or very slowly for at least 40 minutes, so as to lose their unpleasant rubbery texture.) Taste and adjust seasoning before you bring the dish to the table.

Some slices of grilled polenta go very well with this dish.

AGNELLO E CARCIOFI IN
FRICASSEA
Fricassee of Artichokes and Lamb

The word *fricassea* is the Italianization of the French *fricassée*. Fricassea first appeared in Italian recipe books in the middle of the 18th century, about a hundred years after it was first mentioned in *Le Cuisinier François* by La Varenne. Crossing the Alps fricassée abandoned the northern cream to adopt the Mediterranean lemon as one of its ingredients. Fricassea became a favourite method of cooking rabbit, lamb and also vegetables, both in Liguria and in Tuscany.

THE RECIPE

Although the meat and artichokes are cooked together in this recipe, they manage to retain their individual flavours. I like to serve potatoes all'Albina (page 140) with this dish, to produce a nourishing Ligurian course.

For the preparation of the artichokes turn to page 186. If you do not have marjoram, increase the quantity of chopped parsley. Ask your butcher to bone the leg of lamb and to chop the bone into 2 or 3 pieces for you to use in the cooking.

SERVES 6

2 Bréton globe artichokes
900g/2lb boneless leg of lamb
4 tbsp extra virgin olive oil
2 tbsp chopped fresh flat-leaf parsley
2 tbsp chopped fresh marjoram
2 garlic cloves, sliced
150ml/5fl oz dry white wine
salt and freshly ground black pepper
1 egg yolk
the juice of 1 lemon

When you have trimmed all the tough leaves off the artichokes, cut the artichokes into quarters and remove the fuzzy chokes and the prickly purple leaves at the base. Put the cleaned quarters back into the acidulated water. Now go back to the stalks and peel off all the outside part of them, so that you have only the tender marrow left. Cut this into rounds and throw into the acidulated water.

To prepare the lamb, remove fat and gristle from the outside of the leg and any nugget of fat lurking inside. Cut into 2.5cm/1in chunks.

Now that you have prepared the two basic ingredients, you can at last start cooking, which will not take long. Heat the oven to 150°C/300°F/Gas Mark 2. Heat the oil with the herbs

and garlic in a flameproof casserole and sauté until the aroma of the *soffritto* (fried mixture) rises. Throw in the lamb, and the pieces of bone for flavour. Brown the meat carefully on all sides. Splash with the wine and boil for a minute or two.

Drain the artichoke pieces and add to the casserole. Let them *insaporire* (take up the flavour) for about 5 minutes, turning them over frequently. Season with salt and pepper. Cover the casserole and cook in the oven for about 1 hour. Keep a watch on the cooking, and add a little hot water if there is no liquid left.

Remove the pieces of bone from the casserole. Let the dish cool for 5 minutes or so, while you beat together the egg yolk and the lemon juice. Pour this over the meat and stir well. Check seasoning and then serve.

SCIUMETTE

Soft Meringues with Cinnamon and Pistachio

In the summer of 1993 I went to Recco in Liguria to eat at one of the restaurants of my youth, Manuelina. Old Signora Manuelina, now dead, started a lorry drivers' eating place straight after the Second World War. By the early '50s all of us from Milan and Genoa went to Manuelina to eat her splendid Focaccia di Recco and other local specialities. The restaurant and small hotel next door are now run by her granddaughters, who were taught by Manuelina herself. The restaurant has the smart casualness of a well-known place. And the food is typically local, traditional and excellent.

My lunch started with a small tasting of a superb cappon magro (page 138), followed by seppie in zimino. My recipe on page 142 uses calamari, because seppie – cuttlefish – are difficult to find in Britain. But what really excited me were the delicate sciumette. Sciumette are the traditional Christmas pudding of the Ligurians. They also appear on the table during Carnival week, together with the festive sweet ravioli – fried ravioli stuffed with candied pumpkin and candied citrus fruit.

THE RECIPE

Sciumette means little sponges in Genoese dialect. And this is what they look like. They are very similar to the French Oeufs à la Neige, delicate white blobs floating in a sea of yellow custard, speckled with the bright green of the pistachio and veiled with the dusky brown of ground cinnamon.

SERVES 6 TO 8

1.2l/2 pt [US 5 cups] full fat milk
the pared rind of 1 unwaxed lemon
250g/9oz caster sugar [US 1¼ cups + 2 tbsp granulated sugar]
4 whites from size-2 eggs [US extra-large eggs]
1 tsp lemon juice
2 pinches of ground cinnamon plus 1 tsp ground cinnamon to finish
5 yolks from size-2 eggs [US extra-large eggs]
2 tbsp pistachio nuts, blanched, peeled and chopped

Bring the milk very slowly to a boil in a large sauté pan. Add the lemon rind and 2 tablespoons of the sugar and stir gently. Keep an eye on the milk.

Meanwhile, whisk the egg whites until they begin to form soft peaks. Add the lemon juice, 125g/4oz [US ½ cup + 2 tbsp] of the sugar and the cinnamon. Whisk until the mixture is very firm.

When the milk starts to boil, adjust the heat so that the milk is just simmering. Scoop out a few heaped dessertspoons of the meringue and slide gently into the simmering milk. Put in only a few

spoonfuls at a time, as the meringues swell and each mound must be kept separate. Poach for about 1½ minutes on each side, flipping them over very carefully. Use two forks, not spoons which tend to break the meringues. Remove the sciumette from the milk and transfer them to a large tray lined with kitchen paper towel. Repeat this operation until you have used up all the whisked egg white. Re-whisk the whites every time before you poach another batch of sciumette. Make sure that the milk never comes to a proper boil.

Strain the milk and, if necessary, add some extra milk to come up to 700ml/1¼pt [US 3 cups].

Beat the egg yolks in a heavy-based saucepan. Add the remaining sugar and beat very thoroughly until pale and forming ribbons.

Add the milk gradually to the egg yolks while beating constantly with a wooden spoon. Cook until the custard thickens, but do not let the custard come to the boil or it will curdle. If that should happen, pour the contents of the pan into the food processor and whizz for 30 seconds until the custard is smooth. Put the pan in a bowl of cold water to cool. Stir occasionally.

Pour the cooled custard into a large deep dish or a large bowl and carefully arrange the sciumette on top. Scatter the chopped pistachios over the top and dust lightly with cinnamon.

EMILIA-ROMAGNA

Whenever I return from Emilia-Romagna my taste buds tingle with the memory of superb culinary experiences. Each time I am reminded that this region is indeed a paradise for gourmets. From among several great meals I had on a recent visit I must mention a dinner at Fini in Modena, one of the very few Michelin-starred restaurants in Italy able to combine local traditions with *grande cucina*. This dinner was a perfect example of that combination. Having cautiously declared myself not very hungry, I was cajoled into starting with 'just a taste of our *culatello*'. Culatello is made from the rump of a boned pig's thigh. It comes from Zibello, which lies in the flat lands between Parma and the Po and enjoys the damp, warm breezes that are just right for the air-drying of the culatello. This is in marked contrast to the cool, dry winds of the foothills of the Apennines needed for the curing of prosciutto. This difference arises because the large, egg-shaped culatello is very lean, while prosciutto is covered by a layer of fat. Culatello connoisseurs keep it moist before slicing by wrapping it in a cloth moistened with white wine.

After the culatello I chose soup, knowing that nowhere else could I have such perfect tortellini in brodo. In a lake of pale clear stock there were a dozen tortellini, as tiny as if twisted round a child's fingers. The stuffing was rich in flavour and yet incredibly delicate in its mixture of prosciutto, mortadella, pork and turkey, bound by egg and bone-marrow and seasoned with parmigiano-reggiano.

Next, a bollito misto was wheeled in on the traditional drum trolley: chicken, turkey, veal, beef, tongue, cotechino and calf's head, all hot and moist. It was served with four different sauces – salsa verde, a raw vegetable sauce, a tomato and carrot sauce spiked with a dash of balsamic vinegar, and mostarda di Cremona.

The other traditional dish I wanted to try, because it is now served only in old-fashioned restaurants, was the fritto misto. After the luxuriant richness of the bollito, the fritto misto was monastic in its simplicity. A mound of golden courgette [zucchini] sticks was surrounded by fried custard, fried apple rings, tiny lamb chops, sticks of prosciutto and béchamel, and ricotta and spinach fritters. No sauces or dips, just the purity of beautiful fried foods as light as air.

I finished with a slice of *ciambella* (sweet bread) and a sip of Nocino, the local walnut *digestivo* – such an ugly word for such a good drink. All in all, a perfect meal, although in retrospect the tortellini soup of the nearby Villa Gaidello (see recipe for Bensone on page 171) was every bit as good. But the pasticcio di tortellini in crosta dolce (see page 155), which one of my companions had, was unforgettable in its perfection of balance between the sweetness of the pastry and the bold meatiness of the tortellini.

When you start comparing a dish of pasta, stuffed or not, eaten, for instance, in Piacenza, with another tasted in Bologna, you become embroiled in a web of hedonistic pleasures of such complexity that it becomes an intellectual game. Cooking changes subtly but noticeably from one town to the next. Let's just take a piece of stuffed pasta – now universally known as a raviolo – and trace it from the north-west extremity of Emilia to the eastern Adriatic coast of Romagna. In Piacenza the pasta parcels are called anolini and come in a half-moon shape. They contain chopped braised beef (stracotto – see page 163) plus the usual ingredients of any pasta filling. Fifty kilometres down the Via Emilia (the Roman road that bisects Emilia-Romagna horizontally), in Parma, the anolini are still called anolini but they are usually round, and braised meat is represented in the filling only in the bread soaked in its rich juices, produced by cooking the meat for at least 16 hours and then pressing it down. Both these anolini are traditionally served *in brodo* (in clear stock) as are the more famous tortellini of Modena and Bologna, further down the Via Emilia.

Here we meet the authentic square ravioli which nowadays are usually *di magro* (meatless). The part of Romagna that used to be the dukedom of the Este family is the motherland of all cappelletti and cappellacci, made respectively with meat and cheese, and with pumpkin – my favourite. Cappelletti are also the traditional filled pasta of Reggio Emilia, but with a different stuffing, influenced by the Lombard cooking of Mantova.

Squashed between the gastronomically and artistically more fascinating Parma and Modena, Reggio Emilia tends to be forgotten. But not by me, thanks to some dear friends who have lavished on me some of their culinary jewels. After all, Reggio Emilia shares with Parma and Modena the glory of producing two of the greatest jewels: Parmigiano-reggiano and balsamic vinegar. I am often struck by how restrained the use of these two products is in the very places where they originate.

Balsamic vinegar has been made in the provinces of Modena and Reggio Emilia since the Middle Ages. Authentic balsamic vinegar, known officially as 'Traditional', must age for at least 12 years. It cannot contain ordinary vinegar or caramel, and its flavour is very complex and luscious, more comparable to a vintage port than to a normal vinegar. This balsamic vinegar is very expensive, but it lasts a long time. I still have a small bottle given to me by a producer in 1988. It is so precious that I hardly dare use it! Every now and then I have a little tasting, on its own, or I sprinkle a few drops – as if it were holy water – on a dish of warm grilled chicory. Then there is the balsamic vinegar that everybody knows and uses, called *'Industriale'* in Italy. It is rather acidic and it certainly does not taste like old port. Yet the well-made brands have the right balance of sweetness and tartness and add an interesting and pleasant flavour to sauces and roasts. It is for this, and not as part of a vinaigrette dressing for salad, that balsamic vinegar is mainly used in its places of origin. It is added to a roasting bird, to game or to braised vegetables, as well as being used to preserve the vegetables that are to be eaten later in an antipasto. Preserved in balsamic vinegar, the vegetables do not acquire that jarring flavour usually associated with industrial *verdure sott'aceto*.

Parmigiano-reggiano is a great cheese. It was respected by Boccaccio, Molière, Samuel Pepys and the 19th-century writer Giovanni Raiberti, who wrote, 'Parmesan is to all other cheeses what Jupiter is to the rabble of the minor deities.' A chunky sliver of Parmigiano-reggiano is the ideal starter to a meal and an even larger sliver is the perfect finale. This nourishing and very digestible cheese seems to me to embody what the taste buds desire most as an *amuse-gueule*, as well as a *digestivo*. Yet its use must be discreet. Most risotti and pasta dishes, especially egg pasta, benefit from an abundant snowfall of Parmesan, as do cooked vegetables – fennel and leeks being those that come first to mind. It is equally good flaked over some raw salads such as a warm chicory and radicchio salad, a young ceps salad and on freshly grilled vegetables.

The border between Emilia and Romagna is elusive; even the locals are not sure where Emilia ends and Romagna begins. One saying has it that going east from Bologna, Romagna begins at the first farm where, when you ask for a drink, you are offered wine rather than water. The food of Romagna is simpler and more unified than that of Emilia; it is strongly reminiscent of the cooking of Marche. There are historical reasons for this. At the capitulation of the Roman empire Emilia was divided among local lords, while Romagna was dominated by the Byzantine empire, the Este and ultimately by the Vatican, who ruled over the whole of central Italy.

Romagna has a serene arcadian beauty which is hardly known outside the region. The locals are very chauvinistic and dismiss most things from further afield. They certainly dismiss the cooking. I was highly amused when, in the small town of Gatteo Mare, a lovely round Romagnola lady (the women of Romagna are considered among the most attractive in Italy) rebuked me for thinking that the *garganelli* – home-made penne – with prosciutto she was serving at dinner were from a local recipe. 'It is my family's recipe', she declared, 'and I come from Gatteo di Sopra' – a village all of five kilometres up the road.

Romagna is the fruit orchard of Italy, and one of the most luscious in Europe. The best peaches, cherries, pears, and now even the best kiwis, are grown there. Artichokes, broad beans, courgettes and pumpkins are just as excellent and are treated in the simplest way – just grilled. Also melons and watermelons, of which the Romagnoli are inordinately fond. The pasta of Emilia gives way here to a poorer kind of pasta, containing fewer eggs. Romagnolo cooking is marked by a freedom and spontaneity that reflects the character of the people, who are fun-loving, humorous and humane.

The dressed bread dough, which in Emilia is fried in circles or squares to make the exquisite crescentine of Bologna and the gnocco fritto of Modena and Reggio, in Romagna is simply cooked on a hot stone (*piadina*) and then stuffed with the magical *squacquerone*. I came across this melt-in-the-mouth cheese for the first time only a few years ago. Squacquerone is practically unknown outside Romagna – incredible, since it is one of the most lovely fresh cheeses I have ever tasted. Spread on a hot piadina, it melts a little inside, while the rest melts in your mouth. Sometimes the piadina also contains prosciutto, but I prefer to enjoy the taste of the cheese on its own.

The other local product is, of course, fish. The long coastline of Romagna and the richness of the Adriatic waters see to that. It was in search of a Romagnolo fishing port that I had a very interesting experience. It started at the street market in Cento, a typical Po valley town between Modena and Ferrara. The impressive 14th-century castle was the background to the market stalls and barrows, among which I was strolling, looking and smelling. I was attracted by the large stall (actually, like so many others, a converted van) of a fishmonger, where the fish were very fresh and the choice was vast considering the size of Cento. Fish was the passion of this particular fishmonger, who began to extol the importance of buying fish straight from the fishermen.

'You must go to Goro, and be there by four in the afternoon when the auction begins,' he told me. It was midday, just time to have lunch and drive to Goro, a port on the Po delta little known except to those involved with catching and selling fish. Goro's large harbour is home to a huge fleet of fishing boats, and next to the harbour is a vast hangar where the auction takes place.

Small knots of people were standing around piles of boxes and baskets teeming with fish. Coils of large and small eels were undulating gently, octopus and squids were stroking each other with their prehensile tentacles, while a few scampi had managed to crawl lazily, thus upsetting the symmetry in which they were lined up in the box. I looked at a box of small pink crabs and thought of the time I had them last in Cesenatico, just down the coast, cut in half and sautéed in oil with parsley and garlic.

The auction was starting, I was told, and silence fell in the hangar. No shouting, no raising of hands, only a whisper in the ear of the auctioneer. He then knocked the crate of fish down to the person who had whispered the highest offer, an offer nobody else heard. This strange procedure has been adopted because it is much faster, as indeed it was, since all the fish has to be auctioned in two hours so that it can be transported to – in many cases – distant cities and be in the shops by the next day. An attractive girl, the only woman bidder there, had been the most successful bidder that day. 'You have to be tough,' she told me. 'They don't like you.' She was driving to Milan with her crates in time for the 4 a.m. opening of the market. Thanks partly to her efforts, Milan is one of the best supplied fish markets in Europe.

Another landmark of my visits to Emilia-Romagna was a baker's shop in Ferrara. Ferrara is famous for its bread, but of all the bakeries there the Panificio Orsatti was the one I was urged to go and see. They sell 38 different kinds of bread, from the classic *coppia*, which is also called *manina*, to the delicate *farfalle*. Most breads are made with *pasta dura*, a very compact yet soft dough, some dressed with oil or, as in the old days, with pork fat. The Orsatti also sell an array of piadine, pizze, spianate, focacce etc., some local, some from further afield, as well as interesting cakes. Their torta di taglierini, the traditional cake served on special occasions, derives directly from the Renaissance when it was served at the beginning of a dinner. It is a tart filled with an almond mixture over which a few strands of home-made taglierini (very thin tagliatelle) are thrown. These taglierini bake to a crunchy, airy texture which lightens the almond filling.

My favourite Emilian dolci are those of Parma, where the Grand Duchess Marie Louise, the Hapsburg princess who became Napoleon's second wife, reigned supreme for over 30 years. Her legacies are the candied violets, the delicate Parma yellow which makes the palazzi so characteristic, and delicious cakes and desserts. Maria Luigia, as she is called in Parma, brought her pâtissiers from Vienna, but it is thanks to her last chef, Vincenzo Agnoletti, that we know a great deal about the cuisine of the time. Some of Agnoletti's recipes are collected in his book *Manuale del Cuoco e del Pasticcere*. His recipe for zuppa inglese brings this everyday pudding to new heights, and another triumph is a recipe for a kind of half-moon shaped biscuits [US cookie], which has been rewritten by Ugo Falavigna, a famous Parmigiano pâtissier of today. The pastry crescents are stuffed with a mixture containing spinach and almonds. A similar spinach mixture is the ingredient of a Lombard sweet and savoury cake and of a sweet tart from Lucca, where the Swiss chard is sitting on crème pâtissière and topped with pine nuts and bits of chocolate.

But that is Tuscany, and I am in Emilia-Romagna, closing this introduction with the hope that for once you might leave Tuscany and head for this region, where the warm hospitality of its lovable inhabitants renders the delights of its table even more delightful.

Biscotti alla Cipolla Ⓥ
Onion Biscuits

Margherita and Valeria Simili are cookery teachers in Italy. They are twins, but not identical, only '*simili*' – similar – as they say their name explains! They have a school in Bologna and, although they teach most things, their particular speciality is the making of bread, focacce, pizze, biscuits and various doughs, all of which call for different techniques. I was very interested when I heard Margherita saying that each kind of bread must be made with different movements of the hands and body. Quite fascinating.

One of the days I was there, the sisters were concentrating on *stuzzichini* (amuse-gueules). *Stuzzicare*, in fact, means to tickle. And they tickled my fancy so much that when I finished tasting them I had no room for anything else! There were lovely breads stuffed with fresh grapes, in the shape of bunches of grapes, cigars of pasta dough wrapped around anchovy fillets, little savoury chilli knots, deliciously hot and gar-licky, and nutty gruyère biscuits. But my favourites were these onion squares, which incor-porate the traditional flavours of rich Bolognese cooking.

THE RECIPE
This is a translation – with the necessary adapta-tions – of the recipe given to me by Margherita and Valeria Simili. The biscuits [US crackers] are ideal to go with a pre-prandial drink or as an accompaniment to a lovely dish of grilled vegeta-bles or ratatouille.

MAKES ABOUT 40
250g/9oz sweet onion
2 tbsp extra virgin olive oil
salt
250g/9oz [US 2 cups] Italian 00 flour
1½ tsp baking powder
45g/1¾oz [US 3½ tbsp] unsalted butter
1 egg
4 tbsp semi-skimmed milk [US low-fat milk]
butter for the trays

Slice the onion very finely and then chop the slices coarsely. Put the oil and the onion in a heavy-based frying pan and sauté gently, adding a pinch of salt to prevent the onion catching. The onions should not brown, only cook gently for 30 minutes or so. Allow to cool.

Put the flour in a bowl with 1 teaspoon of salt and the baking powder. Cut the cold butter into small pieces and add to the flour mixture. Work with your fingers until the mixture becomes like breadcrumbs, and then work in the onion with its juices.

Lightly beat together the egg with the milk and add gradually to the dough. Work quickly, and as soon as you can gather the mixture into a ball, stop working. Wrap the ball of dough in cling film and refrigerate for at least 30 minutes.

Heat the oven to 190°C/375°F/ Gas Mark 5. Lightly butter 2 oven trays.

Flour the work surface and roll out the dough with a floured rolling pin to a thickness of about 1cm/½in. Cut into 5cm/2in squares and transfer these to the buttered trays. Bake for 15 to 20 minutes, until lovely and golden.

I prefer the biscuits hot, or warm, but they are also good cold.

PASTICCIO DI PENNE E VERDURE AL FORNO Ⓥ

Baked Penne and Roast Vegetables

In 1993 I was invited by the Mulino Spadoni, producers of some of the very best flours, to visit their factory. I was driven from the hotel by Mario and, as always happens when I am in Italy, we talked about food, with me trying to extract as many recipes as possible. One of the recipes Mario told me was this one. 'My wife makes the best pasticcio I have ever eaten,' he said. Oddly enough the dish didn't sound particularly Romagnolo to me. But then back in London I read a very similar recipe in *The Splendid Table of Emilia-Romagna* by Lynne Rossetto Kasper. The book is equally splendid and very reliable. In her introduction the author writes: 'Originally the vegetables were prepared by Adriatic fishermen's wives to eat with the day's catch. Many cooks transform them into a first course by tossing the vegetables with maccheroni.' So it is obviously a traditional local recipe.

THE RECIPE

In Romagna the cheese used is a very soft cheese called *squaccherone*, which is unavailable outside Romagna. Lynne Rossetto Kasper suggests a young pecorino and I agree with her. However, when I can find it I prefer to use *crescenza* because it is much closer in taste and texture to squaccherone. Crescenza is sold in Italian food shops, but being highly perishable only a few will stock it.

SERVES 6

1 aubergine [US eggplant], about 250g/9oz
2 medium courgettes [US zucchini], about 250g/9oz in total
2 sweet peppers, about 350g/12oz in total
6 large ripe tomatoes, about 600g/1¼lb in total, skinned
3 sweet red onions, about 350g/12oz in total
8 tbsp extra virgin olive oil
salt and freshly ground black pepper
3 garlic cloves
30g/1oz fresh flat-leaf parsley, leaves only
1 dozen fresh basil leaves
4 anchovy fillets
1 tbsp capers, rinsed
4 tbsp dried white breadcrumbs
350g/12oz penne
225g/8oz crescenza or mild young pecorino [US romano]

Heat the oven to 200°C/400°F/Gas Mark 6.

Wash and dry the aubergine, courgettes, peppers and tomatoes. Cut the aubergine and courgettes across in half, or into 3 chunks, depending on size, and then lengthwise into 5mm/¼in thick slices. Slice the tomatoes into similar thickish slices. Cut the peppers into quarters, remove seeds, core and ribs, and then cut each quarter in half again. Slice the onions into rings of about the same thickness as the other vegetables.

Grease 2 large oven trays with a little oil and place the sliced vegetables on them, keeping them separate. Brush them with a couple of tablespoons of the oil and season with salt and plenty of pepper. Bake until the vegetables are soft and beginning to brown at the edges, about 45 minutes.

Chop together the garlic, parsley, basil, anchovies and capers. Heat 2 tablespoons of the oil in a large frying pan. When the oil is very hot add the breadcrumbs and fry until lovely and golden. Now mix in the chopped mixture and

sauté for a minute or so over gentle heat. After
that, draw the pan from the heat while you cook
the penne.

When the pasta is still just slightly undercooked, drain it and tip it into the frying pan.
Stir-fry for a minute or two. Taste and check seasoning.

Choose a deep oven dish and grease it with a
little oil. Heat the oven to 180°C/350°F/Gas
Mark 4.

Slice or crumble the crescenza (not an easy job
because crescenza is a very soft cheese) or thinly
slice the pecorino.

Now you are ready to assemble the dish.
Spread a thin layer of pasta in the oven dish, cover
with the courgettes and a few onion rings and
add a little cheese. Put in another layer of pasta,
then the peppers and some onion rings, more
cheese, pasta again, then the aubergine, the rest
of the onion rings, a little more cheese and the
remaining pasta. On the top place the tomato
slices and the remaining cheese. Drizzle with the
remaining oil and bake for 15 minutes or so, until
the cheese has melted.

Do not serve straight from the oven, but let
the dish rest outside for about 5 minutes before
you bring it to the table.

RAGÙ
Bolognese Sauce

Ragù is the perfect example of Bolognese
cooking: rich yet well balanced, lavish and yet
restrained, meaty and yet fresh. There are hundreds of versions of ragù, but the classic one, the
one that everybody identifies with its place of
origin, is the bolognese.

Nowadays ragù is out of fashion – too rich,
unhealthy, bad for the heart, bad for everything,
but certainly not bad for the palate. This recipe is
not too rich, I think. It follows closely the pre-
cepts of a classic ragù, but it is lighter on fat.

Remember that it is very important to chop
the vegetables very finely, so that they are the size
of grains of rice.

MAKES ENOUGH SAUCE FOR 6 HELPINGS OF
PASTA
60g/2oz [US 4 tbsp] butter
2 tbsp extra virgin olive oil
60g/2oz unsmoked pancetta, finely chopped
1 small onion, finely chopped
1 carrot, finely chopped
1 celery stalk, finely chopped
1 garlic clove, finely chopped
1 bay leaf
400g/14oz lean chuck or braising beef, coarsely minced [US ground]
2 tbsp concentrated tomato paste
150ml/5fl oz red wine, such as a Sangiovese or a Barbera
2 pinches of grated nutmeg
salt and freshly ground pepper
150ml/5fl oz meat stock (page 230)
150ml/5fl oz full fat milk

Heat the butter and oil in a heavy-based saucepan
and cook the pancetta for 5 minutes, stirring frequently.

Add the onion, and when it has begun to
soften add the carrot, celery, garlic and bay leaf.
Cook for a further 10 minutes, stirring frequently.

Put in the minced beef and cook until it is
medium brown in colour and nearly crisp, crumbling it in the pot with a fork. Do this over high
heat so that the meat browns rather than stews,
but be careful not to let the mince become too
brown and hard.

Add the tomato paste and continue to cook
over high heat for a further 2 minutes. Still over
high heat, add the wine, nutmeg, salt and pepper,
and the stock. Bring to the boil and then turn the
heat down to very low so that the mixture will
reduce very slowly. This slow lengthy reduction is
of paramount importance. Set the lid askew over
the pan and cook for about 2 hours, adding a
couple of tablespoons of the milk from time to
time. By the end of this time all the milk should
have been added and absorbed, and the ragù
should be rich and thick, like a thick soup.

Taste and adjust seasoning. The ragù is now
ready to dress a dish of home-made tagliatelle,
thus producing one of the greatest dishes of
Emilia.

PASTICCIO DI MACCHERONI IN
CROSTA DOLCE

Macaroni Pie in a
Sweet Pastry Case

In his book *Emiliani e Romagnoli a Tavola*,
Massimo Alberini, the great octogenarian food
historian, describes this dish as follows: 'A recipe
whose Renaissance roots can be seen in the marriage of sweet and salty flavours. A covering of
sweet pastry is filled with a meat sauce and a rum-
flavoured custard.'

The dish can be traced back to Cristoforo da
Messisbugo, steward to Don Ippolito d'Este of
Ferrara. Messisbugo wrote a fascinating book,
Libro Novo, published in Venice in 1557, which
contains many recipes for *torte*. These consisted
of a sweet pastry case filled with various savoury
ingredients – Swiss chard, pigeons, capons,
almonds, etc.

Messisbugo does not mention rum in any of
his dishes – it was probably unknown at the time.
This addition must have come later when rum
became popular. Pellegrino Artusi, writing in the
19th century, also has no mention of rum in his
pasticcio, and has replaced the custard with
béchamel to be more in keeping with the new
tastes. My recipe is based on Artusi's.

Still today, as in Artusi's time, this pasticcio is
the great dish eaten during Carnival week in
Romagna.

A similar pasticcio is made in Emilia, using
tortellini for the filling instead of macaroni. It is
an even grander dish, but because of having to
make the tortellini it is more complicated. So I
have opted for the Romagnola recipe.

THE RECIPE
This is an elaborate dish, the making of which
calls for some experience, and time. However, if
you follow my instructions carefully you should
be able to make it very successfully.

Allow the various elements of the pie to cool before you put them in the tin lined with the dough.

SERVES 8

20g/³⁄₄oz dried porcini
125g/4oz lamb's sweetbreads
125g/4oz fresh chicken livers
40g/1½oz [US 3 tbsp] unsalted butter
4 or 5 fresh sage leaves, snipped
salt and freshly ground black pepper
4 tbsp dry white wine
30g/1oz unsmoked pancetta, preferably in a slab
30g/1oz fatty prosciutto
75g/2½oz small onion
60g/2oz celery
60g/2oz carrot
a bunch of fresh flat-leaf parsley, leaves only
1 tbsp olive oil
2 pinches of ground cinnamon
a pinch of ground cloves
4 tbsp full fat milk
250g/9oz macaroni or penne
a béchamel sauce (page 228) made with 30g/1oz [US 2 tbsp] unsalted butter, 30g/1oz [US 3 tbsp] flour, 500ml/16fl oz full fat milk and 3 pinches of grated nutmeg
1 tbsp dried white breadcrumbs
60g/2oz [US ½ cup] freshly grated Parmesan

FOR THE PASTRY

350g/12oz [US 3 cups] flour, preferably Italian 00
180g/6oz [US 1½ sticks] unsalted butter, cut into small pieces
125g/4oz caster sugar [US ½ cup + 2 tbsp granulated sugar]
a pinch of salt
1 size-2 egg plus 2 egg yolks [US extra-large egg]
butter for the tin

FOR THE GLAZE

1 egg yolk
a pinch of salt
2 tbsp milk

First make the pastry, which is the Italian equivalent of the French pâte sucrée. I make it in a food processor, putting everything in except the egg and egg yolks, which I add through the feed tube while the machine is running. If you do not have a food processor, put the flour on the work surface, make a well in the centre and add the egg, egg yolks, sugar and salt. Mix lightly and then add the butter. Blend quickly together. If the dough is too dry, add a little cold water; if too moist, mix in a little more flour. It is difficult to be precise about quantities because it depends on the flour you are using and even on the humidity of your kitchen. Gather the dough up into a soft ball, wrap it in cling film and put it into the fridge.

Now you must prepare the filling. Soak the dried porcini in boiling water. I have come to the conclusion that some porcini need a lot longer than the 30 minutes usually suggested, so I now prefer to soak any dried porcini for 1 hour. After that lift the porcini out of the liquid, rinse them if necessary and dry them carefully with kitchen paper towel. Chop them and set them aside. Filter the liquid through a strainer lined with a piece of muslin or cheesecloth.

Remove any bits of fat from the sweetbreads. Rinse them and pat them dry with kitchen paper towel. Cut off and discard the gristle and any green spots from the chicken livers. Rinse quickly and pat them very well.

Heat the butter in a smallish frying pan. Throw in the sage leaves and, when they begin to sizzle, add the sweetbreads. Sauté at medium heat for 2 minutes and then add the chicken livers. Sauté for a further couple of minutes, turning the mixture over and over to soak up the butter. Season with salt and pepper. Splash with the wine and let it cook for a few more minutes. Draw the pan off the heat. Lift the offal out of the pan with a slotted spoon on to a chopping board and chop it coarsely. Return it to the pan and set aside.

Now prepare the prosciutto sauce, which in Italian is called *il sugo finto di carne* (the mock meat sauce). Chop the pancetta, prosciutto, onion, celery, carrot and parsley to a granular paste. (I find a food processor ideal for the job. It makes a real *battuto* – pounded mixture – in 1 minute, just as you would have done by chopping by hand for a long time.) Put the battuto in a clean frying pan together with the oil and ½ tea-spoon of salt. Sauté over very low heat for 5 minutes, and then add the chopped porcini. Sauté for a further 5 minutes, stirring very frequently. The mixture should not fry, just gently cook. Stir in the spices and a couple of tablespoons of hot water and continue cooking gently. After 10 minutes or so mix in the milk and a couple of tablespoons of porcini liquid. Continue cooking for a further 30 minutes, adding a little porcini liquid and hot water now and then, mixing and making sure that the mixture does not catch.

While you are watching over the sauce, cook the pasta in plenty of boiling salted water. Drain thoroughly when still slightly undercooked (6 minutes should be enough) and dress immedi-ately with the prosciutto sauce. Mix well and set aside.

Remove the pastry from the fridge to let it warm up a little, so that you can handle it.

Make the béchamel and mix into the pasta very thoroughly. If you are not sure how to make a good béchamel, turn to page 228 for my version. Don't forget to taste and adjust the sea-soning.

Heat the oven to 220°C/425°F/Gas Mark 7.

Now that you have prepared the various ele-ments of the pasticcio it is time to assemble it. Prepare a 20cm/8in spring-clip tin by greasing it with a little butter. Roll out about a quarter of the dough on a piece of floured greaseproof paper [US wax paper]. Turn the dough over on to the bottom of the tin and peel off the paper. (This

pastry dough is difficult to handle. If you roll it out on a piece of greaseproof paper you will find it much easier to transfer.) Roll out another quarter or so of the dough into strips to line the sides of the tin.

Mix the tablespoon of breadcrumbs with 1 tablespoon of grated Parmesan and sprinkle this mixture over the dough covering the bottom of the tin. Lay about one-third of the pasta at the bottom, cover with half the sweetbread and chicken liver mixture, and sprinkle with some Parmesan. Next add another layer of pasta, the remaining sweetbread and chicken liver mixture and more Parmesan. Finish with a topping of pasta and the remaining Parmesan.

Roll out a round of dough to cover the pie and seal the edges well. Make a small flat strip or a thin roll with some of the remaining dough and place it all around the top edge of the pie. Press down with the prongs of a floured fork to seal. With the left-over dough make your favourite pie decorations. The traditional decoration for this pie is a bow. Make a few holes in the dough here and there with a fork to let the steam escape.

Lightly beat together the egg yolk, salt and milk for the glaze. Brush this mixture all over the pie using a pastry brush.

At last, the pie is ready for baking! Bake it at the high temperature for the first 5 minutes, then turn the oven down to 180°C/350°F/Gas Mark 4 and continue baking for 20 to 30 minutes, until the pastry is beautifully golden all over. Leave the pie in the tin to cool down for 10 minutes before you unmould it. Place the unmoulded pie on a lovely round dish and bring it to the table.

RISOTTO COI FUNGHI
DELL'ARTUSI

Mushroom Risotto

Dotted around this book you will find a good
handful of recipes by Artusi. Pellegrino Artusi
wrote his *La Scienza in Cucina e l'Arte di
Mangiar Bene* in the second half of the last
century. The book is deservedly still a best-seller.

Artusi was the first cookery writer to unify
Italy gastronomically, although his recipes tend to
be from the northern Italian tradition, as the
author himself was born in Romagna and lived in
Florence. And it is specifically in the cooking of
these two regions that Artusi found the inspiration for the book.

The book is a large collection of 790 recipes,
most of them valid to this day, always enlivened
by anecdotes, pleasantries and delightful personal
comments. Artusi was very keen on the health-
giving properties of good food, although the
abundant use of butter might make some modern
health gurus shudder.

THE RECIPE

There are as many risotti coi funghi in northern
Italy as there are cooks. Having tried a few from
my family, friends and restaurants, I have decided
that the Artusi one is a version particularly suited
to being made in this country because it can be
totally based on dried porcini, which are always
available. When you buy dried porcini, buy large
pieces sold in clear cellophane bags, so that you
can see what you are buying. Do not buy dried
porcini that look like dried-up brown crumbs
with no mushroom shape left. Dried porcini are
expensive, but they can lift a dish from banality to
excellence.

SERVES 4 AS A FIRST COURSE

30g/1oz dried porcini
2 tbsp olive oil
½ onion, very finely chopped
1 celery stalk, very finely chopped
1 small carrot, very finely chopped
1 garlic clove, very finely chopped
6 parsley sprigs, very finely chopped
1 tbsp concentrated tomato paste
100ml/3½fl oz milk
salt and freshly ground black pepper
*1.2l/2pt [US 5 cups] vegetable stock (page 231), or
light chicken or meat stock (page 230)*
60g/2oz [US 4 tbsp] unsalted butter
*300g/10oz [US 1½ cups] Italian rice, preferably
Carnaroli*
100ml/3½fl oz dry white wine
freshly grated Parmesan

Put the dried porcini in a bowl and cover with
boiling water. Leave to reconstitute for about an
hour (see page 13).

Heat the oil with the onion in a frying pan for
2 or 3 minutes. Add the celery, carrot, garlic and
parsley and sauté gently until the vegetables are
soft, stirring very frequently.

Stir in the tomato paste and fry for a minute,
then pour in half the milk. Continue cooking for
about 7 minutes.

Fish the dried porcini out of the liquid. Rinse
them under cold water and dry them well.

Chop the dried porcini to the size of rice
grains and add to the vegetable mixture together
with the rest of the milk. Season with salt and
pepper and cook for about 10 minutes on very
low heat.

Heat the stock for the risotto and keep it just
simmering all through the cooking of the rice.

Melt the butter in a heavy-based saucepan.
Add the rice and 'toast' it for a minute or so, stirring constantly. Splash with the wine and let it
evaporate while you continue stirring.

Now begin to add the simmering stock, a ladleful at a time, letting each addition be absorbed by the rice before you add the next. About 15 minutes after you have begun to add the stock, spoon in the mushroom mixture with all its juices. Continue cooking and gradually adding the remaining stock until the rice is ready – about 18 minutes.

Transfer the risotto to a shallow bowl or a deep dish and serve with the grated Parmesan on the side.

RISOTTO COL PESCE
Risotto with Fish

All along the Adriatic coast risotto with fish is very popular. This is a risotto I had at the Titon restaurant in Cesenatico, a delightful port in Romagna, a port which has the distinction of having been planned by Leonardo da Vinci. The fish used there was John Dory, but I have also used monkfish, which is more easily available. The cleaned fish should be the same weight as the rice, so that when the risotto is done the predominant ingredient is the rice, since rice increases its volume by about three times during the cooking.

SERVES 4 AS A MAIN COURSE

1.2l/2pt [US 5 cups] fish stock (page 231)

2 tbsp chopped onion

1 tbsp chopped celery

1 garlic clove, chopped

30g/1oz [US 2 tbsp] butter

2 tbsp extra virgin olive oil

2 fresh tomatoes, peeled and coarsely chopped

350g/12oz [US 1¾ cups] Italian rice, preferably Vialone Nano

200ml/7fl oz dry white wine

salt and freshly ground pepper

225g/8oz firm white fish, cleaned weight

4 shelled scallops [US sea scallops]

2 tbsp chopped fresh flat-leaf parsley

Heat the stock in a saucepan and bring slowly to the boil. Keep it simmering very gently all through the cooking.

Put the onion, celery, garlic, butter and oil in a heavy-based wide saucepan and sauté for about 10 minutes, until the vegetables are soft. Do this very gently and stir very frequently. Add the tomatoes and continue cooking for 5 minutes.

Mix in the rice and cook for 2 minutes, stirring constantly. Turn the heat up, pour over the wine and let it bubble away.

Now start adding the simmering stock by the ladleful, letting one ladleful be absorbed before you add the next. Add salt, unless the stock is already salted.

Cut the fish into neat morsels, removing any skin if necessary, and add to the rice after about 9 minutes from the moment you began to add the stock.

Cut the white part of the scallops into morsels of the same size as the fish and throw them into the pan when the rice is nearly done. Cut the coral in half and add to the risotto with the parsley and pepper. Cook for a further minute and then draw off the heat. Taste to check seasoning and transfer to a bowl. Serve immediately.

BOMBA DI RISOTTO ALLA PIACENTINA
Risotto and Pigeon Timbale

Piacenza is a city on the borders of Lombardy and Emilia-Romagna. Its cooking is also delicately poised between the cooking of the two regions. Some dishes originate in southern Lombardy, while others share the characteristics of the fully-fledged rich Emilian cuisine.

There are two traditional local dishes based on pigeon. One is a pasta pie, which is similar to the deliciously rich pasta pies of Bologna, and the other is this risotto timbale, which has strong leanings towards Lombard cooking. The latter was traditionally prepared for the feast of the Assumption of the Virgin on 15th August.

I am not very keen on the pigeons available here; they always seem so tough to me. But they are perfect for this dish. I only use the breast of the pigeons, because I find it is the only part worth eating. Make a gamey stock with the rest. The delicate risotto successfully balances the slightly bitter flavour of the pigeons. Do not overcook the risotto or the pigeons; both receive a second cooking in the oven.

SERVES 6
FOR THE PIGEONS
20g/³⁄₄oz dried porcini
the boneless breasts of 2 pigeons
30g/1oz onion
20g/³⁄₄oz celery
30g/1oz carrot
a small bunch of fresh flat-leaf parsley, leaves only
6 fresh sage leaves
40g/1½oz [US 3 tbsp] unsalted butter
salt and freshly ground pepper
150ml/5fl oz red wine

FOR THE RISOTTO

1.5l/2½pt [US 1½qt] meat stock (page 230)

60g/2oz [US 4 tbsp] unsalted butter

30g/1oz shallot, finely chopped

salt

375g/13oz [US 2 cups] Italian rice (Carnaroli or Arborio)

5 tbsp white wine

2 tbsp freshly grated Parmesan

2 tbsp dried breadcrumbs plus extra for the dish

Put the dried porcini in a small bowl and cover with 200ml/7fl oz boiling water. Leave for about 1 hour (see page 13) and then rinse them. Filter the liquid through a sieve lined with muslin [US cheesecloth].

Chop very finely the onion, celery, carrot, parsley and sage and put them into a sauté pan with the butter and 2 pinches of salt. Let the *soffritto* sauté nicely for 10 minutes or so. The heat must be very gentle and you must stir the soffritto quite often or it will catch.

Wash the pigeon breasts and pat them dry with kitchen paper towel. Season them with plenty of salt and pepper. Place them in the pan and brown them on both sides. Chop the dried porcini and add to the pan. Splash with the wine and bring to the boil. Add the dried porcini liquid. Cover the pan and cook for 5 to 8 minutes, turning the pigeon breasts twice during the cooking.

While the pigeon breasts are cooking, start to prepare the risotto. Put the stock on the heat and bring to a gentle simmer. Keep it simmering all through the cooking of the risotto. Melt half the butter in a heavy-based saucepan and add the shallot and a pinch of salt. Let the shallot cook gently for 5 or 6 minutes, then throw in the rice and sauté it over moderate heat for about 2 minutes, stirring constantly. Splash with the wine and let it bubble away.

Now begin to add the simmering stock one ladleful at a time while you stir very frequently, if not constantly. Let each ladleful be absorbed

before adding the next. Remove the saucepan from the heat when the rice is just a little under-done. Mix in half the remaining butter and the Parmesan. Set aside.

Heat the oven to 220°C/425°F/Gas Mark 7.

Cut the pigeon breasts into strips. Taste the juices and correct any seasoning. If you find the juices not rich enough in flavour, boil to reduce them over high heat (something, however, I have never found necessary).

Generously butter a soufflé dish or deep oven dish of 2l/3½pt [US 2qt] capacity and sprinkle with breadcrumbs to cover all the surface. Shake out excess crumbs.

Cover the bottom of the dish and up the sides with some risotto. Place the pigeon strips in the hole in the middle and pour most of the juices over them. Cover with the remaining risotto so as to make a box. Drizzle with the rest of the juices, sprinkle with the 2 tablespoons of breadcrumbs and dot with the little bit of butter left over.

Place the dish in the oven to bake for 20 minutes or so, until a lovely golden crust has formed on the top. Wait 5 minutes before you bring the dish to the table – let it rest and cool down a little so that the flavours can blend better.

A lighter version of this dish is made by boiling the rice instead of making a risotto. Then the rice is dressed with butter, Parmesan and the juices of the pigeon before being moulded around the inside of the dish and filled with the pigeon meat.

Pesce al Forno alla Romagnola
White Fish Baked in Tomato Sauce

This recipe came originally from a family friend from Cesena in Romagna. However, it has been in my family, both in Milan and in London, for so long that I do not know how many alterations the recipe has gone through, and whether it should, by adoption, be in the Lombardy section.

I use any good fresh white fish, but not one like sea bass or turbot, whose flavour is too good to be submerged in a tomato sauce. Sea bream, whiting (a very underrated fish in this country), hake, grey mullet or a fillet of haddock are all suitable. If you use fillet you should cook it a little less.

SERVES 4

a white fish of about 1.3kg/3lb, cleaned but with the head on
5 tbsp extra virgin olive oil
1 small onion, finely chopped
1 small celery stalk, finely chopped
1 garlic clove, finely chopped
1 tbsp chopped parsley
4 fresh tomatoes, peeled, or canned tomatoes, coarsely chopped
150ml/5fl oz dry white wine
salt and freshly ground black pepper

Heat the oven to 200°C/400°F/Gas Mark 6.

Put 4 tablespoons of the oil, the onion, celery, garlic and parsley into a saucepan and sauté until the vegetables are soft. Add the tomatoes and the wine and cook for 10 minutes or so over a lively heat. Season with salt and pepper and draw off the heat.

Wash and pat dry the fish. Season with salt inside and out. Grease a roasting tin with the remaining oil and place the fish in the tin. Spoon the sauce over the fish and around it and cover with foil. Bake for about 30 minutes, until the fish is cooked. To test, insert a knife into the thickest part of the body, lift out a little of one side and have a peep. The flesh should be opaque but still moist, and it should easily come clean off the bone.

Transfer the fish very carefully to an oval dish and spoon the sauce around it. Alternatively, place the portions directly on individual plates, with a good tablespoon of the sauce on the side – an easier operation.

STRACOTTO DI SAN NICOLÒ
Braised Beef

Not long ago I spent a most interesting morning in Piacenza with a charming lady, Magda Lucchini. She let me into her flat, at the top of a 19th-century house that was typical of northern Italy. Large rooms, lovely mosaic or parquet floors covered with Persian rugs, the walls covered with paintings, and every corner of any flat surface filled with knick-knacks and photographs, some very valuable, some of no distinction, but all expressing the personality of the charming owner.

Magda Lucchini is the Presidentessa dell'Associazione del Fornello, a *fornello* being a kitchen range. The members of this association are up-market ladies who dine together every 2 months. But eating, however deliciously, is not the main object of this group. The members, who are all excellent cooks, want to keep alive and hand down the tradition of a good table around which the family gathers, not only to eat excellent food, but also to express opinions and exchange ideas. They in fact want to foster the family atmosphere, of which the mother is the focal point and her cooking the welcome tie that keeps the family together. The recipe for a piece of beef, slowly braised, is one of Magda Lucchini's favourite dishes from her home town, Piacenza. It is the dish she likes to serve on St Nicholas' Day, the 6th of December.

THE RECIPE
This stracotto is cooked in an interesting way that was new to me. The result is very tender meat with a delicate flavour of wine that is just detectable. The meat is cooked in a pot, preferably earthenware, with another pot, or a deep dish, placed on top so as to seal it. This second dish *must* be earthenware to allow the vapour from the wine, with which it is full, to go through.

The meat must be suitable for braising rather than roasting. I use chuck steak, and make the dish a day in advance so that I can remove the fat easily once it is cold. (I keep the fat to make stewed potatoes.)

The best accompaniment is polenta or boiled potatoes.

SERVES 8 TO 10
a 2kg/4½lb boneless piece of beef
350g/12oz Spanish onions, finely chopped
250g/9oz carrots, finely chopped
225g/8oz celery, finely chopped
3 garlic cloves, chopped
a handful of flat-leaf parsley leaves, finely chopped
the needles from a 5cm/2in fresh rosemary sprig, finely chopped
1 fresh sage sprig, finely chopped
6 fresh thyme sprigs, finely chopped
100g/3½oz [US 7 tbsp] unsalted butter
salt and freshly ground pepper
1 tbsp olive oil
600ml/1pt [US 2½ cups] good red wine
3 cloves
a pinch of ground cinnamon
6 peppercorns
2 bay leaves

Tie the piece of beef neatly in a roll.

Put all the chopped vegetables, garlic, herbs and butter in a pot (see introduction) and sauté for 5 minutes. Season with salt and pepper and sauté for a further 10 minutes or so, stirring frequently.

Heat the oven to 150°C/300°F/Gas Mark 2.

While the vegetables are cooking, heat the oil in a frying pan and, when hot, brown the meat on all sides – also at the two extremities by standing the roll on end. When it is a lovely deep brown colour, season with salt and pepper and place it on top of the vegetables.

Fill the top dish with the wine (see introduction). Add the cloves, cinnamon, peppercorns and bay leaves and set the dish on top of the pot so as to cover it tightly. Cover the top dish with a tight-fitting lid and place this construction of pots in the oven. Cook for 8 hours. Because it is cooked so slowly I find no need to add any liquid to the meat, but should the meat become dry, add a couple of tablespoons of that water.

Remove the meat to one side and skim off as much of the fat as you can. Allow the meat to cool a little and then carve it in thickish slices (an electric knife makes the job much easier). Place the slices on a dish and spoon over a little of the vegetable sauce. Place the rest around the meat, and serve.

POLPETTONE ALLA ROMAGNOLA
Baked Meat Roll

During one of my visits to sunny Romagna I met a chef who was very kind and informative. He took me around the fish market of Cesenatico, and we exchanged recipes and discussed food. Sadly enough I didn't make a note of his name, so I cannot credit him for this very good recipe.

Meat roll in England always seems to me to have undertones of patched-up food made with left-over meat and whatever else is in the fridge. In Italy a polpettone, although '*cucina povera*', is thought of as a very valid and excellent dish – as long as it is well made. In fact a good polpettone can demonstrate the expertise of the cook, who must be able to season and adjust the flavour so as to achieve a well-balanced dish.

THE RECIPE

While most polpettoni are cooked in a sauté pan, this one has the advantage of being cooked in the oven, so that it can be partly ignored without fear of it getting burnt. The use of three different meats gives the dish a more complex flavour. The seasoning must be assertive, with the right amount of salt and pepper.

If you have any left-over polpettone, serve it cold, but not chilled, dressed with a little sauce of chopped parsley, cornichons and capers floating in extra virgin olive oil and sharpened by a few drops of lemon juice (see salsa verde on page 229).

SERVES 6 TO 7

60g/2oz good white country-type bread, crustless
about 120ml/4fl oz milk
250g/9oz lean beef, minced [US ground]
250g/9oz lean pork, minced [US ground]
250g/9oz boned chicken breast, minced [US
ground]
2 eggs
60g/2oz [US ½ cup] freshly grated Parmesan
15g/½oz fresh flat-leaf parsley, leaves only
15g/½oz mixed fresh thyme, rosemary needles and
sage
1 tbsp chopped sweet onion
grated nutmeg
salt and freshly ground black pepper
300ml/10fl oz dry white wine
300ml/10fl oz rich meat stock (page 230)
30g/1oz [US 2 tbsp] unsalted butter
20g/¾oz [US 2 tbsp] flour

Break the bread into pieces, put it in a bowl and cover with milk. Leave to soak up some of the milk and then squeeze the excess milk out and crumble the bread with a fork. Put it in a large bowl.

Heat the oven to 200°C/400°F/Gas Mark 6.

Add the three meats to the bowl, also the eggs, cheese, herbs and onion and mix very thoroughly. I do this with my hands – definitely the best way. Season with nutmeg, salt and pepper. I recommend adding at least 1½ teaspoons of salt, because salt is fundamental to the final result, especially in a dish like this where you cannot satisfactorily add it at the end. Mix and pound again.

Now cut a 30cm/12in square sheet of foil and place it on the work surface. Brush it all over with oil and then transfer the meat mixture on to it. Shape the mixture into a fat salame and pat it together to eliminate any air bubbles and empty spaces. Then roll it up in the foil and pat again. Close the ends firmly, transfer the package to a roasting tin and bake for 30 minutes, until the

polpettone is firm to the touch.

Cut the foil open and pour 4 or 5 tablespoons of the wine over the meat. Place the tin back in the oven. After 10 minutes pour over a little more wine, then repeat the operation once more after a further 10 minutes. Now the polpettone will have cooked for about 1 hour and it should be done. Remove it from the oven and transfer it, without the foil, to a carving board. (Use great care in transferring the polpettone, because it might break in the middle; however if this does happen, don't worry – you have to slice it up in any case!) Keep warm, covered with a clean piece of foil. Be careful to retain the cooking juices in the foil.

Pour the cooking juices collected in the foil and in the tin into a saucepan and bring to the boil. Add the remaining wine and the stock and reduce over high heat by about one-third, until syrupy, rich and full of flavour.

Blend the butter and flour together with the prongs of a fork. Turn the heat down and add the flour mixture (*beurre manié*, to give it its culinary name) little by little to the simmering sauce. When all has been added, taste the sauce and adjust seasoning.

Carve the polpettone into 1cm/½in slices. If you do not have an electric knife – an invaluable tool for this type of dish, as well as for braised meat or roulades – use a very sharp, straight-bladed knife. Transfer the slices to a heated oval plate, overlapping them slightly. Spoon around a few tablespoons of the sauce and serve at once, with the rest of the sauce handed separately in a sauce-boat.

Serve the polpettone with a buttery potato purée and/or with spinach or sautéed courgettes [US zucchini], according to the season.

Cotolette alla Bolognese
Bolognese Veal Steaks

Bolognese cotolette are thicker (about 1cm/½in) than Wienerschnitzel. I sometimes use loin of pork steaks, or I use turkey breast steaks which are just the right thickness.

This is a dish that typifies the exuberance of the local cuisine. To the meat, which has been coated in egg, breaded and fried in butter, is added the delicate prosciutto di Parma, plus the other glory of the region, Parmigiano-Reggiano and, to finish the dish off, a little tomato sauce. When in season, a truffle can be slivered over the meat at the very end. In the past, the truffle used to be put on the meat before it was coated and breaded, a sophisticated touch of the kind that fascinates even the most experienced gourmet. Personally, I find truffles and tomato sauce an unhappy match.

This dish is particularly suitable when you do not want to be in the kitchen at the last minute. You can prepare it totally beforehand and heat it up gently, for a little longer, just before serving it. It is a good dish, when properly made, even if it has been overly exploited by second-rate Italian restaurants. The addition of a little olive oil to the butter is to prevent the butter from burning. An alternative is to use clarified butter.

SERVES 4

a piece of Parmesan
4 veal or loin of pork steaks, about 450g/1lb in total
1 egg
salt
8 tbsp fine dried white breadcrumbs
60g/2oz [US 4 tbsp] unsalted butter
1 tbsp olive oil
60g/2oz prosciutto di Parma, thinly sliced

FOR THE TOMATO SAUCE
15g/½oz [US 1 tbsp] unsalted butter
1 tbsp very finely chopped onion
salt and freshly ground pepper
6 tbsp tomato passata
4 tbsp meat stock (page 230)

First make the tomato sauce. The onion must be chopped really fine, like grains of rice. Put the butter, the onion and a pinch of salt in a small saucepan. Sauté gently for 5 minutes or so and then add the passata. Cook for 10 minutes over gentle heat. Add the stock and bring to the simmer. Taste and adjust seasoning.

Using a potato peeler, sliver 40g/1½oz of shavings from your piece of Parmesan and set aside.

See that the steaks are all of a good shape, and of the right thickness. Also cut off any fat that might be on the edge of the steaks.

In a soup plate beat the egg lightly with 1 teaspoon of salt. Spread the breadcrumbs on a plate next to the egg. Coat the meat on both sides in the egg, let the excess egg fall back into the plate, and then transfer the steaks to the plate of crumbs. Coat each side, pressing the crumbs into the meat with your hands to form a thickish layer.

Now, if you have time, place the steaks in the fridge to chill. It will be easier to fry them properly when chilled.

Choose a frying pan or a sauté pan large enough to hold the steaks one next to the other. Put the butter and the oil into it and heat until the foam has subsided. Put the meat in the fat and fry on a lively heat until the underside is of a golden colour. Turn the steaks over and fry the other side. Be careful not to burn the butter, or the meat will be speckled with black spots instead of being lovely and golden. Turn the heat down if necessary.

Divide the prosciutto into 4 portions and place one over each steak. Do the same with the cheese shavings, placing them over the prosciutto. Spoon the tomato sauce around the meat. Cover the pan with a lid and cook, over low heat, for 7 to 10 minutes. Transfer to a heated dish and serve at once.

SCIARLOTTA DI PERE
Pear Charlotte

In 1988 I went to Parma to receive the Gran Duchessa Maria Luigia prize for my book *Gastronomy of Italy*. After the prize-giving ceremony there was a fantastic banquet in a beautiful palazzo, a banquet in the manner of the Duchess herself. Marie Louise, a Hapsburg princess, was the wife, and later widow, of Napoleon. The Parmigiani adored her and still consider her their only true sovereign. She certainly must have been a fascinating lady who enjoyed life to the full, which is why she decided that rather than join Napoleon in far-flung Elba, she would stay put in delightful little Parma with her dashing Austrian general, Adam Albert Neipperg.

Maria Luigia, as she was called in Parma, loved a good table, and for that she employed one of the best chefs of the time, Vincenzo Agnoletti. She also imported from Vienna many talented pâtissiers, who taught the Parmigiani the art of cake-making, as well as cake-loving.

Parma is still renowned for its pâtisseries, and when I was there the most famous was the Pasticceria Torino. At the banquet I met the man who is the inspiration behind the delicious dolci (sweet things) sold at the Torino, Ugo Falavigna. He was responsible for all the cakes, puddings, friandises and chocolates served at the banquet, which were presented on beautifully moulded chocolate plates (which we soon demolished).

Falavigna gave me a copy of his delightful book, *Arte della Pasticceria a Parma*, which contains the basis of the following recipe for a pear charlotte.

THE RECIPE
If you cannot find Savoiardi, try to make your own sponge fingers, which are called ladyfingers in the US. Bought sponge fingers can be used too. They are sweeter than Savoiardi, so you must make a less sweet syrup. They are also less absorbent, but the result is quite satisfactory.

SERVES 6
1½ unwaxed lemons
800g/1¾lb ripe but firm pears
150ml/5fl oz white wine
180g/6oz caster sugar [US ¾ cup + 2 tbsp granulated sugar]
⅛ tsp ground cinnamon
⅛ tsp ground cloves
2 tbsp Poire William's eau-de-vie or Grappa
approximately 16–17 Savoiardi

Wash and dry the lemon. Using a potato peeler, peel off 3 strips of rind and set aside. Squeeze the lemons and pour the juice into a bowl.

Peel the pears, quarter and core them, and slice them very thinly. Put these slices in the bowl and mix them so that they get coated with lemon juice. This has the double function of preventing the pears from discolouring as well as giving them a lovely flavour. Leave to macerate for 1 hour.

Put the wine and the same amount of water in a large sauté pan. Add the sugar, spices and the strips of lemon rind and heat over low heat until the sugar has dissolved. Stir the syrup constantly. Simmer gently for 5 minutes and then slide in the pears with their juices. Turn them over a few times for the first 2 or 3 minutes or so and then leave to cook over very low heat until they are tender. This will only take a few minutes if you have sliced the pears thinly. Taste and add a little sugar if necessary. It is difficult to give the exact amount of sugar since it depends on the quality of the pears.

Lift the pears out of the pan with a slotted spoon and set them aside. Discard the lemon rind. Turn the heat up and reduce the juices until they are heavy with syrup and rich with flavour. Mix in the liqueur.

Line a 1.2l/2pt [US 5 cup] pudding basin or other dome-shaped mould with cling film. Soak the Savoiardi in the lovely syrup, just enough to soften them, and then line the basin with them. Spoon the pears and their juices into the basin and cover with more Savoiardi soaked in syrup. Pour over any remaining syrup. Cover with cling film and chill for at least 6 hours.

To unmould the charlotte, remove the cover of film and place a pretty round dish over the top of the basin. Turn dish and basin over and lift the basin off. Peel off the film lining.

I decorate the charlotte with some whipped cream and serve some more cream in a bowl at the table. Alternatively I make a mixture of cream and mascarpone in the proportion of 2 to 1, and sweeten it with 2 tablespoons of sifted icing sugar [US confectioners' sugar].

FRUTTA FRESCA ALL'ACETO BALSAMICO
Fresh Fruit and Balsamic Vinegar

In the following two recipes you will find aceto balsamico used to flavour fruit: strawberries and melon. Both recipes are from the provinces of Modena and Reggio Emilia, where aceto balsamico is made. They are extremely simple to make, but, as with all the simplest recipes, you must use a very good aceto balsamico and, of course, top-quality fruit. The balsamic vinegar brings out the flavour of the fruit without imparting any vinegary taste to the fruit.

I have put these two ideas (I can hardly call them recipes) together, but I would never serve them together. Strawberries and melon are definitely not a match. Another fruit that is suited to this treatment is mango – hardly Italian! – and this would be a perfect companion to strawberries.

FRAGOLE ALL'ACETO BALSAMICO
Strawberries with Balsamic Vinegar

SERVES 4
700g/1½lb strawberries
2–3 tbsp sugar
2 tbsp best-quality balsamic vinegar

Cut the larger strawberries in half, or even into quarters. Put them all in a bowl.

About 2 hours before serving sprinkle over the sugar and toss gently but thoroughly. Half an hour before serving sprinkle with the balsamic vinegar and toss again gently and with care. Serve chilled.

MELONE ALL'ACETO BALSAMICO
Melon with Balsamic Vinegar

The most popular melon in Italy is the cantaloupe, but any melon is delicious served in this way, as long as it is ripe.

SERVES 6 TO 8
1 medium melon
1 tbsp caster sugar [US granulated sugar]
2 tbsp best-quality balsamic vinegar

Cut the melon into thin wedges. Peel them and scrape out all the seeds. Place in a lovely glass bowl.

Sprinkle with the sugar and with the balsamic vinegar half an hour before serving. Serve chilled.

SEMIFREDDO SEMPLICE
Plain Semifreddo

'Now I shall let you into a secret; the secret of the Italian meringue.' This is what Signora Cantoni said to me in Bologna when I met her at the cookery school run by the Simili sisters, one of the most renowned cookery schools in Italy. Signora Cantoni is the granddaughter of a famous Bolognese ice-cream maker. So I was delighted that she was happy to pass on to me one of her secrets. She told me that by using Italian meringue one can make delicious semifreddi which, served with different sauces, can take on many different guises. It is one of the gelati she always makes for her grandchildren – lucky them!

THE RECIPE
A semifreddo, as the name tells us, is a half-frozen concoction, very similar to a frozen mousse. It often contains layers of sponge cake, but it can also be made just with a mousse-type mixture.

Italian meringue is a more stable mixture than the usual Swiss meringue, since the egg whites are heated by the hot syrup poured over them.

This semifreddo is made with Italian meringue that is simply flavoured with lemon rind. I find it quite delicious by itself, but a sauce does add to the pleasure. My favourite sauce is a raspberry coulis (see following recipe) flavoured with geranium leaves, a delightfully sensual gastronomic pleasure. A coffee-flavoured chocolate sauce is an excellent alternative, in which case I would substitute a few drops of pure vanilla extract and a pinch or two of ground cinnamon for the lemon rind. When you make the sauce, keep in mind that the semifreddo itself is very sweet.

I prefer to give the amount of egg whites in weight rather than number, because egg sizes differ so much.

The temperature of the sugar syrup is critical, so I feel you do need a jam thermometer.

SERVES 6 TO 8

125g/4oz [US ½ cup + 2 tbsp] sugar
100ml/3½fl oz water
1 tbsp lemon juice
150g/5oz [US ⅔ cup] egg whites
the grated rind of 1 unwaxed lemon

Put the sugar, water and lemon juice in a small saucepan. Heat, slowly at first, and faster when the syrup is clear, until a jam thermometer registers 110°C/225°F. Brush down the sides of the pan frequently with a wet pastry brush.

Now you must begin to whisk the egg whites with the lemon rind. I use a copper bowl and a hand-held electric mixer. Whisk until the whites are stiff but still moist. The snow should remain in position when you turn the bowl upside-down (if you dare to do this!). When the syrup reaches 130°C/250°F, pour it in a steady stream into the bowl, letting it fall into the middle of the egg snow. Do not stop whisking; go on and on until the mixture is cool. (Feel it by pushing a finger down to the bottom of the bowl. It should be no warmer than room temperature.) Line a 1.2l/2pt [US 5 cup] loaf tin with cling film and spoon the meringue into it. Smooth it down, cover with more film and freeze.

When you want to serve the semifreddo, transfer it to a board, remove the film and cut into thickish slices. Place on individual dessert plates surrounded by a pool of the chosen sauce.

This semifreddo can be eaten as soon as it comes out of the freezer.

SUGO DI LAMPONE

A Raspberry Coulis

SERVES 6

450g/1lb fresh raspberries
150g/5oz icing sugar [US 1¼ cups confectioners' sugar], sifted
the juice of 1 lemon
3 or 4 young sweet geranium leaves, torn into small pieces (optional)

Blend together the raspberries, sugar, lemon juice and the optional sweet geranium leaves in a food processor or blender. Taste and add more sugar and/or lemon juice, according to taste. If you want a smooth sauce, strain it through a fine sieve, pushing the purée with a spoon.

SALSA DI CIOCCOLATO

A Chocolate Sauce

SERVES 6

200g/7oz bitter chocolate with a high cocoa butter and cocoa solids content
120ml/4fl oz strong espresso coffee
6 tbsp caster sugar [US granulated sugar]
120ml/4fl oz double cream [US heavy cream]

Break the chocolate into small pieces and place in a heavy-based pan. Add the coffee and the sugar and dissolve over very gentle heat, stirring constantly. Mix in the cream and keep on the heat until the sauce is smoking. Pour into a sauce-boat and serve immediately.

Bensone di Villa Gaidello
Sweet Focaccia

Villa Gaidello is a charming guest-farm near
Modena, owned by Paola Bini. Paola was born
there and has inherited the farm from her grandmother. To make it possible for her to keep it, she
has refurbished the barn, the house and out-
houses into a sort of hotel *cum* restaurant. The
surrounding countryside has the placid serenity of
the Po valley, at first sight seemingly a little dull
although appreciation of it grows with time.
Appreciation of Villa Gaidello's food, however, is
immediate.

Paola has a brigade of local women who, following her guidance, cook for her. She decides on
the menu according to what is best in the shops
or in the vegetable gardens. The menu is fixed.
You sit in the large conservatory-like dining room
(it used to be the barn) with a pile of six white
plates in front of you. After each of the six courses
a waitress comes round with a large basket into
which she whisks the dirty top plate in readiness
for the next course on the clean plate beneath. I
thought it was the best local food I had ever had,
comparable to the marvellous meals I have
enjoyed at the homes of my many friends in
Reggio Emilia and Parma. The soup, a stock in
which a few perfect tortellini were gently floating,
was particularly memorable – an unforgettable
delight.

Traditionally, bensone is an S-shaped cake,
often eaten warm with chilled sweet Lambrusco.
You break your piece of bensone into the glass of
Lambrusco and you eat it with a spoon. Paola
Bini's bensone, although a little different, is also
excellent for dunking; when dunked it softens and
absorbs the flavour of the liquid, but without dis-
integrating.

THE RECIPE
At the Villa Gaidello the bensone was shaped in
individual rounds and served with fruits preserved
under spirit. I suggest you serve it, as I do, with a
lovely eggy crème anglaise. If you prefer to serve
it with wine – still a perfect way to enjoy it – I
suggest a Moscato d'Asti or a heavenly Albana
from Romagna, although only Lambrusco has
that slightly sharp fizzy flavour that makes it the
ideal accompaniment. But alas, *good* sweet
Lambrusco is not easily found outside Italy, or
even outside Emilia-Romagna.

MAKES 8
*300g/10oz [US 2½ cups] white flour, preferably
Italian 00*
*150g/5oz caster sugar [US ¾ cup granulated
sugar]*
2 tsp baking powder
a pinch of salt
150g/5oz [US 10 tbsp] unsalted butter, melted
1 size-2 egg [US extra-large egg]
the grated rind of ½ unwaxed lemon

Heat the oven to 180°C/350°F/Gas Mark 4.

Mix together the flour, sugar, baking powder
and salt on the working surface. Make a well and
add the butter, the egg and the lemon rind. Stir
them with a fork to blend, gradually adding the
dry ingredients that form the well. Knead quickly
into a ball, avoiding beating or overworking the
dough as this would toughen it.

Wipe the work surface clean and then lightly
flour it. Divide the dough into 8 portions. Roll
out or pat each portion into a round.

Lightly butter two baking trays and place the
rounds on them, spacing them out as they will
spread when baking. Place the trays in the oven
and bake for 15 to 20 minutes, until pale gold.
Transfer to a wire rack and let them cool for
about 10 minutes before serving.

TOSCANA

The Tuscan contadini are sober; their meals are healthy and varied; the bread, the best of nourishment, is excellent, of pure wheat, grey yes, but free of husk . . . One must remember that the Tuscan contadino makes his own oil not only for lighting his lamps, but also to dress the vegetables on which he feeds, thus making them more tasty and nourishing.' This passage comes from a book, *Delle Condizione degli Agricoltori in Toscana*, written in 1860 by G Sismondi. Apart from the lighting of lamps, this passage could have been written yesterday.

The well-known sobriety of the Tuscans has at times been confused with avarice, as the journalist Indro Montanelli has pointed out. 'The Tuscan countryside is bare, lean, disdainful of trivialities and the superfluous. The cooking, too, is lean, made of three or four essentials. And their parsimony is leanness, which should never be confused with meanness, because it is a mental attitude rather than a financial calculation.' Once again, and maybe more obviously than in most other regions, the cooking reflects the character of the people.

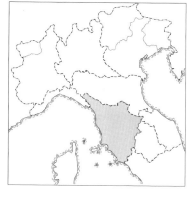

Another factor that underlines this sobriety is that Tuscany is not as fertile as most people imagine. Only a small part of this large region is lowland; other parts are hilly, but most is mountainous. The soil is poor, yet nature here seems to make up in quality what is lacking in quantity. With this sort of quality it is no wonder that only the minimum is necessary to dress it up. This minimum usually consists of the olive oil, which, on the table, is the symbol of Tuscan cooking, as the olive tree is that of the countryside. Olive oil is the only condiment used in Tuscany, and perhaps this is why traditional Tuscan cooking has no risotti and very few pasta dishes in its repertoire.

But let me take you around Tuscany, the way I recently went, from the Ligurian border to the southern Maremma. The cooking of northern Tuscany and that of Liguria have very strong links. The best place to appreciate this is at the Trattoria Bussè in Pontremoli, where Antonietta Bartocchi reigns in the kitchen and her brother Luciano entertains the guests with his remarkable knowledge of local food.

It is there that I was first introduced to *testaroli*. Testaroli are made of a water-based batter poured into flat, round, cast-iron or earthenware moulds which have been heated to a very high temperature by being placed between hot embers. The embers should contain dried chestnut leaves for their aroma. The fire is lit in a room next to the house, called the *gradile*, a room where bread is made too. The testaroli, which are about 40cm/17in in diameter, are kept there. When they are to be served they are cut into squares and thrown into boiling salted water, just like lasagne, and then dressed with a light pesto – the Ligurian influence.

As an alternative, the torta di bietole – Swiss chard tourte (for a similar dish see page 135) – is more Ligurian than Tuscan, the pastry being the poor man's pastry of flour, oil and water characteristic of Liguria.

The *involtini di vitello* which follow at Bussè again show great similarity with the Ligurian *tomaxelle*, slices of veal wrapped around a delicate mixture of sweetbread and minced veal. Antonietta cooks her involtini in a beautiful shallow earthenware dish for at least two hours. While I was enjoying them I remembered a passage from one of the autobiographies I enjoyed most in recent years, *A Tuscan Childhood*. The author, Kinta Beevor, grew up before the Second World War in the Fortezza della Brunella in nearby Aulla. When Kinta tried to reproduce in England the Tuscan involtini of her childhood, to keep them rolled up she used toothpicks bought from a chemist, which turned out to be medicated!

But involtini are the food of the wealthy, while Lunigiana and the adjacent valley of Garfagnana are rich only in their wealth of peasant dishes. The flour from the superb local chestnuts is used to prepare castagnaccio (page 197), nowadays mostly eaten in the street straight from the baker, or polenta, which with its sweetish flavour matches perfectly the pork or sausages that traditionally accompany it.

The new wave of restaurateurs now make pappardelle with chestnut flour, and delicious they are indeed, especially when dressed with stewed hare or a ragù of wild boar. Pappardelle are one of the only two traditional Tuscan pastas, the other being *pici*, a sort of thick hand-made spaghetti. Pici, which near Montalcino are called *pinci*, are made with a poor man's dough, just water and plain flour, and are traditionally dressed with a ragù of wild mushrooms.

The subject of mushrooms brings me back to my journey through Tuscany, where the next stop is in Chianti. We had a house there for a long time, but decided to sell it after I counted no less than seven British cars parked in our local village of Gaiole. Chianti had become Chiantishire! I used to go mushroom hunting with the locals, who disdained all fungi other than boletes, a preference I fully endorse. Later on, when a friend and I ran a cookery school in Chianti, we used the different species we found for a risotto (as on page

158), but the fungi which gave the best flavour to the dish were undoubtedly the boletes which shot up overnight in the woods to welcome the bright autumn sun.

In Chianti as in Lucchesia the choice for a first course should be soup. A ribollita (page 181) made with black cabbage, a pappa col pomodoro, and a zuppa di farro (page 179) are three examples of superb soups in which bread or beans stand in for pasta or rice. Hot, warm or even cold in the summer, soup brings together two of the strongest elements of Tuscan cooking: bread and vegetables. The vegetables, more than anything else, confirm the fact that quality is of paramount importance. The small broad beans eaten raw with young pecorino (which 'should never be peppery but only sapid' as the gastronome Giovanni Righi Parenti writes), the noble cardoons (called *gobbi* – hunchbacks – in Tuscany because of the way they are grown there), the small succulent artichokes of Caterina de'Medici fame (the old tyrant ate so many that she was sick for days), the fat garlic with which the Senesi prepare the delicious fried garlic on St John's Day, 24th June, and of course the beans . . . and the beans . . . and more beans. Not for nothing are the Tuscans called *mangia fagioli* (bean eaters).

But the Tuscans also eat wonderful meat and even better chicken and game. The best way to appreciate the quality of the meat and chicken is to have it in a *grigliata* – mixed grill, which usually includes fegatelli – slices of pig's liver wrapped in 'crépine' and flavoured with wild fennel seeds.

Oh, the herbs of Tuscany! You go for a walk and you pass through mist after mist of different scents, according to what you are treading on or brushing against. *Nepitella*, a kind of wild mint; *finocchietto*, wild fennel; *ramerino*, rosemary – the constant partner to roast meat; *pepolino*, wild thyme, for the rabbit; and even *dragoncello*, tarragon, which is hardly used in other regions. The best foil for the herbs are the delicious schiacciate (see page 177) – Tuscan focacce – scented with herbs and moistened, though never dripping, with the green olive oil of this perfect country.

Going south you arrive in the Maremma, a land of biblical beauty in its wide green valleys and steep dramatic hills topped by old crenellated towns. The vineyards and the olive groves have given way to fields of tomatoes, sunflowers and cereals, but the lines of cypresses, the landmark of the Tuscan countryside, are still there. And the food is still similar, with its accent on simplicity and quality: vegetables and bean soups again, such as *acquacotta*, literally 'cooked water', the Cinderella of all soups.

Acquacotta is made with whatever vegetables are ready, wild or cultivated, plus the beans, of course, and water, which should be *di fonte* (spring water). 'I cook the eggs gently in a little of the soup stock and put them on top of the soup; that's easier than the more usual method of breaking the eggs over the soup and putting the stockpot in the oven for the eggs to cook.' This is what I was told by Lorenzo Seghi, chef of the Taverna del Borgo Vecchio in Massa Marittima, a town well worth a detour also for its incredible beauty.

Acquacotta is also popular in Arezzo and its surrounding villages, but there it does not contain eggs and the soup is ladled on to bread. 'Acquacotta is made with natural ingredients and this is why the Italians love it.' This short passage precedes the recipe written by a six-year-old girl who, in typical Tuscan fashion, confuses Tuscany with Italy! The recipe appears in a book edited by Guido Gianni, the delegate of the Accademia Italiana della Cucina in Arezzo. All the recipes were written by primary school pupils in the province of Arezzo. They are recipes the children have learnt from mothers and grandmothers, and they are an interesting social comment on the local food. I was fascinated by the book and its charming drawings; but, alas, I only had it on loan.

After much thought I decided not to include a recipe for acquacotta because, more than any other soup, it needs vegetables grown in earthy soil and ripened by the sun, and not pale imitations of vegetables grown in water and ripened in air-conditioned greenhouses. I feel an acquacotta made in Britain would taste just like its name implies: 'cooked water'.

A word about the fish that are caught and cooked all down the coast, from the river Magra to Orbetello. Simplicity, again, in the grilling or roasting of the fish, or in the boiling of prawns and langoustines. These are dressed with local olive oil, and sometimes combined with cannellini beans, in one of the most creative fish salads ever, known as *i ricchi e i poveri* (the rich and the poor). Only *cacciucco* – fish soup – and *triglie alla livornese* (page 187) demand a complicated treatment and the skill of the cook. Of all Italian fish soups, cacciucco (of which it is said that the soup should contain five different fish, one for each c in its name) is the most similar to bouillabaisse. As with bouillabaisse one of the fish must be rascasse rouge – scorpion fish – for the flavour. Cacciucco, however, does not contain saffron, and the piquancy is given by *zenzero*, as they call chilli in Tuscany (in Italian zenzero is ginger, and chilli is peperoncino; so do not be fooled when you are told that cacciucco contains ginger!).

Another Tuscan speciality are *cee*, a Tuscan contraction of *cieche*, meaning blind, elvers. The incredible story of the elvers swimming to Europe from the Sargasso Sea fascinated me so much when I first heard it as a child that I sat motionless and speechless in front of a dish of the most exquisite *cee alla salvia* in Viareggio, unable to touch them. What also disturbed me deeply was that these tiny translucent fish, blind as I was told they are, are alive until thrown into the boiling oil, so alive that when they touch the hot oil, they regain their full strength to such an extent that the cook must quickly cover the frying pan with a lid and keep it firmly on. Now I can eat cee with delight, but it is a rare treat indeed since they are astronomically expensive. This, I have been told, is due to the fact that the government has prohibited the catching of elvers because they are in danger of extinction. But, inevitably, they are still caught – in the middle of the night – to be served in expensive restaurants.

And how do you finish your meal in Tuscany? Like the Tuscans, with pecorino and pears, when they are in season, or with an almondy cantuccio di Prato dipped in Vinsanto. As for me, I love their country tarts, where the soft shell of sweet pastry is brought alive by its contrast with the sharp home-made jam (page 199). A real treat in a repertoire that abounds with good, simple things.

Schiacciata con le Noci Ⓥ
Flat Bread with Walnuts

Schiacciata is to Tuscany what focaccia is to Liguria, a kind of dressed flat bread. The traditional schiacciata is made with flour, yeast, water and rendered pork fat instead of the oil used in the Ligurian focaccia. Nowadays oil usually replaces the pork fat for the benefit of health, but to the detriment of the flavour. There are many different schiacciate, most of them slightly sweet, such as the schiacciata fiorentina which is eaten in Florence during Carnival.

Schiacciata means squashed flat, but quite a few shiacciate are deliciously light and puffy. Paolo Petroni, in his excellent book *La Cucina Fiorentina*, suggests that the name might derive from the meaning of *shiacciare* in relation to the eggs, i.e. to break the eggs, since schiacciate were also made at Easter time. After Lent, when the eating of eggs was forbidden, every larder was bursting with eggs. An arguable theory, to which I cannot subscribe since quite a few schiacciate are made without eggs, as, for instance, this one. I think that the name simply comes from the shape. The dough is rolled out to about 2cm/¾in thick and is baked in a rectangular oven tray. The result is a bread usually no thicker than 2–3cm/1–1½in.

THE RECIPE
Of the several different schiacciate I have tried, this is the one I like best. The recipe, which contains maize (polenta) flour, appears in the fascinating book *Italy in Small Bites* by the American food writer Carol Field. I adapted my previous recipe because I found that the added maize flour in Carol Field's recipe gives the schiacciata a sweet flavour and a gritty texture that is particularly appealing.

I use easy-blend yeast because I find it easier. It does not need dissolving and it mixes better.

SERVES 8 AS AN APPETIZER
60g/1oz [US ½ cup] walnut kernels
150g/5oz [US 1¼ cups] white flour, preferably Italian 00
60g/2oz coarse-ground maize (polenta) flour [US ½ cup coarse cornmeal]
1 tsp fine sea salt
1 tsp easy-blend dried yeast [US rapid-rise dry yeast]
2 tbsp extra virgin olive oil
½ tbsp chopped fresh rosemary (optional)
coarse sea salt

Heat the oven to 180°C/350°F/Gas Mark 4.

Spread the walnuts on a baking tray and, when the oven is hot, place them in the oven to toast for about 10 minutes. You will know when they are ready because of the lovely smell that will pervade your kitchen.

Put the walnuts on a chopping board and chop them very coarsely. I do not like to use a food processor for this recipe because the walnuts will either become ground, if you process for too long, or if you process for only a few seconds some kernels will be ground and others will be whole.

Mix the two flours, fine sea salt and yeast together on the working surface. Make a well and pour into it 1 tablespoon of the oil. Gradually add 150ml/5fl oz of lukewarm water while gathering the dry mixture from the inside walls of the well. When all the water has been added, begin to knead as usual for about 4 or 5 minutes. Knead in the chopped walnuts. (If you do not like kneading you can make the dough in a food processor, but transfer the dough to a working surface to knead in the walnuts quickly.)

Place the dough in a bowl that has been lightly greased with olive oil and cover with a damp linen towel. Put the bowl in a warm corner of the kitchen, out of any draught. Leave for about 1 hour.

Roll out or stretch the dough to fit a 30 × 25cm/ 12 × 10in baking tray. Cover again with the towel and leave to rise for another 50 minutes or so.

Turn on the oven to 200°C/400°F/Gas Mark 6 half an hour before baking.

Mix the remaining oil with 1 tablespoon of water. Just before you put the dough in the oven, moisten your fingers in the oil mixture and make dimples in the top of the dough. Sprinkle with the optional rosemary and some coarse sea salt and bake until golden, about 20 to 25 minutes.

Schiacciata is excellent hot or at room temperature. If you are eating it at room temperature, transfer it to a wire rack after baking.

SALVIATA Ⓥ

Sage Omelette

There are two traditional Tuscan omelettes, one with mint and the other with sage, both characteristic of the freshness and simplicity of Tuscan cooking.

To make the dish more complete you can present salviata as they do at the prestigious Enoteca Pinchiorri in Florence. The salviata is cut into thin strips and dressed with a fresh tomato sauce. This is, in fact, an old Roman dish called Uova in Trippa, which is traditionally made with a cheese omelette.

SERVES 4

6 size-3 free-range eggs [US large eggs]
1 tbsp flour
2 tbsp milk
1 tbsp chopped fresh sage
1 small garlic clove, very finely chopped
6 tbsp freshly grated Parmesan
½ tsp salt
freshly ground black pepper
2 tbsp olive oil

Lightly beat the eggs with a fork. Mix together the flour and the milk and then beat into the eggs. Add the sage, garlic, Parmesan, salt and pepper.

Heat the oil in a large non-stick frying pan – I use a 25cm/10in frying pan – and when hot pour in the egg mixture. Turn the heat down immediately and let the mixture cook very gently. When the omelette is nearly all set, but still shows a pool of uncooked eggs at the top, place it under a low grill [US broiler] until the top is set too.

Serve hot, warm or cold; it is equally good.

ZUPPA DI FARRO DELLA VECCHIA OSTERIA DI PONTE A BOZZONE Ⓥ
Emmer and Pulses Soup

Farro – emmer wheat – is the ancestor of present-day durum wheat. It was the food on which the Roman soldiers won their empire. I can see why they were such great conquerors: they fought hard so as to survive for their next dish of farro. At that time farro was mainly milled into flour – *farina* in Italian – and eaten mixed with water in a porridge-like mixture called *puls*, the predecessor of maize polenta.

The origins of emmer wheat are shrouded in mystery. Elizabeth David, in her book *English Bread and Yeast Cookery*, writes '. . . in the Mediterranean world wheat exported from Alexandria was much prized for the good bread it made. It is thought to have been this variety, later known to us as emmer wheat, which was the ancestor of our European grain.' However, emmer is a species of durum wheat, not of the soft wheat that is usually the one used in this country to make bread.

For centuries farro was the food of the poor Lucchesi and other Tuscans. But in the last 10 years it has become one of the foods of discerning gourmets, and zuppa di farro is now the most chic soup ever, served even at the three-Michelin-star restaurant, the Enoteca Pinchiorri in Florence.

Like the best olive oil, its natural companion, zuppa di farro originally comes from Lucchesia, and it is in that zone that the recipes abound. However, my recipe is from Siena. I had this soup for the first time some years ago when we were looking for good, and not too expensive, restaurants where we could take the pupils of our cookery school in Tuscany. One of our chosen restaurants was the Vecchia Osteria, just north of Siena, where Cinzia presides over the kitchen and

Gianfranco looks after his impressive cellar. This *simpatico* couple is outstandingly knowledgeable, each in their own field. Cinzia knows all about the history and traditions of Tuscan cooking, which she follows carefully while adding light personal touches of her own. And here is Cinzia's recipe.

THE RECIPE

You can now buy farro in a few specialist Italian foodshops. However, if you cannot find it, whole wheat grain or pearl barley are good substitutes. If you use whole wheat grain you must soak it overnight; pearl barley does not need soaking. The soup is thick and of a consistency that fills your mouth with the earthy flavours of the pulses and the gluey sweet texture of the farro.

SERVES 6 TO 8

225g/8oz [US 1 cup] farro
150g/5oz [US scant 1 cup] dried cannellini beans
100g/3½oz [US ½ cup] dried chick-peas
1 dried chilli
4 garlic cloves
4 tbsp extra virgin olive oil
3 small fresh rosemary sprigs
300g/10oz [US 1½ cups] canned peeled tomatoes, chopped, with their juice
600ml/1pt [US 2½ cups] vegetable stock (page 231)
salt and freshly ground black pepper
extra virgin olive oil for the table

The evening before you want to cook the soup, put the farro, the beans and the chick-peas in 3 separate bowls. Cover with water and soak overnight. I usually add a flour paste, for which you will find the instructions on page 15, to the water for the chick-peas. The next day drain the lot and rinse under cold water.

Put the beans, chick-peas and farro in 3 saucepans and cover with cold water by no less than 5cm/2in. Bring slowly to the boil and simmer, covered, at the lowest heat, until very tender. The times can vary, but as a guide I can say that the chick-peas will take 2 to 2½ hours and the cannellini 1 to 1½, while the farro will cook quite quickly – in about 20 minutes. Whatever you do, please do not undercook them. The contemporary mania among smart restaurateurs to serve pulses that are like bullets is totally deplorable. Anyhow, for this recipe you must cook the pulses thoroughly, since you have to purée them later. Drain and keep the liquid.

Process the cannellini beans with half the chick-peas until smooth. If you want a more homogenized purée, without any bits of skin, you must pass the mixture through a food mill set with the small hole disc.

Chop the chilli and 2 of the garlic cloves; bruise the other 2 with the side of a broad-bladed knife. In your stockpot make a little *soffritto* (frying mixture) with the oil, the chopped and bruised garlic, rosemary and chilli and fry gently until the garlic begins to turn gold. Mix in the tomatoes and cook for 15 minutes. Fish out the bruised garlic cloves and discard them. Mix in the farro and the whole chick-peas and stir them around to *insaporire* (take up the flavour) for a couple of minutes. Add the purée of pulses and enough vegetable stock for the soup to be the right consistency. You will probably need about 300ml/10fl oz of the stock, but it depends on how much liquid was left in the pan after the pulses and the farro were cooked. Bring gently to the boil. Season with salt and pepper and then taste the soup and correct the seasoning. Fish out the rosemary sprigs. Cook for a further 15 minutes and then ladle the soup into individual bowls.

Pass around a bottle of your best extra virgin olive oil so that everyone can 'christen' the soup with it.

Pappa col Pomodoro ⓥ
Bread and Tomato Soup

As its name implies, this soup is like a pap you give to babies. The taste, however, is worthy of the most discerning palate.

Like minestrone, or any other peasant soup, pappa col pomodoro can be made in countless different ways. But two ingredients that are always present are the best-quality extra virgin olive oil and good, properly baked bread. I use a Pugliese loaf, which you can buy in most supermarkets.

This is a soup to be made during the summer, when you can get really good tomatoes. ('Grown for their flavour', as they are so absurdly advertised in supermarkets. Whatever else does one grow tomatoes for?) If you cannot find good tomatoes, use best-quality Italian canned tomatoes.

You can now find good bouillon cubes on the market that contain no monosodium glutamate, or only a small amount which is neither dangerous to health nor predominant in the flavour.

SERVES 6 TO 8

150ml/5fl oz extra virgin olive oil
1 sweet onion, very finely chopped
3 garlic cloves, very finely chopped
1 small leek, very finely chopped
1–2 dried chillies, according to strength and taste,
very finely chopped
salt
1kg/2¼lb fresh ripe tomatoes, or best-quality canned
peeled tomatoes with their juice
500ml/16fl oz vegetable stock (page 231) or 2
vegetable bouillon cubes dissolved in the same
amount of water
300g/10oz country-type bread, such as Pugliese, 2 or
3 days old
extra virgin olive oil for serving

Put the oil, onion, garlic, leek and chilli in a heavy
stockpot. (I use my earthenware soup pot which
goes directly on the heat because it is ideal for
slow cooking.) Sprinkle with salt and sauté for 10
minutes over low heat, stirring very often.

Meanwhile, purée the tomatoes through a
food mill set with the small hole disc.

Add the tomato purée to the *soffritto* (frying
mixture). Let it come slowly to the boil and then
add the stock. Bring the liquid back to the boil
again.

Break the bread into small pieces, or slice it
thinly, and throw it into the pot. Break it up with
a fork and bring to a simmer. Cook very gently
for about 1 hour, mixing occasionally. By the end
of the cooking the soup should be quite thick,
like a porridge. If it is too thick, add a little
boiling water; if too thin let it boil on higher heat
a little longer. Taste and check salt. Add pepper if
you wish.

Ladle the soup into individual bowls and let it
sit until it has cooled a little. This soup is also
delicious served at room temperature. Whatever
you choose, do not serve it either piping hot or
chilled.

At the table hand around a bottle of your best
olive oil for everyone to give the soup the necessary *battesimo* (christening) by dribbling a little
oil into their soup.

LA RIBOLLITA Ⓥ

Tuscan Bean Soup

'Ribollita' means 'boiled again', and boiled again
this soup should be since it is traditionally made
the day before it's eaten. La Ribollita contains
two of the most characteristic ingredients of
Tuscan cooking: cannellini beans and *cavolo nero*.
This is a kind of cabbage that has a less cabbagey
flavour than a common cabbage and it is now
available in a few specialized greengrocers. Spring
greens are a good substitute.

This peasant soup is very thick, and it makes a
good meal on its own. It can be served hot, warm
or at room temperature.

SERVES 6 TO 8

225g/8oz [US 1¼ cups] dried cannellini beans
100ml/3½fl oz extra virgin olive oil
1 Spanish onion, sliced
1 or 2 dried chillies, seeded and chopped
2 ripe tomatoes, peeled, seeded and coarsely chopped
1 tbsp concentrated tomato paste
3 medium potatoes, cut into small cubes
2 medium carrots, cut into small cubes
1 small leek, both white and green part, cut into
small pieces
3 celery stalks, cut into small pieces
350g/12oz greens, cut into thin strips
2 garlic cloves, sliced
3 or 4 fresh thyme sprigs
salt and freshly ground pepper

FOR COOKING THE BEANS
1 medium onion, cut into quarters
1 small celery stalk
fresh sage, rosemary and parsley sprigs
3 garlic cloves
salt

FOR THE REHEATING
1 or 2 Spanish onions
6–8 slices of country-type bread, such as Pugliese
2 garlic cloves, cut in half

Soak the beans overnight in cold water. The next day, drain and rinse them and put them in a heavy pot with all of the ingredients for cooking the beans. Cover with cold water by about 5cm/2in and bring slowly to the boil. Add 2 teaspoons of salt, cover the pan and cook very gently until the beans are well done, about 1½ to 2 hours. Lift all the beans out of the liquid and purée three-quarters of them into a bowl using a food mill with the large hole disc fitted. (If you do not have a food mill – a most valuable tool – you can purée the beans in a food processor, but you will get a very coarse purée with unpleasant bits of skin in it.) Leave the remaining beans whole. Transfer the cooking liquid to another bowl.

Put three-quarters of the oil, the onion and the chillies in the pot in which you cooked the beans. Sprinkle with a pinch of salt and sauté for 10 minutes or so. Add the tomatoes and the tomato paste, cook for 2 or 3 minutes and then mix in the bean purée. Let it take up the flavour for a couple of minutes while you stir it around, and then add all the other vegetables, the garlic and the thyme.

Measure the bean liquid and add enough water to make it up to about 1.5l/2½pt [US 1½qt]. Add to the pot and bring to the boil. Cook over the lowest heat for about 2 hours. Check seasoning and leave until the next day.

The next day, mix in the whole beans. Heat the oven to 180°C/350°F/Gas Mark 4. Slice very finely enough onion to make a nice thin layer all over the surface of the soup. Put the pot in the oven and cook until the onion is tender, about 1 hour.

Rub the bread with the garlic cloves, then toast under the grill [US broiler]. Put the bread into individual soup bowls and ladle the soup over it. Dribble the remaining oil over each bowl.

RISOLATA Ⓥ
Risotto with Cos Lettuce

The odd name of this recipe comes from the elision of two words, *riso* and *insalata* – rice and salad. But when you eat the dish there is nothing that would remind you of a salad. It is a soft risotto with a slightly bitter flavour – a soft, creamy dish that brings comfort and health.

I am quite sure this is a modern recipe, but I feel no qualms about including it because it is well within the traditions of Tuscan cooking. The dish is one of the delights of the restaurant La Baraonda in Florence. Duccio, its owner, is a real Florentine: quick, witty and extremely good at promoting his fare, which is certainly worth promoting. We used to take the students at our cookery school to eat there, and that was after thorough research into the best value for money.

THE RECIPE
You should use only the green outside leaves of a cos lettuce, which has a stronger flavour than any other.

You can add a little chopped parsley at the end, but I prefer it without.

SERVES 4 AS A MAIN COURSE, OR 5 TO 6 AS A FIRST COURSE

350g/12oz cos lettuce [US romaine], the green outside leaves only
2 shallots, very finely chopped
1 garlic clove, very finely chopped
1 tbsp very finely chopped celery leaves
2 tbsp extra virgin olive oil
40g/1½oz [US 3 tbsp] unsalted butter
salt and freshly ground black pepper
1½ tsp concentrated tomato paste
1.5l/2½pt [US 1½qt] vegetable stock (page 231)
350g/12oz [US 2 cups] Arborio rice
6 tbsp freshly grated Parmesan plus more Parmesan for the table

Wash the lettuce leaves and cut them across into 1cm/½in strips.

Choose a heavy-based saucepan that is large and deep; the rice in a risotto increases its volume by nearly three times. Heat the shallots, garlic, celery leaves, oil and half the butter in the pan, adding 2 pinches of salt to help the onion and garlic to cook without browning. Stir frequently, and after about 5 minutes mix in the tomato paste. Cook for 1 minute.

While the onion is cooking, bring the stock to simmering point. As with all risottos, the stock must be gently simmering all the time the rice is cooking because it must be boiling when added to the rice or the rice will cook unevenly.

Slide the rice into the pan with the vegetables and 'toast' it, as we say in Italy (meaning that the outside of the grain should be exposed to a lively heat) for a couple of minutes. Then throw the lettuce into the pan and sauté for 1 minute, stirring the whole time.

Now you must begin to add the simmering stock by the ladleful. Wait until one ladleful is absorbed before you add the next one. And add even less stock when the rice is nearly done, or there will be too much liquid in the pan when the rice is ready.

When the risotto is ready, remove from the heat. Check seasoning and add the remaining small bit of butter and the Parmesan. Put the lid on the saucepan and leave for a minute or two. This allows the butter and the Parmesan to melt. Now give the risotto a good stir and transfer it to a heated dish. Bring to the table, with more grated cheese on the side if you wish.

FAGIOLI ALL'UCCELLETTO Ⓥ
Cannellini Beans with Garlic, Sage and Oil

'Uccelletto' means little bird. But why this dish of beans is called all'uccelletto is anybody's guess. I, along with other cookery writers, think the dish has acquired its name because it is the traditional accompaniment to uccelletti, of which the Tuscans are inordinately fond. The writer Paolo Petroni suggests that the name probably derives from the fact that the dish contains sage, a herb always included in the cooking of birds.

Fagioli all'uccelletto are the accompaniment de rigueur to the arista. The beans are served warm, while the meat is usually served cold.

THE RECIPE
In Tuscany the dish is made with fresh cannellini, which are not available in Britain. I make it with dried beans.

There are two versions of the recipe, one with tomatoes and one without. I give you the option of either in the recipe below, since the method is fundamentally the same.

SERVES 4 AS AN ACCOMPANIMENT
225g/8oz [US 1¼ cups] dried cannellini beans, soaked overnight, or 700g/1½lb canned cannellini beans
a flavouring of garlic, rosemary, sage and onion, if using dried beans
3 tbsp extra virgin olive oil plus more for serving
1 beautiful fresh sage sprig
2 garlic cloves, bruised
3 fresh tomatoes, peeled and chopped, or 3 canned tomatoes, chopped (optional)
salt and freshly ground black pepper

If you are using dried cannellini, cook them with the usual flavouring of garlic, rosemary, sage and a piece of onion until tender; rinse and drain canned cannellini. Put the olive oil in a sauté pan with the sprig of fresh sage and bruised garlic cloves. Sauté until the sage begins to sizzle and the garlic aroma rises. At that point remove and discard the garlic. If you want your fagioli to be red, add the tomatoes. Stir for a minute or so, then add the beans and flavour them in the cooking juices. Pour in enough water or stock just to cover the bottom of the pan, about 4 to 6 tablespoons. Season with a little salt and a lot of pepper and cook until most of the liquid has been absorbed. Now you can remove and discard the sage, although I leave it because I like to eat it.

Transfer the beans to a dish or bowl and let them cool: they should be eaten just warm. Pour over a couple of tablespoons of extra virgin olive oil before serving – this is the touch that makes all the difference!

ZUCCHINE IN UMIDO O AL
FUNGHETTO Ⓥ
Braised Courgettes

This is a recipe from a cookery book I discovered
recently, and which has now become one of my
favourites. It is *La Cucina di Casa Mia* by
Zenone Benini, written in the 1950s. In Benini's
recipes quantities are sometimes approximate,
since he assumes that his readers are familiar with
the basics of cooking. The style is chatty, not
didactic, which I find much more appealing, and
the book is full of useful suggestions. I give her a
literal translation so as to convey the flavour of
the original. The comments in square brackets are
mine.

'I am not here to talk to you about boiled
courgettes, because everyone knows how to do
them. You put them in salted boiling water and
they are cooked in 20 minutes. [Note the length
of time needed to cook courgettes grown out-of-
doors and not in greenhouses or in water as are
most of the courgettes we buy these days.
Besides, al dente vegetables are an altogether
non-Italian concept.] They are usually served
cold. Nor is there much to say about fried courgettes. They are cut into sticks, floured and fried
in boiling oil, a few at a time.

'I'd like to linger a little on courgettes cooked
in a sauté pan. They can be cooked in two ways,
"al funghetto" and "in umido". To tell you the
truth the difference between these two methods
is not great. It consists of a modest addition of
tomato at the beginning of the cooking of the
courgettes in umido. Therefore, take 1kg (2lb) of
medium size courgettes. Brush them, wash them
and cut them in four lengthwise. Then cut them
into pieces of about 2cm (¾in). Put them in a
sauté pan with 6 tablespoons of olive oil [extra
virgin] over moderate heat together with a small
clove of fresh garlic and a sprig of *nepitella* (a
kind of mint with small leaves and a more delicate
flavour, popular in Tuscany and Rome). No

water: they make enough themselves. Let them
boil, covered, for 20 minutes or so, stirring every
now and then.

'As I said before, to cook them in umido add,
right at the beginning, a little fresh or canned
tomato or concentrated tomato paste. And if you
can't find nepitella, do without it and use a few
leaves of mint, its close relation.'

When I make this recipe with 900g/2lb of
courgettes [US zucchini], I add 300g/10oz of
good fresh tomatoes, peeled, or, rather than not
so good fresh tomatoes, the same quantity of
canned peeled tomatoes without the juice. If you
want to use concentrated tomato paste, 1 tablespoon is the right amount to be added, diluted
with 120ml/4fl oz of hot water. This recipe is
enough for 6 people.

CARCIOFI IN TEGAME ⓥ
Artichokes Stewed in Milk

In Italy, artichokes are one of the most popular vegetables. From January to April there are mountains of different kinds of artichoke displayed in every street market, in every town. The thin and thorny Spinoso Sardo and the fatter Spinoso of Palermo are the first to appear, followed by the round and plump Romanesco, very reminiscent of the Bréton. The Violetto of Tuscany, with its beautiful mauvy shades appears shy and sombre in comparison with the acid green of the Precoce di Chioggia. None, however, is as pretty or as delicious as the small Castraura of the Venetian lagoon, which makes Easter in Venice an even more glorious occasion.

Artichokes were first grown in southern Italy, where they arrived from North Africa with the Arab name of *Al-kharsuff*. Once carciofi became established in Italy, they soon became known north of the Alps and won the approval of the French, who took to them and began to develop local species, of which the Bréton we buy in this country is the most popular.

But undoubtedly it is in Italian cooking that these beautiful sculptural vegetables find their best fulfilment. The recipes for artichokes are numerous. They can be stewed, stuffed or eaten raw. They can be fried and used to make delicious risotti or vegetable pies or timbales or stuffing for fish and chicken. In every recipe they are superb; very seldom are they just boiled, as they are in France and Britain.

Having said all that, I must mention the one snag, which is that they are difficult to prepare. In what follows I explain how to go about it.

HOW TO PREPARE ARTICHOKES

Buy fresh-looking artichokes without blemish or brown parts. If they have leaves these should be silvery-green and alive-looking.

Before you start, rub your hands with half a lemon to protect them from the artichoke juice, which would otherwise make them black. Cut off the artichokes at the base and rub the cut parts with the lemon. Hold the artichoke in one hand and with the other break off the tough outer leaves. It is hard to say how many layers of these tough leaves must be discarded, since it depends on the age and quality of the artichoke. Next snap off the green part of each leaf by bending it back with a sharp movement. This leaves the tender part attached to the bottom. Continue snapping off the tough tops until you get to the central cone of paler leaves.

With a very sharp knife cut off about 2.5cm/1in straight across the top of the cone. What is left is the edible part of the artichoke, without the stringy parts that will remain uneatable however long you cook them. Every time you cut this edible part, rub immediately with the lemon, and, finally, drop into a bowl of cold water to which you have added the juice of ½ lemon.

THE RECIPE

This recipe, the one used in my home in Milan, is actually from Tuscany, but carciofi in tegame are made all over northern Italy, every cook having his or her own recipe. My mother's contains milk instead of the more common water or vegetable stock. Artichokes cooked in this way are excellent by themselves or as an accompaniment to roast meat or roast or grilled fish.

If you have any carciofi left over, make a frittata di carciofi, one of the best frittate ever. See page 143 for the frittata recipe.

SERVES 6
10 globe artichokes
4 tbsp olive oil
4 tbsp chopped fresh flat-leaf parsley
½ garlic clove, finely chopped
2 tsp flour
salt and freshly ground black pepper
a cupful of milk

Prepare the artichokes as described above, removing all the tough leaves, which would be woody and uneatable however long you cook them.

Cut each artichoke into quarters lengthwise and remove the fuzzy chokes and the prickly purple leaves at the bottom. Put them back into the acidulated water until you are ready to cook them.

Heat the oil in a sauté pan. Drain and roughly dry the artichokes. Slide them into the pan and sauté nicely for 5 or 6 minutes. Add the parsley and garlic and cook for a further minute. Sprinkle with the flour and let it cook for a minute or so, stirring constantly.

Season with salt and pepper and then, when the artichokes begin to release their liquid, add a little of the milk – about 6 or 7 tablespoons. Cover the pan tightly and let the artichokes stew gently until tender. The cooking time varies a lot according to the kind and freshness of the artichokes. To test whether they are done, pierce the core with a fork, or taste an outside leaf. If they are not ready and there's no liquid in the pan, add a couple more tablespoons of milk. When tender, check salt and pepper before serving them.

TRIGLIE ALLA LIVORNESE
Red Mullet in a Piquant Tomato Sauce

Red mullet is one of the most highly prized Mediterranean fish. Unfortunately it has quite a few bones, and I expect this is one of the reasons why it is unpopular in this country. This may also explain why, oddly enough, it is always served filleted in restaurants. To do this is odd because, as any connoisseur knows, red mullet must be cooked whole so that the liver, which is the best part, remains in place. It is for this reason that red mullet is sometimes known as the woodcock of the sea. Besides, it is such an attractive fish that it seems a pity not to enjoy its full beauty on the plate.

Red mullet is always cooked very simply, with the minimum of flavourings, so as not to distract from the delicate taste of its meat. There are innumerable versions of triglie alla livornese. Some people flour the fish before frying it; others cook it straightaway in the tomato sauce. Onion is sometimes added to the *soffritto* (frying mixture); chilli is sometimes left out. Whatever you choose, use a very light hand when you add any flavouring.

SERVES 4
4 fresh red mullet, about 225g/8oz each
salt and freshly ground pepper
4 tbsp extra virgin olive oil
½ garlic clove, very finely chopped
3 tbsp chopped parsley
1 small celery stalk, preferably with its leaves, very finely chopped
1 dried chilli , very finely chopped
225g/8oz [US 1 cup] best-quality canned tomatoes, coarsely chopped

Whether or not you have cleaned them, wash and dry the red mullet. Sprinkle with salt and pepper inside and out.

Heat 2 tablespoons of the oil in a small frying pan with the garlic, half the parsley, the celery and chilli for about 2 minutes and then pour in the tomatoes. Cook for 10 minutes or so at a lively simmer to concentrate the flavour.

While the tomato sauce is cooking, heat the rest of the oil in a large frying pan in which the fish can fit in a single layer. When the oil is very hot, slide in the fish. Cook for 3 minutes and then turn them over very gently and cook for a further 2 minutes.

Spoon the tomato sauce over the fish, and cook the fish for a further 10 minutes. Taste and check seasoning.

Sprinkle the rest of the parsley over the top and serve at once. Triglie alla livornese are traditionally served in the pan in which they cook.

POLPI ALLA VERSIGLIESE

Stewed Octopus from Versiglia

I hesitated before including this excellent recipe. Octopus are not popular in Britain and not easily available. Yet we Italians love octopus and eat them a lot. So I decided that a serious book on Italian cooking should contain at least one octopus recipe.

I also hope to popularize this underrated, although unalluring, cephalopod. After all, squid – no prettier – were hardly known in Britain 10 years ago and now they appear on the shelves of most fishmongers and good supermarkets. Perhaps octopus will be next.

In northern Italy octopus are usually just boiled and eaten as an antipasto, dressed with a light extra virgin olive oil and lemon juice. This recipe from the coast north of Livorno is typical of the way the Tuscans of that area cook their fish: in oil flavoured with garlic, parsley and a soupçon of *zenzero* – dried chilli in Tuscan parlance, but ginger in proper Italian, something that always causes confusion.

THE RECIPE

Octopus are quite plentiful during the summer around the coasts of southern England, where they come after spending the winter in deep waters. Your fishmonger will clean the octopus, but he might not skin it or beat it. So when you get home you must remove the skin from the body and the thicker part of the tentacles, an easy job, and then beat it with a meat pounder to tenderize it. Some cooks swear that a cork placed in the pot with the octopus will make it tender. Frankly, I've tried cooking half an octopus with the cork and the other half without, and found no difference!

The best octopus are the *veraci*, which have two rows of suckers on each tentacle. Small octopus are better than large ones for this recipe.

Squid can be cooked in the same way; they are more tender than octopus, but to my mind less tasty.

SERVES 4

1.3kg/3lb octopus

a lovely bunch of fresh flat-leaf parsley

4 garlic cloves

1 or 2 dried chillies, according to strength and taste

100ml/3½fl oz extra virgin olive oil

salt

100ml/3½fl oz dry white wine

Beat the octopus (see above), skin it and wash it thoroughly, taking care to squeeze out the specks of dirt from the suckers. Cut the body into short strips and the tentacles into morsels.

If you have one, use an earthenware pot of the sort you can put straight on the heat, otherwise use a heavy flameproof casserole. Chop together the parsley, garlic and chilli and put them in the pot with the oil and 1 teaspoon of salt. Let this sizzle for a minute and then throw in the octopus. Cook for 5 minutes or so, turning the pieces over and over. Add the wine and bring to the boil.

Now turn down the heat so that the liquid is bubbling gently. Cook, uncovered, for about 30 minutes and then cover the pot and continue cooking until tender. The cooking can take from under 1 hour to 2 hours, depending on the size of the octopus.

At the end of the cooking, taste and adjust seasoning. If the liquid is a bit watery, turn the heat up and boil rapidly in the uncovered pot to reduce.

In the summer I prefer to serve this dish warm or even at room temperature, never hot.

POLLO ALLA DIAVOLA

Grilled Devilled Chicken

Why this dish is called devilled chicken I cannot make out. Pellegrino Artusi, the great 19th-century writer, called it 'Pollo al Diavolo' and gave this amusing explanation. 'It is so called because it should be dressed with a lot of cayenne pepper and served with a very piquant sauce, so that whoever eats it, when his mouth is on fire, would like to send the chicken and the cook to hell.' Marcella Hazan is also of the opinion that it is so called because of 'the diabolical quantity of black pepper'. Whatever the name, the recipe is quick and easy, and the result excellent.

Here is the Tuscan version, which uses chilli instead of black pepper as in Rome.

I prefer to buy a poussin for this dish. Being small, they are easier to handle and they cook more quickly without becoming too dry.

SERVES 2

a fresh poussin [US squab chicken] of about 700g/1½lb

4 tbsp extra virgin olive oil

3 tbsp lemon juice

2 good pinches of chilli powder, or more according to strength

salt

2 garlic cloves, bruised

Ask your butcher to split the chicken open from the back and pound it flat. If you are doing this yourself, place the poussin on a work counter, breast-side down. Split it open along the backbone with a large chopping knife or a cleaver. Crack the breast bone and open the chicken up flat, using the palm of your hands. Now pound the poussin as flat as you can, using a meat pounder.

Mix together with a fork the oil and 2 table-spoons of lemon juice to form an emulsion. Add the chilli powder and salt and mix again.

Lay the chicken on a dish, pour over the oil mixture and then add the garlic. Leave to marinate for about 2 hours. Turn the chicken over and baste it from time to time.

Preheat a cast-iron frying pan until very hot. Place the poussin in it, skin side down, and cook over high heat until brown, not just golden, pressing it down against the bottom of the pan with a fish slice. Now turn the bird over and brown the underside.

Choose a lid that is smaller then the pan so that it drops inside the pan and sits on the bird. Turn the heat down. Add the marinade, cover with the lid and place a weight on the lid. Cook for about 15 minutes. Turn the bird over and continue cooking, covered, until done, another 10 minutes or thereabouts. When the chicken is ready dribble over a few drops of fresh lemon juice and serve.

If you prefer to cook over charcoal, light the fire in good time and, once browned, turn the bird frequently until it is cooked, basting it with the marinade, or, if you have run out of marinade before the chicken is cooked, with a little extra virgin olive oil.

CONIGLIO IN DOLCEFORTE

Rabbit in Sweet-and-Sour Sauce

The cooking of food in a sweet-and-sour sauce is characteristic of Venice, Tuscany and Sicily. Each region tends to specialize in one type of ingredient. Venice offers recipes for various different fish in a sweet-and-sour sauce, while Sicily is more concerned with vegetables. In Tuscany it is meat – hare and wild boar, which are cooked most successfully in this way, and rabbit too. In the past it would have been a wild rabbit, but nowadays most rabbits eaten in Italy are domestic ones. I have come to the conclusion that these are the only rabbits worth cooking, and the same applies in this country. The wild ones are too unreliable: often too tough and sometimes with an unpleasant flavour.

Please, use good vinegar, remembering that cheap vinegar is made from ultra-cheap wine and the flavour of your dish will be affected.

This dish is even better made a day in advance. If you have some left over, remove all the meat from the bone and cut into small pieces, then use the sauce to dress some pappardelle or tagliatelle. But add a tablespoon of butter to the sauce before you reheat it. The pasta needs the sweetness of the butter. This sauce is particularly good with chestnut pasta, and you will find the basic proportions for that at the end of this recipe.

SERVES 4
a rabbit of about 1.3–1.5kg/3–3¼lb, cut into
pieces
30g/1oz sultanas [US 3 tbsp golden raisins]
1 carrot
2 celery stalks
1 garlic clove
a handful of fresh flat-leaf parsley
1 tbsp fresh rosemary needles
60g/2oz prosciutto
5 tbsp olive oil
1 tbsp flour
salt and freshly ground black pepper
300ml/10fl oz meat or chicken stock (page 230)
120ml/4fl oz good red wine vinegar
20g/¾oz candied peel, cut into tiny pieces
30g/1oz bitter chocolate, broken into small pieces
30g/1oz [US ⅓ cup] pine nuts
1½ tbsp brown sugar, preferably Muscovado

Wash and dry the rabbit pieces.

Soak the sultanas in a cupful of hot water to plump them up.

Make a *battuto* (chopped mixture) with the carrot, celery, garlic, parsley, rosemary and prosciutto.

In a heavy flameproof casserole sauté the rabbit in the oil together with the battuto. Turn the rabbit pieces so that they brown well all over. After this sprinkle with the flour and with salt and pepper. Add the stock and cook, covered, for about 1 hour.

Meanwhile, prepare the *dolceforte*. Drain and dry the sultanas, and put them in a small saucepan with the vinegar, candied peel, chocolate, pine nuts and sugar. Cook gently, stirring constantly, until the chocolate and the sugar have melted, then pour the whole mixture over the rabbit. Turn the pieces over and over, and cook for a further 30 minutes or so, stirring and turning the pieces over occasionally.

Serve from the casserole, with polenta or with chestnut pasta.

For chestnut tagliatelle, you need 100g/3½oz [US scant 1 cup] chestnut flour, 125g/4oz [US 1 cup] Italian 00 flour and 2 size-2 eggs [US extra-large eggs]. Do not roll out this dough as thinly as you would a traditional pasta dough.

FAGIANO ALLA MAREMMANA
Pheasant Stewed in Vinegar and Oil

Cooked this way, the pheasant has a fresh, lively flavour – a welcome change from the usual roast pheasant.

SERVES 3
a hen pheasant
150ml/5fl oz olive oil
4 tbsp white wine vinegar
salt
1 small onion
1 carrot
2 celery stalks
1 garlic clove, peeled
2 bay leaves
1 small fresh sage sprig
1 small fresh rosemary sprig
a handful of parsley, preferably flat-leaf
6 fresh basil leaves
4 or 5 fresh thyme sprigs
a pinch of ground cinnamon
4 juniper berries, bruised
6 black peppercorns, bruised

Skin the pheasant and remove the yellow fat. Cut the pheasant up into 6 pieces: 2 drumsticks, 2 thighs and 2 breasts. The pieces are small, which is what you want. Use the wings and the back to make a rich game stock, adding all the flavouring vegetables, spices and herbs that you like.

Mix together 4 tablespoons of the oil and 1 tablespoon of the vinegar. Add ½ teaspoon of salt and coat each piece of pheasant in this mixture. Put all the pieces in a bowl and pour over any left-over oil and vinegar mixture. Leave to marinate outside the fridge for 4 or 5 hours.

Cut the onion, carrot and celery into small pieces and throw them into a flameproof casserole with all the other ingredients in the list. Season with 1 teaspoon of salt. Bury the pheasant pieces in this mixture and pour over the remaining oil and vinegar, plus 5 tablespoons of water. Put the casserole on a low heat and cook for about 45 minutes, until the pheasant is done. Remove the pieces to a heated deep dish and keep warm.

For the sauce, pick out and discard the bay leaves and all the woody stems of the herbs. Pass the vegetables and the juices through a food mill set with the small disc. You are bound to throw away some of the vegetables after all the juices have been pressed through into the sauce. Return the sauce to the casserole. Thin the sauce to the desired consistency with some game stock (keep the rest of the stock for a soup). Taste and check seasoning. Heat the sauce, then spoon over the pheasant. You may prefer to coat the pheasant with a little of the sauce and serve the rest separately in a sauce-boat.

Il Lesso

Boiled Beef

'The food of the gods and of all true people.' This is how the Tuscan Zenone Benini describes this dish in his invaluable book *La Cucina di Casa Mia*. While bollito misto is traditionally one of the great meat dishes of Piedmont, Lombardy and Emilia-Romagna, lesso is more popular in Tuscany, although in my Milanese home, for instance, lesso was prepared more commonly than bollito misto. And this is for a very good reason: lesso is made with two or three cuts of beef rather than with the beef, veal, tongue, cotechino and chicken that go to make an ideal bollito misto. Lesso is, therefore, much more suitable for an average family, being either finished at one sitting or leaving enough left over for a meal of polpette or of 'lesso rifatto' – re-made lesso (see recipe following).

The suitable cuts for lesso are of beef, and the meat should be that of a young ox or a heifer. This might be a tall order for the modern cook who often buys meat cut and wrapped and ready at supermarkets (a habit of which I disapprove). You should see that the meat is not too fresh, i.e. the colour should not be bright red, but verging on a browny-red, and the fat, which should be there, should be the colour of butter and not white. The best cuts are brisket, silverside, chuck, shank and shin, all in one piece. I also put in some bones, but only a few or the broth, which I use for soups, will take on an unpleasant flavour.

In my home lesso was made every Monday for lunch, so that there was always some stock handy for the week. It was served with boiled vegetables, salsa verde and mostarda di Cremona. In Tuscany it is served with *peperonata* – peppers stewed in tomato sauce – stewed cannellini, vegetables under vinegar or oil, radishes and spinach, everything dressed in plain olive oil and that's all. Still, what more does one want?

MACARONI PIE IN A SWEET PASTRY CASE
(PAGE 155)

CLOCKWISE FROM LEFT:
FLAT BREAD WITH WALNUTS (PAGE 177);
CHEESE BREAD (PAGE 205)
CHICK-PEA FLOUR PANCAKE (PAGE 127)

BEAN AND BARLEY SOUP
(PAGE 115)

POT-ROASTED SHIN OF PORK (PAGE 83),
SERVED ON STEWED SAVOY CABBAGE
(PAGE 98)

SLOW-ROASTED SQUABS
(PAGE 224)

SERVES 7 OR 8
1 large onion, stuck with 2 cloves
2 carrots
2 celery stalks
1.8kg/4lb different cuts of beef (see introduction)
2 ripe tomatoes
a few flat-leaf parsley stalks
6 peppercorns
2 bay leaves
salt

In your stockpot, or other large heavy pot, put the onion, carrots and celery. Add about 5l/9pt [US 5qt] of water and bring to the boil. Slowly immerse the meat in the boiling water and bring back to the boil. Adjust the heat so that the liquid is just simmering. Remove the scum that comes to the surface during the first few minutes.

Now add the tomatoes, parsley, peppercorns, bay leaves and salt. Cover the pan and continue cooking at the lowest simmer for at least 4 hours, although 5 would be better. The secret of a good lesso is very long cooking at the lowest possible simmer.

When the meat is tender – you should be able to cut lesso with a fork – slice it and arrange it on a dish. Do not slice more meat than you think will be eaten at one sitting. Keep the rest of the lesso in the stock and slice more if necessary.

LESSO RIFATTO ALLA SENESE
Left-over Boiled Beef

This is the best and simplest use of left-over lesso.

SERVES 4
450g/1lb left-over lesso
700g/1½lb sweet onions, very finely sliced
5 tbsp extra virgin olive oil
450g/1lb ripe tomatoes
½ dried chilli, crumbled
salt

Cut the meat into thick slices and set aside. Sauté the onions in the oil for about 10 minutes, then add the remaining ingredients and cook for 20 minutes or thereabouts.

Mix in the meat and let it slowly absorb the lovely flavour of the tomato sauce for 15 minutes. Turn the slices over gently every now and then.

BISTECCA ALLA FIORENTINA
Grilled Steak

The steak used in Florence for this famous dish comes from the Chiana breed of cattle, a breed that produces very tasty meat in ample quantities, even from an animal no more than 2 years old. Buy the best Scottish meat, and you will eat something similar to the original steak from Florence.

La Fiorentina is always cooked on a charcoal or wood fire.

SERVES 2 OR 3
*a T-bone steak of about 600g/1¼lb, at least
2.5cm/1in thick*
salt and freshly ground black pepper
olive oil or lemon juice

Season the steak with pepper on both sides, rubbing it into the meat.

Grill the steak over a charcoal or wood fire. When one side is done (the steak must be served rare), sprinkle the cooked side with salt, turn the steak over and grill the other side. Each side takes about 3 to 4 minutes to cook.

Some cooks dribble 1 tablespoon of extra virgin olive oil over the meat just before serving, while others prefer a light squeeze of lemon juice.

ARISTA ALLA FIORENTINA
Florentine Roast Pork

The origin of the name 'arista' has always been a matter of dispute. Does it relate to the comment made by one of the Byzantine patriarchs at the Ecumenical Council held in Florence in 1439? While he was tasting the meat he is supposed to have said '*Aristos!*', meaning 'the best' in Greek. A nice little story, but not true, since arista is referred to in a short story by Franco Sacchetti written before that, in the 14th century. Another possibility, as Paolo Petroni writes in *Il Libro della Vera Cucina Fiorentina*, is that *arista* does indeed come from the Greek: quite a few Greek merchants had lived in Florence since the 13th century and might have christened the Florentine roast they enjoyed eating.

But I have another theory. Arista is the Latin for the beard on an ear of corn, thus the word was also used to mean 'harvest'. Perhaps, then, this roast pork was the food served as part of a harvest feast. After all, arista is usually eaten cold in Tuscany, and it could easily be a July dish (harvest time in Italy), served with the fagioli all'uccelletto – stewed beans – which are just ready in July.

Whatever the origin of its name, I recommend arista heartily. Not only is it excellent, but it seems to be particularly well suited to a good English loin of pork.

THE RECIPE
Ask the butcher to remove the bones, keeping the loin bone in one piece. Ask him also to remove the rind. Bring the bone and the rind home.

SERVES 6

4 garlic cloves, finely sliced

the needles of 3 fresh rosemary sprigs, each about 10cm/4in long

salt and freshly ground black pepper

a 1.6kg/3½lb loin of pork (weight with bone)

2 cloves

3 tbsp olive oil

Chop together the garlic and the rosemary, add ½ tablespoon of salt and plenty of pepper, and mix well. Make small incisions in the pork and push a little of the mixture into the meat. Stick the meat with the cloves and rub with half the oil.

Pour the rest of the oil into a roasting tin. Place the bone in it and spread over half the remaining rosemary mixture. Now place the meat on the bone, spread the rest of the rosemary mixture over the meat and cover with the rind. Marinade for a few hours, preferably outside the fridge, unless the weather is very hot.

Heat the oven to 180°C/350°F/Gas Mark 4.

Place the tin in the oven and roast for about 2 hours, basting and turning the pork every 20 minutes or so. The meat is ready when it is quite tender. Lift the piece of rind and remove it. Turn the oven up to 220°C/425°F/Gas Mark 7 and brown the meat for about 10 minutes, then transfer to a wooden board.

Remove as much fat from the cooking liquid as you can. Add 4 tablespoons of hot water to the pan and boil briskly while loosening the delicious bits at the bottom of the tin.

Carve the meat into 1cm/½in slices, spoon over the cooking juices and serve.

You can serve the roast cold; it is equally succulent and delicious.

BUGLIONE DELL'ALBERGO GUASTINI

Lamb Stewed in Wine

Buglione is a very odd name. In his *La Cucina Maremmana*, Aldo Santini writes that it is an ancient word meaning *brodo* (stock), of the same etymology as bouillon. The name certainly describes the dish, a very liquid stew, which in the Maremma is served in a wide soup bowl and eaten with a spoon. However, it only appears there in a few restaurants, being the sort of dish that has gone out of fashion, partly because it is 'slow food'.

But I wave the flag for slow food. After all, you can prepare it all one or two days in advance. Besides, slow food is only slow in cooking, which it does by itself without you having to watch over it. It is the ideal food to serve for a group of friends, when you don't want to be banished to the kitchen to cook last-minute 'fast food'.

Buglione is made with red wine in Grosseto and in the northern Maremma, while in the southern part it is made with white wine. The reason is simple: the wine of southern Maremma is predominantly white, the best known being the Bianco di Pitigliano.

It is indeed Pitigliano that this recipe comes from. (If you want to know more about this beautiful town, turn to page 197.) There I met a charming young-looking grandmother, Signora Loreta Guastini, the owner of the hotel of the same name, which stands on the town bastion made of *tufo*, the local volcanic rock. After a perfect traditional lunch, starting with bread gnocchi dressed with wild boar, and finishing with a homely plum tart, Signora Loreta sat at our table and with great generosity gave me her recipe, which I now pass on to you.

THE RECIPE

I prefer to make buglione with lamb neck fillets, which become beautifully tender by the end of the cooking, as indeed the meat was in Pitigliano. There, however, the leg was used, but the lambs in Tuscany are killed when they are much younger.

SERVES 6

2 or 3 dried chillies, depending on size and strength
1.25–1.3kg/2¾–3lb lamb neck fillets
3 tbsp extra virgin olive oil
4 garlic cloves, peeled
salt
500ml/16fl oz dry white wine
2 garlic heads, unpeeled
1 tbsp chopped fresh rosemary
2 tbsp concentrated tomato paste

Put the chillies in a small bowl and cover with hot water. Leave them in the water until you need them.

Remove most of the fat from the lamb fillets and cut into smallish chunks.

Heat the oil with the peeled garlic cloves in a large sauté pan. When the garlic aroma rises, take out the cloves and discard them. Now brown the meat on all sides without crowding it or it will stew instead of browning. If your sauté pan is not large enough, fry the meat in two batches. When you see drops of blood seeping to the surface, the meat is ready to be seasoned with salt and covered with the wine.

Divide the garlic heads into cloves and remove only the outer layer of skin. Throw the unpeeled cloves into the pan together with the soaked chillies, which should be broken up into tiny pieces. Bring to the boil and simmer, covered, for half an hour.

After that mix in the rosemary and the concentrated tomato paste, turning the meat over. Continue cooking gently, with the lid still on, for a further hour. The meat should cook in plenty of liquid and still have quite a lot of juices at the end of the cooking, so you must pour in small additions of boiling water whenever necessary. It is impossible to state how much water to add, since it depends on the heat, the quality of the meat (nowadays meat often contains a lot of water that comes out during the cooking) and how well the lid fits on the pan. The meat should be very tender indeed. Don't forget to taste and check the seasoning before you bring the stew to the table.

If you are serving the buglione in the traditional way, place one or two slices of toasted bread in each bowl. Otherwise, serve buglione with polenta. The polenta should be freshly made, not grilled, so as to absorb the sauce better.

CASTAGNACCIO
Chestnut Flour Cake

An original speciality of Lucchesia, the province of which Lucca is the capital. Slices of castagnaccio are sold in bakers' shops and often eaten in the streets.

You can buy chestnut flour in the best Italian food shops. As chestnut flour does not keep long, it should be stored in the freezer and used within 6 months.

The original recipe does not contain sugar, but I find that the chestnut flour we can buy here does not have the same depth of flavour as the flour one can get in Tuscany. A little sugar brings out the flavour.

SERVES 6

75g/2½oz sultanas [US ½ cup golden raisins]
300g/10oz [US 2½ cups] chestnut flour
a pinch of salt
2 tbsp caster sugar [US granulated sugar]
3 tbsp extra virgin olive oil
40g/1½oz [US ½ cup] pine nuts
1 tbsp fresh rosemary needles

Soak the sultanas in warm water for 20 minutes, then drain them.

Heat the oven to 200°C/400°F/Gas Mark 6.

Sift the chestnut flour into a bowl. Add the salt and sugar and about 400ml/14fl oz of cold water to make a smooth soft batter. Add 2 tablespoons of the oil and the sultanas and stir well.

Grease a metal tin with oil. The tin, which traditionally should be rectangular, must be large enough to allow the mixture to spread to a thickness of about 2cm/¾in. Pour in the chestnut batter and sprinkle the top with the pine nuts and rosemary needles. Dribble the rest of the oil over and bake until the top is crisp and cracked and a lovely deep brown in colour, about 35 to 40 minutes.

SFRATTI
Honey and Walnut Sweets

It is difficult to describe sfratti in one word since they are neither sweets nor biscuits. They look like sticks and, in fact, they take their name from the stick used to evict (*sfrattare*) the *contadini* who could not pay their rent.

Sfratti are the best known of the dolci made by the Jews who used to live in the Tuscan Maremma. However, some food historians claim that sfratti precede the Jewish settlement and were a speciality of the Etruscans who first civilized this area. Whichever is the case, they have been around for a long time.

The principal place where sfratti are made is Pitigliano, a town in southern Tuscany which has all the characteristics of an Etruscan town. Pitigliano, sometimes called the little Jerusalem, became a Jewish settlement at the beginning of the 14th century, and remained a flourishing town with a strong and well-integrated Jewish population up to 1940, when Mussolini joined the Nazis in their persecution of the Jews.

Pitigliano is a beautiful town, built on a high ridge of *tufo* – the local volcanic rock – with a magnificent 16th-century aqueduct and an impressive castle. But these architectural splendours, however stunning, are quite common in Italy, and especially in Tuscany. What sets Pitigliano apart from other beautiful towns is its Jewish ghetto, a fascinating network of tiny dark alleys, through which, every now and then, comes a shaft of bright sunshine and a glimpse of the dramatic surrounding countryside. There is also a beautiful small synagogue, the inside of which unfortunately I have never been able to see. Edda Servi Machlin, in her fascinating book *The Classic Cuisine of the Italian Jews*, vividly describes the life of this small Jewish community, of which her father was the rabbi.

While wandering idly through this maze of alleys I was suddenly assailed by the delicious scent of freshly baked bread. Following my nose, I finished in a tiny shop, under an archway, where a delightful girl was behind the counter selling hot bread to her customers. Catia Franci showed me the specialities, but sadly 'No,' she did not know how the various breads were made, and mother and father weren't there. But her sweet face lit up when I asked about the sfratti. 'Ah,' she said triumphantly, 'I make those myself,' and she gave me the recipe. And here it is.

THE RECIPE
Make this dessert for Christmas when you are sure to find good fresh walnuts in the shops. I like to serve sfratti with a good dessert wine.

MAKES 3 SFRATTI, CUT INTO 36 SLICES

FOR THE PASTRY
250g/9oz [US 2 cups] Italian 00 flour
90g/3oz caster sugar [US ½ cup granulated sugar]
a pinch of salt
30g/1oz [US 2 tbsp] unsalted butter, just melted
6 tbsp dry white wine
½ tbsp brandy
5 drops of pure vanilla extract

FOR THE FILLING
250g/9oz [US ¾ cup] honey
250g/9oz [US 2 cups] walnut kernels, coarsely chopped
grated nutmeg
a pinch of ground cloves
¼ tsp ground cinnamon

Put the flour, sugar and salt on the work surface and mix lightly. Make a well in the centre and put in the butter and wine. Gradually mix with a fork, incorporating the flour around the well. Add the brandy and the vanilla and enough cold water (about 3 or 4 tablespoons) to form a ball of

dough. (You can make the dough in a food processor.) Knead for a few minutes, then wrap the dough in cling film and refrigerate.

Now make the filling. Heat the honey in a 20cm/8in sauté or frying pan. Bring it to a vigorous boil and then boil fast for 3 minutes or until a jam thermometer registers 130°C/250°F – the soft ball stage. Now add all the other ingredients and cook for 5 minutes exactly. Place the pan in a sink of shallow cold water to cool the mixture. Stir it constantly or the mixture at the bottom of the pan will solidify while the top is still hot.

As soon as the mixture is cool enough to handle, divide it into 3 portions and make a 30cm/12in long sausage out of each portion. Now leave to cool completely.

Heat the oven to 190°C/375°F/ Gas Mark 5.

Take the pastry dough out of the fridge and divide this too into 3 portions. On a floured board, and with a floured rolling pin, roll out each piece of dough into a 10 × 33cm/4 × 13in strip. Place one of the sticks of filling over each strip of dough and roll the dough around it, without overlapping it too much. Pinch the ends tightly together and place on a well-floured baking tray, with the pastry seam down. Bake for 35 to 40 minutes, until golden. When cold cut each sfratto into about 12 slices.

To store, keep the sfratti whole, wrapped in foil, and cut just before you want to serve them.

CROSTATA DI MARMELLATA
Jam Tart

Although *crostata* is the Italian for a tart, this crostata is in fact very different from an English tart. It is more like a compact and buttery sponge cake. The mixture contains a small amount of baking powder and a higher proportion of egg than would be used for pastry. When the crostata comes out of the oven it has jam on top in the middle, surrounded by a wide circle of puffy sponge.

This type of crostata is very popular in Tuscany, although it can also be found in Emilia Romagna and in Marche. It is served at the very end of a meal, always with a glass of Vinsanto or other dessert wine. It is definitely a country cake, often made to use up the home-made jam.

SERVES 8

75g/2½oz [US 5 tbsp] butter, at room temperature
150g/5oz caster sugar [US ¾ cup granulated sugar]
2 eggs
200g/7oz [US 1¼ cups] flour, preferably Italian 00
a pinch of salt
1 tsp baking powder
the grated rind of 1 unwaxed lemon
200g/7oz [US 1 heaped cup] plum or apricot jam

Heat the oven to 180°C/350°F/Gas Mark 4.

Beat the butter and sugar together in a bowl – use a fork first to start amalgamating them and then, if you have one, a hand-held electric mixer. When the butter and sugar have properly amalgamated, drop in the eggs one at a time and continue beating until the volume has increased.

Sift the flour, salt and baking powder together and gradually fold into the egg-butter mixture. Also mix in the lemon rind.

Butter a 22cm/9in tart tin and spoon the mixture into the tin. Spread it out, leaving a thicker edge of about 2.5cm/1in all around. Spoon the jam into the centre, leaving the edge clear. Bake for 35 to 45 minutes. Let the crostata cool in the tin, then gently unmould and transfer to a serving dish.

UMBRIA

I f I had to choose one word to describe Umbria, it would be 'magical'. Magical in the hazy blue colour of its landscape, magical in its towns built on gnarled and jagged hills girded with silvery olive trees, magical in its romantic valleys, in its sunny aquamarine lakes and in its warm, welcoming people who produce magically good food out of the humble ingredients that grow there in abundance.

Umbria is a small region of central Italy, straddling the Appennines between Tuscany to the west, Marche to the east and Lazio to the south. Although it shares a lot with its neighbours, artistically, culturally and gastronomically, the distinctive Umbrian mark is always there.

I drove into Umbria from Le Marche during June recently, crossing the Appennines at one of the range's highest points. I was heading for Todi in southern Umbria via Castelluccio, where I wanted to see the fields of lentils. I knew that Castelluccio lentils were among the best in the world, but what I was not prepared for was the magic of the plain on which they grow, the Piano Grande. It is a wide, flat expanse, chequered with pale greeny-blue fields of lentils, while all around the mountain tops rise up to enclose it. In the middle of the plain, perched on a little hill, sits the small town of Castelluccio. The fields of lentils were broken here and there by others, crowded with the red, blue  and white of poppies, cornflowers and marguerites. For a while I forgot that I was there for the lentils as I walked among the myriad wild flowers.

I did justice to the lentils, however, at lunch time. They were cooked very simply, as in the recipe on page 206. I also had ricotta salata – salted ricotta – another speciality of Castelluccio, and a rich assortment of the local *salumi*, cured pork meats.

These salumi, in fact, would not be considered local in Italy, since they came from Norcia, which is all of 30 kilometres away. The pork butchers of Umbria, and in particular those of Norcia, are master salumi makers, so much so that a *norcino* is the butcher who, after the killing of the pig, is there in his important role of maker of all the many pork products. Among the best known of these salumi are *capocollo*, salame made with the upper part of the pig's neck (as its name implies) and flavoured with pepper and garlic; *finocchiella*, salame flavoured with wild fennel; and *coppa di testa*, a succulent kind of pig's brawn, [US head cheese], flavoured with orange and lemon peel (page 211).

Norcia is well worth a detour, and not only for the salumi. Leaving its handsome square behind me I went straight to the Salumeria Ansuini which, as I approached, proclaimed its speciality by means of three large stuffed boars' heads gazing at me soulfully from outside the shop. Once inside, one of the Ansuini brothers showed me all the different salami they make, from pig, from wild boar and from a mixture of the two. From wild boar they also make prosciutti. These are thinner than the usual prosciutti, dark red, strong and full of gamey flavour. In one of the windows a large wooden bowl was piled high with a rising spiral of small, fat sausages, all strung together in a long coil. And in between these mouthwatering specialities, stuffed baby boars looked mutely on in their striped fur coats, supervising their future!

As it was June I missed another of Norcia's famous products, the black truffle, *tuber melanosporum*, identical to the better known truffe de Périgord. The tartufo nero, unlike the Piedmontese white truffle, requires slight heating to express its pungent aroma and subtle richness. Its best use is in a sauce for spaghetti consisting of grated truffles and chopped anchovy fillets, or in a humble dish of scrambled eggs.

My voyage through Umbria eventually took me to my destination, a restaurant on Lake Corbara, near Todi, where I was going to eat and to talk to the owner, Gianfranco Vissani. I found Lake Corbara rather gloomy, but Vissani's food amply compensated for the lack of natural beauty. His restaurant is famous all over Italy, and people drive up from Rome, something like 1½ hours away, just to eat there. Vissani is a local man who has been able to bring the simplicity of Umbrian cooking to the level of *grande cucina*, 'grande' here denoting excellence rather than sophistication.

As an example, I had a dish of pasta dressed with a sauce of young white onions and marinated fresh anchovies. Perfection! The sauce has its origin, Vissani told me, in a local dish, a frittata made with young onions served with a sauce of marinated fresh anchovies. The original combination of ingredients was therefore still there, albeit in a different guise. The pasta was an egg pasta, which Vissani makes with only the yolks of the eggs, thus accentuating the egginess. Neither butter, nor cream, nor *fonds de cuisson* enter into Vissani's kitchen, yet his sauces, made with the best local oil and stock, are rich and full of flavours. These flavours usually include lemon rind and chilli, a traditional Umbrian combination that is also very popular in nearby Marche.

Another dish that Umbria shares with Marche is made with squabs (see recipe on page 224). These, locally called *palombacci*, are destined for the pot before they can fly, that is, when their cotton wool coat begins to turn into feathers. Vissani, following the old custom, does not clean his squabs. 'I starve them for two days before I put them on the spit, insides and all, and I tell you that the inside is my favourite bit.'

I had another great dish during that trip, in the town of Montefalco. It was a plate of tagliatelle dressed with field mushrooms and chilli, the mushrooms very finely chopped. The point of interest was that the tagliatelle were made with flour, egg and Sagrantino. This is a wine made only around Montefalco from local black grapes. Victor Hazan, in his excellent book *Italian Wine*, writes, 'A dark, strong red made near Perugia in the Montefalco appellation zone. The small black grape was originally thought to have been brought to Umbria by one of St Francis of Assisi's followers, but it is now believed to have existed all along. The grapes are partly shrivelled before crushing. . . It is high in alcohol and slightly bitter in taste.' It certainly gave an unexpected and undefinable flavour to the large tagliatelle, and cut perfectly into the heavy sweetness of the mushroom sauce.

In the true country tradition, Umbria excels in vegetable dishes. Vegetables are seldom served as an accompaniment to meat or fish; they are a dish in their own right, and Umbrian vegetables certainly deserve to be treated as such. The cardoons are exceptional – often prepared 'alla parmigiana', parboiled, fried and then layered with tomato and cheese – as are the tiny peas from Bettona. The tender broad beans are cooked with pancetta and Swiss chard in a dish called scafata (page 207), while the cheerful and patriotic la bandiera – flag – is so called because of the red of the tomato, the white of the onion and the green of the excellent local sweet peppers (page 208).

La bandiera is ideal as an accompaniment to porchetta, the most famous of all central Italian dishes. A lean young pig weighing about 40–50 kilos is boned and stuffed with wild fennel, garlic, salt and pepper. It is stuck through with a spit and traditionally cooked in the bread oven. A long-handled container called a *leccarda* is placed under it to collect the rich juices. The cooked porchetta, golden brown and glistening, is one of the most appetizing sights at village feasts or on market stalls. Juicy pieces of the meat, sandwiched between slices of thick country bread, make the perfect 'elevenses'.

Meats are cooked either in wood-fired ovens, on the spit or under the grill, the three oldest methods of cooking. Olive, myrtle, rosemary and other scented woods fuel the fire and impart a hint of their aroma to the meat through the ointment of the local oil. The green Umbrian oil is regarded as one of the best in Italy; it has the right balance of fats and a pronounced flavour, without being too pungent. In the old days fresh pork fat was used but nowadays, for health reasons, oil is the predominant cooking fat. This change produces a lighter touch in the finished dish, but a lack of that sensual porky flavour so necessary in some dishes.

In recent years I have had endless discussions with local people and chefs about the use of pork fat. It is mainly restaurateurs who prefer to use only oil. In homes I have found pork fat still in use, in moderation perhaps, but still there to give the desired touch to a dish of spaghetti, to a soup of rice and lentils, or to a coniglio in porchetta – rabbit cooked in the manner of a porchetta. This dish results from the locals' love for their porchetta, which is so great that they have created a version that can be made at home, using a small homely rabbit instead of a large festive pig.

In my rambles through Umbria so far I have rather neglected the beginning and the end of the meal. Umbria is rich in paste, pizze, savoury *torte*, minestre and polenta dishes. There are quite a few home-made paste peculiar to the region. These include *umbrici* or *ciriole*, thick spaghetti traditionally dressed with *sugo finto*, imitation meat sauce and pecorino; *fiocchetti*, bow-ties made with an egg dough flavoured with lemon rind and nutmeg and dressed with tomato sauce and Parmesan; and *stringozzi*, so called because they look like shoe laces (*stringhe*). They are dressed with an incredibly delicious wild asparagus sauce.

The pizze are not what is generally meant by that term. They are the predecessors of the Neapolitan pizza, which is of a more recent date. The original pizze, usually called pizze rustiche, are nothing more than pies. The dough can vary, being made with butter or oil or pork fat, with eggs or with water and no eggs, and sometimes with sugar. Yes, sugar in savoury pies, a relic of Renaissance cooking when sweet and savoury intermingled in very successful combinations. Some of these pizze are no more than savoury bread; sometimes they contain a rich filling of cheese and salumi. Tomato hardly ever appears in the pizza rustica – after all, tomato is a newcomer.

As in every country where the cooking is still fundamentally *casalinga* (homely) soups take an important place. There is a soup the name of which alone makes me want to eat it: blò blò. This name describes the noise the soup makes while gently boiling! It consists of very thin fettuccine made with an eggless dough cooked in a broth based on lard, fresh marjoram and garlic, reddened by home-made tomato passata.

At the end of my meal in Montefalco, at the charming Coccorone restaurant, I was served the traditional local finale, *torzetti* dipped in a glass of chilled Sagrantino. Torzetti are very hard almond biscuits [US cookies] which you have to dunk before you can take a bite. The resulting flavour in your mouth is that of very tipsy almond crumble. All Umbrian dolci are of this kind: homely and rustic, more like sweet breads than cakes. These breads are often studded with dried fruits and nuts, in the manner of the best-known spiced breads, the panforte of Siena and the *spongata* of Emilia-Romagna. Sweets of this type are the oldest in Italy. It is a testimony to the cultural traditions of Umbria that anything from the past survives more strongly there than in any other region.

There are also some biscuits made in the shape of shin bones. These are called *stinchetti* (*stinco* is the Italian for a shin bone) or *ossa di morto* – dead man's bones. They contain marzipan flavoured with cocoa. We, as children, found the idea of eating dead man's bones fascinating, a passion not shared by Paul Valéry, who wrote in his *L'Italie Confortable*: '*Cet horrible bonbon, qui a sa moëlle comme les ossements humains, rappelle, par sa forme et son nom, l'ancienne réputation de férocité des habitants, heureusement fort adoucie!*' Valéry clearly did not know the superstition which said that eating bone-shaped biscuits would strengthen one's bones.

Finally, mention must be made of the most famous Umbrian sweet, the *Bacio* – kiss. It was introduced in 1922 by Perugina, who still produce some of the country's best factory-made chocolates.

Although most people will find Umbria magical because of the works of Raphael and Pintoricchio, I hope I have demonstrated that there is something quite out of the ordinary in Umbrian cooking as it still is to this day.

PIZZA AL FORMAGGIO Ⓥ
Cheese Bread

'Pizza' means savoury bread. There are many different kinds of pizza, of which the Neapolitan is the only one known around the world. This pizza al formaggio predates the Neapolitan one by quite a few centuries.

In Umbria and in Marche this pizza is eaten at Easter with the new salame, which is just ready by then. I had it in Marche on an occasion when four beautiful pizze had the place of honour in the most magnificent display of antipasti I had seen in a long while.

Provolone is not easily available; if you cannot find it you can use a good farmhouse Cheddar instead.

SERVES 8 TO 10 AS AN ACCOMPANIMENT TO
AN ANTIPASTO
30g/1oz fresh yeast
*350g/12oz [US 3 cups] white flour, preferably
Italian 00*
2 size-2 eggs [US extra-large eggs]
45g/1½oz [US 6 tbsp] freshly grated Parmesan
*45g/1½oz freshly grated pecorino [US 6 tbsp freshly
grated romano]*
2 tbsp extra virgin olive oil
1 tsp salt
freshly ground black pepper (optional)
60g/2oz provolone, cut into 1cm/½in cubes
40g/1½oz gruyère, cut into 1cm/½in cubes

Put the yeast in a bowl and add 3 tablespoons of warm water. Leave it for 10 minutes and then mix it until creamy.

Measure 100g/3½oz [US just under 1 cup] of the flour and place it in a mound on the work surface. Make a well, pour in the yeast and knead to make a ball of dough. Place the dough in a bowl, cover with a heavy linen towel and leave in a warm corner of the kitchen. In about 1 hour the dough will have doubled in size.

Break the eggs into a bowl and mix in the grated cheeses.

Put the remaining flour on the work surface, make a well and pour the oil into it. Add the salt, optional pepper and the risen dough ball. Knead to incorporate, while adding the egg and cheese mixture. Add enough warm water (about 3 to 4 tablespoons) until you can form a ball. The dough should be soft. Incorporate the little cubes of cheese. (You can use a food processor for all of this.) Now knead for about 10 minutes – if you can! Shape the dough into a neat ball.

Brush an 18cm/7in cake tin with olive oil and place the dough in it. Cover with the towel and leave for 2 hours in the warm.

Heat the oven to 200°C/400°F/Gas Mark 6. Bake the bread for 20 minutes, then turn the oven down to 180°C/350°F/Gas Mark 4 and bake for a further 20 minutes, until the bread sounds hollow when you tap it on the base. Place on a wire rack to cool a little before serving.

LENTICCHIE IN UMIDO COME A
CASTELLUCCIO Ⓥ

Stewed Lentils

Castelluccio is a small town in Umbria, high up in
the Appennines, built on a hilltop that rises out of
the Piano Grande, a plateau equally famous for its
lentils and its wild flowers. The view of the Piano
Grande, when it comes into sight after turning
the last hairpin, is breathtakingly beautiful. A
wide expanse of brilliantly coloured wild flowers
spreads out in front of you, and it is among these
that the lentils grow in symbiosis. The lentil plant
is small and its flower pale blue, as humble a plant
as is its fruit.

Castelluccio lentils are very small, similar in
size to the equally good Puy lentils, and, like
those, they do not need soaking. They keep their
shape while cooking and, unlike most other continental lentils, they do not have that unpleasant
papery skin that sticks between your teeth.
Unfortunately they are rather difficult to find.

THE RECIPE
This is my interpretation of a splendid dish of
lentils I had for lunch at the Ristorante Sibilla in
Castelluccio. If you cannot find Castelluccio
lentils, I suggest you buy Puy lentils, which are
similar.

Actually this is hardly a recipe. In all its simplicity it is utterly delicious, as long as you use
top-quality lentils, good country bread and the
best extra virgin olive oil from Umbria or
Tuscany. It should be a rich fruity oil with a well-
balanced peppery flavour and a full after-taste.

SERVES 4 AS A FIRST COURSE
*400g/14oz [US 2 cups] lentils (or 100g/3½oz per
person)*
1 celery stalk, cut into pieces
4 garlic cloves plus halved cloves to rub the bread
salt and freshly ground black pepper
4 or 8 thick slices of good country-type bread
*extra virgin olive oil, preferably Tuscan or
Umbrian*

Rinse the lentils under cold water carefully,
picking out any pieces of grit or husk lurking
among them. Put them in a saucepan. (I always
use earthenware pots to cook my pulses, the type
of earthenware you can place directly on the heat,
because earthenware is the ideal material for slow
cooking.) Add the celery, whole garlic cloves, 1
teaspoon of salt and a generous grinding of
pepper. Add enough cold water to come level
with the lentils and bring to the boil.

Cook, uncovered, over a very low heat until
the lentils are tender. It is difficult to state exactly
how long they take; you must taste them. But
please let them cook until they are really tender.
Forget the undercooked lentils served in some
fashionable pseudo-Italian restaurants in this
country. Add a little boiling water whenever the
lentils are cooking without any liquid, but add it
gradually and never drown the lentils. By the time
the lentils are cooked there should be hardly any
liquid in the pot.

Meanwhile, gently toast the slices of bread
under the grill [US broiler] so that the outside
becomes just crusty. Rub them with a cut clove or
two of garlic and place them in soup bowls.
Dribble ½ tablespoon of olive oil over the bread
and then, when the lentils are lovely and tender,
ladle them over the bread. Now you must
perform the christening of the dish by pouring
another tablespoon or so of oil in each bowl.

SCAFATA
Broad Beans and Swiss Chard Stewed in Tomato and Wine

While touring Umbria in search of good food, good recipes and kind people to probe, I went to see Alastair Little at his summer cooking school near Orvieto. The school is in a most beautiful spot even by the standards of that most beautiful part of Italy. The school is held in a farmhouse which is part of an *azienda agrituristica* – a farming plus tourism enterprise – owned by Avvocato Belcapo and his wife Clara, who cooks for the guests in her villa. Over a cup of coffee she very kindly gave me her recipe for this local broad bean dish.

THE RECIPE
I have tried this recipe with fresh broad beans and frozen ones. Of course, small fresh broad beans – which is how they should be – are better because their skin is tender. But if you cook large, or frozen, broad beans long enough, as in fact this recipe demands, you will find that the skin will soften and the final dish will be good.

SERVES 6

1.8kg/4lb fresh broad beans [US fava beans] or 700g/1½lb frozen broad beans [US fava or lima beans]
1 or 2 dried chillies, according to taste and strength
100g/3½oz unsmoked pancetta, cut into pieces
1 small carrot
1 onion
1 celery stalk
1 fresh rosemary sprig
2 tbsp extra virgin olive oil
150ml/5fl oz dry white wine
225g/8oz [US 1 cup] tomato passata
salt
450g/1lb Swiss chard

Pod the fresh broad beans or thaw the frozen ones.

If you have an earthenware dish that you can put directly on the heat, use this; otherwise use a heavy-based saucepan.

Put the chillies in a bowl and cover with hot water to soften.

Now make the *battuto* (chopped mixture) by hand or in the food processor, which I find makes a wonderful job when the battuto contains pancetta. Chop or process the pancetta, carrot, onion, celery, rosemary needles and drained chilli. If you do this by hand, chop to a very fine consistency.

Put the mixture in the pan with the oil and sauté gently for about 10 minutes. Throw in the broad beans, stir them around for a couple of minutes to take up the flavour of the *soffritto*, and then pour over the wine. Bring to the boil and boil for 5 minutes. Now add the passata and salt, keeping in mind that broad beans, like French beans, need more salt than other vegetables. Cover the pan and cook very gently for 1½ hours. Check the pan every 20 minutes or so and add a little boiling water if the dish gets too dry.

Wash the Swiss chard and remove the green leaves from the white stalks (keep the stalks for another dish such as the one on page 34). Cut the green leaves into 1cm/½in strips. Pack them into the pan and as soon as they have wilted turn them over and over to mingle with the broad beans. When the mixture is back to the boil, cover the pan again and cook for about half an hour longer, stirring occasionally and adding a little boiling water whenever necessary. Taste and check salt. Serve hot.

Scafata is a lovely vegetable dish in its own right, just as it is good as an accompaniment to a roast, or some grilled chops.

La Bandiera di Vera Ⓥ
Roasted Vegetables

This bandiera (meaning flag) does not look like the traditional dish of the same name, because it is made with more vegetables. The original bandiera contains only green peppers, tomatoes and onion, thus combining the three colours of the Italian flag.

My Umbrian friend Vera Collingwood has given me the recipe for her bandiera, which I think is much nicer. It contains more vegetables, but the cooking and the presentation are similar to the traditional dish.

SERVES 3 TO 4

1–1½ red sweet peppers
200g/7oz aubergine [US eggplant]
150g/5oz courgettes [US zucchini]
200g/7oz large waxy potato
5 tbsp extra virgin olive oil
225g/8oz sweet onion, very finely sliced
225g/8oz [US 1 cup] tomato passata
salt and freshly ground pepper
1 tbsp chopped fresh mint
1 tbsp fresh rosemary needles
½ tbsp dried oregano
2 tbsp chopped fresh flat-leaf parsley
2 garlic cloves, finely sliced

First prepare the vegetables. Wash and dry the peppers and cut in half. Remove seeds, core and ribs, and cut into quarters. Wash and dry the aubergine and cut it in half. Cut each half lengthwise into thickish slices – about 5mm/¼in. Do the same with the courgettes and with the potato, peeled, of course. See that the slices are more or less the same size.

Heat the oven to 180°C/350°F/ Gas Mark 4.

Oil a rectangular oven dish, about 30 × 20cm/ 12 × 8in. Spread the onion over the bottom and drop on 2 or 3 blobs of passata. Season with salt and a generous grinding of freshly milled pepper, and add about 5 to 6 tablespoons of water. Place the pepper quarters down the length of the dish in a tidy overlapping strip. Do the same with all the other vegetables, so that at the end you have an attractive looking dish of four parallel strips of vegetables.

Sprinkle the mint over the courgette strip, the rosemary over the potato, the oregano over the peppers and the parsley over the aubergine. Season with the garlic, salt and pepper. Spoon the remaining passata here and there over the vegetables and drizzle with all the remaining oil.

Bake until the vegetables are soft, about 1½ hours, basting occasionally. You will find that the strange thing is that the courgette will take just as long to cook as the potatoes. Don't worry if the aubergine cooks first; it will be even nicer soft, and rich with the juices.

Serve hot, warm or even at room temperature – it is equally good.

IMPASTOIATA ⓥ
Polenta and Cannellini Beans

The name of this dish is descriptive; *impastare* means to knead and impastoiata is a mixture similar to a dough. It is one of the more esoteric polenta dishes, since the dressing of stewed beans is added to the polenta while it is still cooking, for a final cooking all together. It is a lovely earthy dish, and very healthy too.

I derived this recipe from one of my favourite books, *Un Secolo di Cucina Umbra* (A Century of Umbrian Cooking) by Guglielma Corsi. In the original recipe the polenta is made with water, but I find stock gives more flavour to the dish.

SERVES 5 TO 6
2 tbsp olive oil
1 small onion, finely chopped
1 garlic clove, finely chopped
4 fresh sage leaves, chopped
the needles of a 10cm/4in fresh rosemary sprig
salt and freshly ground pepper
400g/14oz canned tomatoes, coarsely chopped, with their juice
1.5l/2½pt [US 1½qt] vegetable stock (page 231) or 2 vegetable bouillon cubes dissolved in the same amount of water
225g/8oz maize (polenta) flour [US 2 cups coarse cornmeal]
300g/10oz cooked or canned cannellini beans

First make the sauce. Put the oil, onion, garlic, sage, rosemary, 1 teaspoon of salt and plenty of pepper in a saucepan and cook for 10 minutes over low heat. Add the tomatoes and cook until the sauce has thickened and the oil comes to the surface, about 20 to 25 minutes.

While the sauce is cooking, make the polenta. Heat the vegetable stock. When it begins just to show bubbles at the side, add the maize flour in a very thin stream, while beating hard with a large balloon whisk or a wooden spoon. Cook, stirring constantly at the beginning, and then very frequently, for about half an hour.

Now throw the cannellini into the tomato sauce, mix well and let them cook for 10 minutes or so.

When the polenta has cooked for half an hour mix the cannellini stew into it and cook the whole thing together for a further 10 minutes. Taste and check seasoning, and then spoon this nourishing and tasty mixture into individual soup bowls. Pass around a bottle of your best extra virgin olive oil for everybody to drizzle a little over the impastoiata.

Il Coniglio della Zia Lidoria
Old-fashioned Rabbit (or Chicken) from Umbria

Zia Lidoria is a cousin of a great friend of mine. She lives near Orvieto in Umbria. I have never met the lady, but judging by some of the dishes of hers I have had at her cousin's house, she must be a great cook.

I have also made this recipe with chicken, maybe a less tasty meat than good rabbit, but just as suitable. I've discovered that the best rabbits here are French – expensive but as good as the Umbrian ones. Wild rabbits are too unreliable, sometimes perfectly all right, sometimes having an unpleasant wild flavour, and at other times so tough that no length of cooking can make them eatable. I shall always remember once in the country at a friend's house when the leg of a lovely bunny shot across the table as one of the guests tried in vain to cut into it.

SERVES 4

a domestic rabbit of about 1.6kg/3½lb, cut into small pieces

12 fresh sage leaves

3 garlic cloves

6 tbsp extra virgin olive oil

150ml/5fl oz white wine vinegar

salt and freshly ground pepper

60g/2oz [US ⅓ cup] capers

1 unwaxed lemon

4 canned anchovy fillets, drained, or 2 salted anchovies, rinsed and cleaned

½ tbsp potato flour

Wash and dry the rabbit pieces.

Make a little *battuto* (chopped mixture) with the sage and the garlic. Heat the oil in a large sauté pan, add the battuto and cook for 1 minute or so. Add as many of the rabbit pieces as will fit in a single layer and sauté them until dark golden and slightly caramelized. If your pan is not large enough, do this in two batches. This is a very important step in the recipe since you need the meat to be really deep golden to get that particular flavour out of it. When you have finished browning all the pieces, put them all back in the pan together. Pour over the vinegar mixed with the same quantity of boiling water. Season with salt and pepper and cook gently, with a lid on, for 40 minutes.

Test if the rabbit is done by pushing the point of a small knife into the thick part of the leg. The knife should penetrate easily. Take the rabbit pieces out of the pan, place them on the serving dish and keep warm, covered with foil. Taste the cooking juices and boil to reduce, if necessary, until rich and full of flavour.

Rinse and dry the capers. Wash the lemon and pare off a thin layer of rind from half the fruit. Chop finely the capers, anchovy fillets and lemon rind and put this mixture in a small bowl. Add the potato flour and dilute with 2 or 3 tablespoons of the rabbit juices. Beat well with a fork and then pour this mixture into the pan with the rabbit juices. Bring to the boil and cook for 1 minute. Spoon the sauce over the rabbit and serve with boiled new potatoes (skin removed) or potato purée to mop up the delicious juices.

Coppa di Testina di Maiale
Pig's Head Brawn

Although this recipe is not to everyone's taste, I
decided to include it because it is very representative of the cooking of Umbria and Marche. This
is an Umbrian recipe, although the Marche one
would be very similar.

The brawn is full of the flavour of the herbs,
spices and orange.

SERVES 8
half a pig's head
3 tbsp coarse salt
3 bay leaves
a few parsley stalks
1 onion, unpeeled, stuck with 2 cloves
1 large celery stalk
1 carrot
3 juniper berries, bruised
1cm/½in cinnamon stick
7 peppercorns
a generous grating of nutmeg
2 cloves
a small piece of dried chilli
½ tbsp fennel seeds
1 garlic clove
1 tsp sugar
4 tbsp red wine vinegar, preferably aceto balsamico
salt
the rind of 1 unwaxed orange and 1 unwaxed
lemon, without any of the white pith
30g/1oz [US ⅓ cup] pine nuts
30g/1oz [US 3 tbsp] pistachio nuts, blanched and
peeled

Ask the butcher to chop the half head into 2 or 3
chunks. Burn away all the hairs from the pig's
head and scrape the rind thoroughly. Rub the
coarse salt all over the pieces of meat and then
put them in a bowl with 2 of the bay leaves and
the parsley stalks. Leave for 24 hours.

Rinse the meat chunks, put them in a stockpot
and cover with cold water. Bring to the boil and
boil for 5 minutes. Drain and put the head back
in the stockpot with the onion, celery, carrot,
juniper berries and remaining bay leaf. Cover with
cold water, bring to the boil and simmer steadily
for about 4 to 4½ hours, until the meat comes
away easily from the bones. Allow to cool a little.

As soon as you can touch the meat, remove all
the meat pieces and set aside. Strain the liquid,
reserve and cool. Remove the bones from the
pieces of meat, cut the meat into bite-size pieces
and transfer to a bowl.

Pound together in a mortar the cinnamon,
peppercorns, nutmeg, cloves, chilli, fennel seeds,
garlic and sugar, moistening the mixture with the
vinegar. Stir into the meat pieces and add salt in
generous quantity, remembering that when cold
the flavourings will become much milder. Cut the
orange and lemon rind into tiny pieces and add to
the bowl together with the pine nuts and the pistachios. Add the reserved cooking liquid. Mix
very thoroughly with your hands. Taste and
adjust seasoning.

Lay a clean linen towel on the work surface
and transfer the meat mixture on to it. Roll the
meat up tight like a Swiss roll, with the help of
the cloth. Tie both ends with string and put the
meat roll on a wooden board. Place another
board and a weight on it and leave until cold.
When it is cold, put the coppa in the fridge to
chill well.

To serve, unwrap the coppa and cut it into
thin slices. Serve covered with a thin salsa verde
(page 229), or simply with a little vinaigrette
sauce.

MARCHE

U p to a few years ago Marche was an uncharted territory for me. Of course, I knew Urbino with its incredible ducal palace and its soft surrounding hills. I had been to Ancona, a sad city destroyed by the bombardments of the Second World War, and to the extraordinary sanctuary of Loreto, built by five of the greatest Renaissance architects around the Holy House of Mary, which had been miraculously transported there from Nazareth by a host of angels. But I did not know the fascination of Marche's hinterland, nor the warmth and hospitality of its inhabitants, nor indeed the pleasures of its cooking.

This new knowledge has come to me recently, since my daughter Julia and her husband bought Faveto No. 65. Why 65 is a mystery, since Faveto is a tiny hamlet of 10 or 12 houses, dotted around three different roads, in the southern province of Ascoli Piceno, judged by André Gide 'the most beautiful town in Italy'. Faveto sits in the foothills of the Appennines, which rise steeply to Monte Vettore, the most beautifully shaped mountain I know, especially when seen in the morning lit by the rising sun. The hills are gentle and green, and speak of all the food they provide. The older generation still works these fields that are divided between different crops and dotted with fruit trees. The pattern of their lives is set by ancestral rhythms which keep them sane and serene.

Last time I was there it was June. The cherries were ready and we spent hours dealing with them. Some were preserved under alcohol or wine, others went for jam. I was so overwhelmed by the quantity of cherries that I shared a lot with Magda, Matilda and Maud, Julia's three Livornese hens, and the six beautiful but nameless white ducks. Every day one of the neighbours arrived with a gift: a quarter of pecorino or a bowl of freshly made ricotta, a home-made salamino, half a pizza dolce (rich fruit cake), a young rabbit, a pot of *strutto* – melted pork fat for us to sauté the potatoes that were just beginning to be dug up. But best of all was the gift of *olive ascolane*. These are giant local green olives that are pitted and stuffed with minced veal and pork and then breadcrumbed and fried in oil.

Olive ascolane are the characteristic centrepiece of any antipasto all over the region, as I noticed when I went to the medieval town of Staffolo, near Ancona, in September 1994. That occasion was for me unforgettable, not only because

I was awarded the Verdicchio d'Oro prize, but also for the many excellent things that I managed to eat in two days. The banquet after the prize-giving ceremony took place at a restaurant called La Ciminiera, and I was assured by the many knowledgeable members of the Accademia Italiana della Cucina who surrounded me that the food was typical of the best Marchigiano cooking. In recounting what we ate I can give you a good idea of the cooking of Marche.

The alfresco lunch started with an immense spread of antipasti. The small pieces of fried food were breadcrumbed, as is traditional in the region, rather than the more usual coating in batter. The most interesting was the *crema fritta* – fried squares of crème pâtissière which are served as part of an antipasto. Their sweetness is a very pleasant and welcome contrast to the richness of the salame di Fabriano or the prosciutto di Carpegna, two outstanding local pork products. Sage leaves were gently fried, and they served as a palate cleanser. Three or four pizze al formaggio (page 205) were lined up as centrepieces instead of bread or focaccia. Pizza al formaggio is very different from Neapolitan pizza. It is a panettone-shaped bread of a feathery-light consistency, studded with morsels of mild young pecorino.

After two excellent *primi*, the *secondi* brought the climax of the meal, with a succulent porchetta and a coniglio in porchetta. That select group of people judged the coniglio in porchetta to be the best dish. It is rabbit cooked in the manner of a porchetta, the melt-in-the-mouth suckling pig that is the best known traditional dish of Tuscany, Umbria, Marche and Lazio. The rabbit in question was just as melting in the mouth, with that incredible sweet and yet assertive flavour of wild fennel.

It reminded me of the previous time I had eaten coniglio in porchetta at my daughter's house. The rabbit had been given, ready for the oven, by a much older Giulia, a Faveto neighbour, and I went to see how she prepared it. She had made two *battuti* (pounded mixtures); one was more like a paste with a good amount of *strutto* – fat from her last year's pig – mixed with lemon rind, lemon juice, garlic, wild fennel, rosemary, vinegar and *vincotto* – a kind of syrup made with new must from sweet grapes. The other battuto was a herb one, containing a stock cube (see page 16) which she pushed into small cuts in the thighs and placed in the inside of the rabbit, which was already thickly lined with home-made prosciutto. And what amazed me was the amount of salt she put in the battuto: 'it needs it, or the dish will be *sciocco*' (insipid). I was fascinated by the care and tenderness with which Giulia proceeded to pat the first battuto all over the rabbit's body. Not a single scrap of meat was left uncovered: pat, pat, pat in every nook and cranny. Then she put the rabbit in the roasting dish and gave it to me, just as she would have handed me her first-born baby.

It was a triumph, and we sucked every little bone, and scraped every little crust attached to the tin. It was so good that I forgot to keep a little for Giulia for her to taste the next day and have proof of her triumph. I have her recipe, but when I made it here it wasn't what I expected. The rabbit was not good, the lard was different, vincotto is not to be had here, nor is wild fennel. So rather than write a patched-up recipe, I prefer to leave it and just keep the memory of a coniglio in porchetta of supreme perfection. There are other recipes for rabbit in this book which can be made here without loss.

With its long coastline, Marche enjoys a rich harvest of fish, supplying 10 per cent of the national catch. The ports of San Benedetto del Tronto, Fano, Porto San Giorgio and Civitanova Marche are packed with fishing boats which disgorge on the quay grey mullet and hake, sole and turbot, squid and cuttle-fish, anchovies and mackerel, prawns and mussels, red mullet and gurnard and even lobster. No *brodetto* (local fish shop) is worthy of its name unless it con-tains 13 different species of fish.

At Pedaso one day, before going to the beach, I discovered a large firm spe-cializing in the purification of mussels. The mussels are 'planted' in the wild, not in farms, and are then purified by keeping them for 24 hours in tanks of sea water pumped from the sea 600 metres out from the coast. This sea water is highly oxygenated by ozone to achieve the right balance. The mussels are then packed into plastic bags marked with a 'sell-by' date set at five days after leaving the firm as well as the name of the technician responsible for the cleans-ing. A very impressive operation. But what surprised me most was that there was no fishy smell in the factory.

An even more interesting visit was the one I made to a buffalo farm near Faveto. The breeder, Francesco Tofoni, started his farm four years ago with 82 buffaloes imported from Battipaglia, the original buffalo breeding area in Campania. Tofoni has very cleverly increased the production by keeping some Marchigiane cows as well, for suckling the buffalo calves, thus keeping all the buffalo milk for delicious mozzarella made by the local dairy. The buffaloes, slim, active and inquisitive, with their large eyes half hidden by their centre-parted brown locks, don't seem to mind having to give up their new-born calves to placid white cows, who indeed looked better suited to their role of wet nurse.

I could go on writing about the food of Marche for ever, but my editor would cut it out! So I'd better round off this introduction with a mention of the dolci. The Marchigiani have a very sweet tooth, nearly as much so as the Sicilians. Ugo Bellesi, a local gastronome, writes that in the province of Pesaro alone some 70 recipes for different dolci have been discovered. The variations are slight, but they exist. There are two reasons for the abundance of Marchigiani sweets. Firstly, there – more than in most other regions – dolci are closely linked to the feast days of the calendar or celebrations of special occasions; and secondly because in Marche the dolci from northern Italy and those from the South are both present. Thus there are the bready and cakey dolci of the North and the dolci based on candied fruits and nuts of the South; and even the two mixed together, which call to mind similar dolci from Sardinia.

Another reason for the abundance of dolci could be that the sugar beet of Jesi has the reputation of being the best in Italy. As a sweetener it superseded honey earlier than in most other regions, although old recipes for dolci made with honey are still in use. These latter dolci often contain soft pecorino.

As with all other dishes, they are dolci made with the produce of the region, and this is one of the glories of Marchigiano cooking – a natural, traditional cooking still based on local produce. It has not been spoiled by tourism, either from the big cities or from abroad. No spaghetti bolognese or sauerkraut there, nor beer, but tons of sausages and gallons of Verdicchio.

FETTUCCINE COL SUGO ALL'ASCOLANA

Fettuccine with Sausage, Mushroom and Green Olive Sauce

In his dish from Ascoli Piceno, the sauce is used to dress home-made fettuccine. If you do not have the time or inclination to make your own pasta, buy some fresh tagliatelle from an Italian food shop or from a good supermarket, or a good-quality dried pasta (Spinosi and Cipriani are the best brands). The sauce combines sausage, mushrooms, green olives and lemon rind, a very popular local flavouring. The local olives, fat and meaty with their exciting and lively flavour, are a perfect foil to the sensuality of a rich pork sausage, while the whole dish is enlivened by the pleasing bitterness of the lemon rind. It is a superb sauce.

SERVES 4

home-made fettuccine (page 232) made with 3 eggs and 300g/10oz [US 2½ cups] Italian 00 flour, or 450g/1lb best fresh tagliatelle, or 300g/10oz dried egg tagliatelle

20g/¾oz dried porcini

225g/8oz coarse-grained pure pork sausage, Italian or French

1 tbsp olive oil

60g/2oz [US 4 tbsp] unsalted butter

90g/3oz cultivated brown mushrooms, thinly sliced

salt and freshly ground pepper

2 tbsp chopped parsley

1 tsp grated rind from an unwaxed lemon

1 garlic clove, very finely chopped

12–18 green olives, large and sweet, pitted and cut into strips

2 tbsp extra virgin olive oil

If you are making your own pasta, do this first. My instructions are on page 232.

Cover the porcini with boiling water and leave to soak for about an hour (see page 13). Drain, rinse under cold water and dry them. Chop them coarsely and set aside.

Cut the sausage into thin rounds and put in a frying pan with the oil. Fry for 10 minutes, stirring frequently.

Choose another frying pan large enough to hold the cooked pasta later. Heat the butter and add the mushrooms and the dried porcini. Sauté for 5 minutes over a lively heat. Season with salt and pepper and stir in the parsley, lemon rind and garlic. Cook for 1 to 2 minutes and then add the sausage. Turn the heat down and continue cooking for a further 5 minutes, stirring very frequently.

Add the olives and cook for 1 minute. Taste and check seasoning.

Meanwhile, cook the fettuccine in plenty of salted boiling water. Drain, but do not overdrain, and reserve a cupful of the pasta water. Turn the pasta into the large frying pan and pour over the extra virgin olive oil and a couple of tablespoons of the reserved pasta water. Cook for 1 minute while tossing constantly and lifting the strands up high so that they are all glistening. Serve immediately, preferably from the pan.

VINCISGRASSI

Lasagne with Ceps and Parma Ham

The name of this dish from Macerata is odd to an Italian, and I, together with many other cookery writers, had previously attributed its etymology to the name of the Austrian general, Windisch Graetz, who was stationed in Ancona in 1799, and in whose honour this dish was said to have been created. However romantically alluring that may sound, the facts point to something quite different. In Antonio Nebbia's book *Il Cuoco Maceratese*, published in 1784, a similar dish had already appeared, called Princisgrass.

THE RECIPE
I have made and written recipes for vincisgrassi, and been quite happy. But then I tasted Franco Taruschio's dish at his restaurant, The Walnut Tree, near Abergavenny in Wales, and it was even better. This is his recipe.

I would like to suggest just one alteration to Franco's recipe. The pasta for vincisgrassi should contain Vinsanto or dry Marsala. So substitute about 3 tablespoons of the wine for 1 egg. This makes a pasta with a more positive flavour to balance the taste of the porcini.

If you can't find fresh porcini, use the same quantity of cultivated mushrooms plus 30g/1oz dried porcini, which you must soak (see page 13).

SERVES 6

FOR THE PASTA
500g/1lb 2oz [US 4½ cups] Italian 00 flour or strong plain bread flour
2 whole eggs plus 4 egg yolks
1 tsp salt

FOR THE SAUCE
150g/5oz [US 10 tbsp] butter
60g/2oz [US 6 tbsp] flour
1.2l/2pt [US 5 cups] milk
400g/14oz fresh ceps, sliced
4 tbsp extra virgin olive oil
200g/7oz Parma ham, cut into julienne
200ml/7fl oz single cream [US light cream]
3 tbsp finely chopped parsley
salt and freshly ground black pepper
150g/5oz [US 1¼ cups] freshly grated Parmesan
truffle oil, or if possible a little shaved white truffle

Make a dough from the pasta ingredients (see page 232). Knead well and roll through a pasta machine as you would for lasagne. Cut the pasta lengths into 12.5cm/5in squares. Cook the squares in plenty of boiling salted water, a few at a time. Place on linen towels to drain.

For the sauce, melt 60g/2oz [US 4 tbsp] of the butter, add the flour and blend in well. Add the milk, which has been previously heated, a little at a time, beating well with a balloon whisk. Cook the porcini in the olive oil and add to the béchamel. Stir in the Parma ham. Add the cream and parsley, season and bring to the boil. Remove from the heat.

Heat the oven to 220°C/425°F/Gas Mark 7.

To assemble the vincisgrassi, butter a gratin dish and cover the bottom with a layer of pasta. Then spread over a layer of béchamel, dot with butter and sprinkle with some Parmesan cheese. Continue the process, making layer after layer, finishing with a béchamel layer and a sprinkling of Parmesan cheese. Bake for 20 minutes.

Serve with a little truffle oil splashed on top or, better still, with shavings of white truffle, and a little Parmesan cheese.

FINOCCHI E GAMBERI IN SALSA DI VINO

Fennel and Prawns in a Winey Sauce

This is definitely not a traditional recipe. It is an excellent modern one that could come from anywhere up and down the coast of northern Italy. But since I had the inspiration from a similar dish I ate at the Ristorante Davide, in Porto San Giorgio, I have decided to place the dish in the Marche region.

SERVES 4
450g/1lb bulb fennel
200ml/7fl oz dry white wine
1 layer of onion
1 garlic clove
½ celery stalk
1 bay leaf
6 peppercorns
salt
350g/12oz raw king or tiger prawns in shell [US raw large shrimp]
4 tbsp sweet extra virgin olive oil, such as Ligurian

If necessary remove the bruised part of the fennel as well as the stalks and the fronds. Wash and dry the fronds and set aside for decoration. Cut the fennel lengthwise into quarters and then into thin segments, being careful that each segment is attached to the central core so that it will keep whole during the cooking. Wash them well and drain.

Pour the wine into a sauté pan. Add the fennel, onion, garlic, celery, bay leaf, peppercorns and 1 teaspoon of salt. Add enough water to cover the fennel. Bring to the boil and cook, uncovered, until the fennel is tender but still crunchy. Turn it over every so often during the cooking. Lift it out of the liquid with a slotted spoon into a deep serving dish.

Throw the prawns into the liquid and cook for 2 minutes. Fish them out, peel them and remove the black veins. Put about half a dozen of the best looking prawns in the fridge in a covered container. Cut the rest into 1cm/½in pieces. Mix these pieces into the fennel.

Now you must boil the cooking liquid over high heat to reduce it until its flavour is concentrated and rich. When you think it is just right, add a little more salt if needed. Pour this lovely juice and half the oil over the fennel and prawn mixture and toss lightly. When the dish is cold, cover with cling film and refrigerate.

About 2 hours before you want to sit at table, take the dish and the whole prawns out of the fridge. They must have time to come back to room temperature before you serve them.

The last thing to do is to scatter the whole prawns over the top. Pour the remaining oil all over the dish to give a lovely fresh sheen. Snip the fennel fronds with your kitchen scissors directly here and there over the dish.

I PISELLI DI TARSILIA
Drunken Peas

Tarsilia is one of my daughter's neighbours at Faveto, the remote hamlet in the foothills of the Marchigiane mountains where she has a house. The day after we arrived on our last visit we were, as always, immediately asked for lunch. I make a point of writing down all we eat in these people's houses, and one of these days I'm going to write a book on the subject which will contain every dish Tarsilia cooked for us. But here I can only include her 'drunken peas', which are an interesting alternative to the usual boiled peas with mint and butter. The colour won't be as pretty, but the flavour will be a hundred times more interesting.

Do use a good wine (a good Verdicchio di Jesi was what Tarsilia used) and, please, cook the peas properly and not al dente.

SERVES 4

1.3kg/3lb fresh young peas
4 tbsp extra virgin olive oil
100g/3½oz unsmoked pancetta, very finely chopped
1 tbsp chopped onion
salt and freshly ground black pepper
dry white wine

Pod the peas.

Heat the oil and the pancetta in a large sauté pan. Add the onion and sauté for 5 minutes or so, stirring frequently. When the onion is beginning to get soft throw in all the peas. Turn them over and over for a couple of minutes and season with salt and pepper.

Pour enough wine into the pan to come level with the peas. Cook, uncovered and over gentle heat, for 15 to 20 minutes, until the peas are tender, stirring occasionally. Vegetables cooked in this way take longer to be ready than if boiled or steamed. The wine will have partly evaporated and partly been absorbed by the peas. But if there is too much liquid in the pan once the peas are ready, transfer the peas to a heated bowl with a slotted spoon and boil the liquid rapidly to reduce. Pour the reduced liquid over the peas and serve. On the other hand, if the peas are not cooked when all the liquid has gone, add a couple of tablespoons of boiling water.

CAVOLFIORE STRACINATO DI TERESA Ⓥ

Stewed Cauliflower

Teresa Cesaritti is a charming lady who was my hostess in Jesi, near Ancona, when I was invited there to receive the Verdicchio d'Oro prize.

Teresa, in her warm and spontaneous manner, gave me this recipe: 'It is so simple and so delicious that I must pass it on to you.'

SERVES 4

a cauliflower head of about 600–700g/1¼–1½lb
5 tbsp extra virgin olive oil
2 garlic cloves, bruised
½ or 1 dried chilli, according to size and strength
3 tbsp chopped fresh flat-leaf parsley
salt
100ml/3½fl oz dry white wine

Remove the end stalk and the outside leaves of the cauliflower, leaving only the young and tender leaves surrounding the head itself. Divide the head into very small florets and cut the stalks and the tender leaves into neat small pieces. Wash and drain the lot.

Heat the oil with the garlic in a sauté pan. When the garlic begins to brown at the edge, fish it out and discard it. (If you like garlic flavour you can leave it in and search for it at the end of the cooking. To make this task easier, pierce the garlic cloves with a wooden toothpick. Alternatively, you can chop the garlic, add it and forget about it.) Add the chilli, 2 tablespoons of the parsley and the cauliflower florets and sauté gently for 5 minutes to *insaporire* – take up the flavour. Now add enough water to come about half-way up the cauliflower. Season with salt and bring to the boil. Half cover the pan and cook for 5 minutes or so.

Pour in the wine and cook until the cauliflower is tender. Taste a piece of thick stalk as these take longer to cook. It should be *tender*, not crunchy.

It is not possible to say how long a cauliflower takes to cook. If it is grown in the old-fashioned way it takes twice as long as a cauliflower grown with the hydroponic method, which also releases a lot of water during the cooking. The liquid should have nearly all evaporated. If there is still too much liquid when the cauliflower is ready, transfer the cauliflower to a bowl and boil to reduce the juices briskly until full of flavour.

Pour the juices over the cauliflower and sprinkle with the remaining parsley before serving. Check the salt before you remove the cauliflower from the pan.

PESCE ARROSTO ALLA MARCHIGIANA

Baked Fish with Herbs and Black Olives

When I was staying at my daughter's house in the foothills of the Appennines I realized that I was very close to Campofilone, a small town I knew of only because my favourite egg pasta, Spinosi, is made there. So I rang the Spinosi and they immediately asked me to lunch and to visit their pasta and ravioli factory, of which Sandro Spinosi is rightly very proud.

Campofilone is a pretty little town about 3 kilometres from the coast, 3 kilometres up rather than along, on a hill that dominates the surrounding countryside. Lunch at the Spinosi's was based on fish, as is quite usual near the sea. First course was a huge seafood salad, perfect in its simplicity – many different kinds of seafood dressed with excellent olive oil and lemon juice. The main course was a baked sea bass, another simple triumph, and here is Paola's recipe, which she told me she uses also for salmon.

THE RECIPE
You can use any large fish. On different occasions I have used codling (how sad that it is so difficult to find), hake and grey mullet, and they were all good. A sea bass, of course, would be better than a grey mullet or a codling. But the most important thing is that the fish should be fresh.

It was in Marche that I learnt to soak the dried chilli for certain dishes. The chilli becomes soft and easy to de-seed and chop; it also becomes just a little less hot.

SERVES 4

1 dried chilli

a fish of about 1.2kg/2½lb, head and tail on

a bunch of fresh flat-leaf parsley, leaves only

the needles of 2 fresh rosemary sprigs, each about 10cm/4in long

1 garlic clove

salt and freshly ground black pepper

1 unwaxed lemon

6 tbsp extra virgin olive oil

4 tbsp dried white breadcrumbs

1 dozen plain black olives

8 tbsp dry white wine

Soak the chilli for 10 minutes in hot water and then de-seed it.

Heat the oven to 200°C/400°F/ Gas Mark 6.

Wash the fish and wipe the cavity clean with kitchen paper towel. Dry the whole thing. Chop the herbs, garlic and chilli. Season with salt and put this mixture into the cavity of the fish. Stitch up the opening of the cavity with one or two wooden toothpicks.

Scrub the lemon under cold water and then dry it. Grate the rind from one half into a bowl. Squeeze the whole lemon and pour the juice into a small jug to bring to the table. Add half the oil, the breadcrumbs, salt and pepper to the lemon rind and mix well. Pat this mixture all over the body of the fish and then place the fish in a roasting tin together with the olives. Pour the rest of the oil, the wine and 4 tablespoons of water around the fish, but not over it or you will wash away the crumb mixture. Bake for about 20 minutes, basting two or three times with the cooking juices during the cooking. The fish is ready when the flesh near the backbone can easily be detached. To find out, just push a small knife into the thickest part of the body and peer down.

Now you can either transfer the fish carefully to a heated oval dish to bring to the table, or you can 'plate' the fish in the kitchen, which is easier as you don't risk breaking the fish in two when you transfer it. Spoon the delicious juices around the fish and place a few olives on each plate.

Put a bottle of your best olive oil on the table, as well as the little jug with the lemon juice. Someone may like to add a drizzle of one or the other, or even both.

POLLO IN POTACCHIO
Chicken with Tomato and Rosemary Sauce

Potacchio is the odd name of a sauce that is added to chicken or rabbit for a final cooking. It has the characteristic aroma of the cooking of Marche: garlic, chilli and lemon rind, joined here by abundant rosemary.

Do remember that rosemary, just like any other herb, is sweeter in the spring, with its new shoots, and it gets stronger later in the year. So use this knowledge and your discretion when you add the rosemary – or any other herb, for that matter.

SERVES 4 TO 6

a free-range chicken of about 1.5kg/3¼lb, cut into pieces
½ lemon
2 tbsp olive oil
60g/2oz [US 4 tbsp] unsalted butter
150ml/5fl oz dry white wine
1 onion, finely chopped
2 garlic cloves, finely chopped
salt and freshly ground pepper

FOR THE POTACCHIO SAUCE

1 small onion or 3 shallots
2 or 3 fresh rosemary sprigs, each 12cm/5in long
the rind of 1 unwaxed lemon
½ to 1 dried chilli, according to strength
3 tbsp extra virgin olive oil
450g/1lb fresh tomatoes, peeled and coarsely chopped, or 400g/14oz canned plum tomatoes, drained and coarsely chopped

Wash and dry the chicken pieces. Rub each piece with the half lemon. Heat the oil and the butter in a large sauté pan. When the butter foam begins to subside put in the chicken pieces and fry on all sides until they are nicely browned. Add the wine, bring to the boil and boil for 1 minute. Turn the heat down and throw in the onion and the garlic. Season with salt and pepper, then cover the pan and cook for 20 minutes.

While the chicken is cooking, prepare the sauce. Chop very finely together the onion or shallots, rosemary needles, the rind of the lemon and the chilli. Put the oil in a frying pan and when it is hot add the chopped ingredients. Sauté gently for 5 minutes or so and then add the tomatoes and a little salt. Cook over lively heat for about 15 minutes, stirring frequently.

Now that the potacchio is done, scoop it into the sauté pan with the chicken and mix it with all the lovely cooking juices at the bottom of the pan. Let the whole thing cook together for another quarter of an hour so that the chicken will *insaporire* – take the flavour of the sauce.

Test the chicken for doneness by pricking the thigh with the point of a small knife or a thin skewer. The juices that run out should be clear. Correct the seasoning before bringing the dish to the table.

PICCIONCINI DI MAFALDA
Slow-roasted Squabs

In Umbria, Tuscany and Marche, squabs are still raised with loving care just for the pleasure of eventually eating them. Mafalda is one of my daughter's septuagenarian neighbours in the remote and hilly countryside of Marche. Having abandoned their old house, Mafalda and her husband Beppe now live in their modernized upstairs flat, complete with plastic flowers, above the store-rooms where oil, wine, ham, pulses, salami, liqueurs and preserved vegetables are all, in their turn, stored away through the year, to last until the next supply is made.

It was June when we had squabs for lunch, so the store-rooms were fairly empty, although there was still plenty of oil and salame and, of course, wine, which is always plentiful. Wine, after all, is the only commodity that does not have to be finished within the year. The rest, as any good *massaia* (housewife) knows, must be used up before the new crop comes in.

We were asked to go round on the previous day to 'choose' the squabs. My Italian origins and my interest in food helped me to overcome the acquired British attitude of not wanting to connect the lovable living creature with the appetizing dish on my plate. I feel that either you become a vegetarian or you must be prepared to accept the link. The squabs, 10 in all, were chirping away in the cage. '*Guarda come son belli,*' Beppe said, '*bisogna proprio mangiarli.*' (Look how lovely they are, they are just ready for the pot – squabs must be eaten while still fledglings.) They were lovely indeed in their, by now, nearly full plumage of different tender browns, greys and whites. Mafalda touched, pinched, caressed, fondled all the birds in turn and then pointed out the chosen six to her husband.

Next day we arrived and, after the obligatory salami and tagliatelle, the piccioncini were brought to the table, surrounded by *patatine,* in a beautiful old copper *teglia* (roasting tin). This must have been one of the few of its kind to have escaped the Fascist net when every bit of copper had to be given to the State to try to counteract the consequences of the sanctions imposed on Italy at the time of the Abyssinian war.

The squabs were just magical. My dish, when I made it here in London was, inevitably, not quite up to the same standard. After all, I don't rear squabs in my back garden, nor grow olives to press in my local *frantoio* in Barnes.

THE RECIPE
Squabs are milk-fed domestic pigeons, ready for the pot before they begin to fly. They have a gamey flavour and a darkish skin, but they are very tender, unlike pigeon, of which I find only the breast is edible. Until recently they were imported from France, but now there are some squabs reared in Britain which are equally good, and cheaper. They can be bought, or ordered, from the best butchers.

This recipe can also be used for poussins. In either case you will need one bird per person, but remember that poussins take less time to cook. If you have time, prepare the stuffing a few hours in advance so the flavours can mix and blend.

The squabs are cooked slowly and for what you might think is too long. The timing is correct. 'They must be cooked for a long time', Mafalda explains, 'and not . . . *bom, bam, bin in due minuti come é di moda adesso*' (and not in 2 minutes as is the fashion these days).

SERVES 4

4 squabs
salt and freshly ground black pepper
2 tbsp olive oil
4 tbsp extra virgin olive oil
the juice of 1 lemon
2 tbsp good red wine vinegar

FOR THE STUFFING

125g/4oz fatty prosciutto, very finely chopped
150g/5oz minced pork [US ground pork]
6 tbsp freshly grated Parmesan
2 tbsp chopped fresh flat-leaf parsley
the grated rind of 1 unwaxed lemon
1 tbsp chopped fresh rosemary
2 garlic cloves, very finely chopped
½ tsp salt
2 pinches of freshly ground black pepper
2 eggs, size 3

To prepare the stuffing, put the prosciutto and minced meat in a bowl and add all the other ingredients except the eggs. Mix very well – hands are the best tool – and then drop in one egg. Mix the egg in, which will take some time to incorporate. Do the same with the second egg. Once the mixture is perfectly well blended, but not before, cover the bowl with cling film and refrigerate until you need it.

Squabs often have livers and hearts left in the cavity. Take these out, chop them and mix into the stuffing. Wash the birds and dry them thoroughly.

Heat the oven to 180°C/350°F/ Gas Mark 4.

Divide the stuffing roughly into 4 portions and stuff a portion into each cavity. 'A bird should never be over-stuffed or it will burst, and the stuffing will appear too uniform when the bird is carved.' These are the instructions given by Baron von Rumohr in his invaluable book *The Essence of Cookery*, first published in 1822. Sew up the opening or stitch with two wooden toothpicks. Rub salt and pepper all over the birds.

Now you must brown the birds in the hot olive oil. I use a cast-iron frying pan and turn them over to brown on all sides.

Transfer the birds to a roasting tin and pour the extra virgin olive oil into it. Add enough hot water just to cover the bottom of the tin and then roast for 15 minutes.

Take the tin out of the oven and pour half the lemon juice over the squabs. Turn the birds on to their breasts, return the tin to the oven and roast for 15 minutes. Pour over the vinegar. After a further 15 minutes of roasting, add the remaining lemon juice. Now turn the birds on to their backs and let them cook for at least a further 45 minutes to 1 hour, basting them every 15 minutes or so. Squabs must, as this recipe demands, be cooked slowly and at length.

Place a squab on each heated plate, surrounded by the cooking juices.

If you want to serve some potatoes with the birds, parboil them in their skins for 10–15 minutes. Then peel and cut them into cubes and put them around the squabs for the last 30 to 40 minutes. Be gentle when you turn the potatoes over or they might break. Use a waxy, rather than a starchy, variety of potato.

COSTOLETTINE DI AGNELLO CON
LE OLIVE NERE

Lamb Cutlets with Black Olives

The culinary imprint of Marche consists of lemon rind, chilli and garlic. This mixture goes into many dishes, especially in southern Marche which is affected by its proximity to the southern cooking of Abruzzi, where chilli and garlic reign supreme.

The olives must be plain, not dressed with other superfluous ingredients. I always buy olives with the stone still in, for the simple reason that they are better.

SERVES 4

12 best end lamb cutlets [US lamb rib chops]
6 tbsp extra virgin olive oil
3 garlic cloves, thickly sliced
1–2 dried chillies
the grated rind of 1 unwaxed lemon
1 tsp dried oregano
salt
2 tbsp lemon juice
about 15 large black olives, or 20 small ones, pitted and sliced

Remove all fat from around the cutlets and flatten them down gently. Place them in a large dish. Pour over 4 tablespoons of the oil and add the garlic, chillies, lemon rind and oregano. Season with salt on both sides and leave to marinate for about 1 hour. Do *not* refrigerate. Meat to be cooked must be at room temperature.

Heat a very large frying pan – or two pans – until hot. Add the remaining oil. If you are using two pans you must add an extra ½ tablespoon of oil. When the oil is hot, add the cutlets and cook them for about 2 minutes on one side, shaking the pan occasionally so that they do not stick. Turn them over and cook for 1 minute. Now scoop in all the bits of the marinade from the dish, and add the lemon juice and the olives.

Cook for about 5 minutes for rare cutlets, or a little longer if you prefer lamb well cooked. The timing also depends on the thickness of the cutlets. A sign to look for is when blood rises to the surface of the meat; this means that the meat is no longer bloody inside.

While the cutlets are cooking, add a couple of tablespoons of hot water, so that the meat cooks in a little liquid. When you think the lamb is done the way you like it, transfer to a serving dish and keep warm.

Remove and discard the chillies. If the cooking juices are too syrupy and thick add a little hot water and boil, stirring, for a minute. Taste and adjust seasoning, then spoon the juices around the lamb.

Ciambelline Marchigiane
Little Ring Biscuits

You see trays of ciambelline in almost every baker's shop in Marche. They can be flavoured with fennel seeds, with orange rind or with pine nuts; the recipe is the same. The recipe I give here is for ciambelline with pine nuts, which are the more difficult to make. For the other two versions you simply add the crushed fennel seeds or the grated orange rind to the egg mixture.

The preliminary blanching of the biscuits, or cookies, helps keep them soft inside, while it hardens the outside during the baking, as with American bagels.

MAKES ABOUT 60

600g/1¼lb [US 5 cups] flour, preferably Italian 00
salt
3 size-2 eggs [US extra-large eggs]
180g/6oz caster sugar [US 1 cup granulated sugar]
the grated rind of 1 large unwaxed lemon
a pinch of ground cinnamon
100g/3½oz [US 7 tbsp] unsalted butter
6 tbsp milk
butter for the trays
30g/1oz [US ⅓ cup] pine nuts

Sift the flour with 2 pinches of salt on to your work surface and make a well.

Whisk 2 of the eggs and the white of the third one with the sugar until the mixture thickens. This will take quite a time unless you have a hand-held electric mixer. Add the lemon rind and the cinnamon.

Now melt the butter over very low heat. Just melt it; do not let it sizzle. Pour gradually into the well of flour. Keep pouring, alternately, the egg mixture and butter, while with the other hand you begin to incorporate the flour from the inside wall of the well. When you have poured in all the butter, heat nearly all the milk in the same small saucepan and pour this into the flour too. When the egg mixture, butter and milk have all been incorporated into the flour, knead the dough for 5 minutes or so, until lovely and smooth. Wrap the ball of dough in cling film and chill for half an hour to harden, so that it becomes easier to shape.

Pinch some dough off the ball – about the size of a walnut – and roll it out with floured hands into a little sausage, about 7.5cm/3in long and 1cm/½in across. Bend the little sausage around to form a ring and seal the two ends very thoroughly. Continue taking dough from the ball and making rings until you have used all the dough.

While you are shaping the biscuits, bring some water to the boil in a large sauté pan. When it is boiling gently lower just enough little rings in to cover the bottom of the pan, where they will sink. After about 3 minutes of simmering they will begin to float to the surface. Lift them out of the water with a slotted spoon and place them on kitchen paper towel to dry well. Blanch all the rings in this way, and dry them.

Heat the oven to 190°C/375°F/Gas Mark 5.

Place the rings on well-buttered baking trays. Lightly beat the remaining egg yolk with the little milk you left aside. With a small pastry brush, glaze the little rings all over. Place 5 or 6 pine nuts on each ring and press them in gently to prevent them falling off. Now the rings are ready to be baked in the preheated oven for about 20 minutes, until golden.

Cool on a wire rack and then store in an airtight tin.

Rustic and simple they may be, but ciambelline are very good.

BASICS

SUGO DI POMODORO
Tomato Sauce

I use good fresh tomatoes when they are in season. When they are not I prefer to use good canned tomatoes rather than out-of-season fresh tomatoes, which do not taste like tomatoes and have an unpleasantly thick and woolly pulp. Unless the tomatoes are really good I like to add 1 teaspoon of concentrated tomato paste to give depth to the sauce. I should point out that northern Italian tomato sauces have a richer flavour compared with the freshness beloved by the Southerners.

MAKES ABOUT 600ML/1PT [US 2½ CUPS]
2 tbsp extra virgin olive oil
30g/1oz [US 2 tbsp] unsalted butter
150g/5oz Spanish onion, sliced
1 celery stalk, cut into pieces
1 carrot, cut into pieces
1 garlic clove, peeled
1 tsp concentrated tomato paste
a handful of fresh flat-leaf parsley
6 fresh basil leaves
200g/2lb fresh ripe tomatoes, cut into quarters, or canned plum tomatoes with their juices
salt and freshly ground pepper

Heat the oil and the butter in a saucepan. Add the onion, celery, carrot and garlic and sauté for 10 minutes. Mix in the concentrated tomato paste, if you are using it, and cook for 1 minute, stirring constantly. Then add the herbs, the tomatoes, salt and pepper and cook at a moderate heat for 30 minutes.

Pass the sauce through a food mill or a sieve. If you want to use a food processor you must first peel the fresh tomatoes and squeeze out some of the seeds.

SALSA BESCIAMELLA
Béchamel Sauce

Béchamel is not an Italian sauce and it did not appear in Italian recipes as such until the 19th century. It came from France, where it was allegedly created in the seventeenth century by Louis de Béchamel, steward to Louis XIV. However, a similar sauce, based on such everyday ingredients as milk, butter and flour, must have already existed both in France and northern Italy. After all, béchamel is the ideal partner to home-made pasta and it is inconceivable that the creative Emiliani would not have 'discovered' this combination earlier.

Béchamel is an easy sauce to make. Its density can vary according to its use. I prefer to make a thin sauce when I use the béchamel in combination with pasta and a thicker sauce whenever I use it as a binder. The sauce here is a medium thickness.

I like to flavour my béchamel differently according to the dish in which it is used. If it is for a pasta dish I add some grated nutmeg, or I infuse one or two garlic cloves or a layer of onion in the milk. If the béchamel is to be added to fish or meat I like the milk to be flavoured with a bay leaf and maybe with a light grating of nutmeg too.

MAKES ABOUT 450ML/15FL OZ
600ml/1pt [US 2½ cups] milk
60g/2oz [US 4 tbsp] unsalted butter
45g/1½oz [US ¼ cup] flour, preferably Italian 00
salt

Heat the milk until it just begins to bubble at the edge.

Meanwhile, melt the butter in a heavy-based saucepan over low heat. Blend in the flour, stirring vigorously. Remove the pan from the heat and add the hot milk, a few tablespoons at a time.

228

You must let the flour mixture absorb each addition thoroughly before adding more.

When all the milk has been absorbed and the sauce is lovely and smooth, return the pan to the heat. Add salt to taste and bring to the boil. Cook over the gentlest heat for at least 10 minutes, stirring frequently. I use a flame diffuser, or else I put the saucepan in a larger saucepan containing 5cm/2in or so of simmering water, so that I do not need to stir the whole time.

This lengthy cooking is not really necessary, but it does give the sauce a more delicate flavour.

SALSA VERDE

Green Sauce

In Lombardy and Piedmont this is the traditional accompaniment to bollito misto, lesso (page 192) and boiled calf's head; it is also used on hard-boiled eggs. The oil should be a sweet oil from Liguria or Lake Garda, not a *fruttato* (peppery one).

MAKES 150ML/5FL OZ

15g/½oz [US ⅓ cup] fresh white breadcrumbs
1 tbsp red wine vinegar
1 garlic clove
about 15g/½oz fresh flat-leaf parsley
2 tbsp capers
½ dozen cornichons (very small gherkins – if unobtainable use 1 extra tbsp capers)
1 hard-boiled egg, shelled
4 anchovy fillets, or 2 salted anchovies, boned and rinsed
2 tsp Dijon mustard
120ml/4fl oz extra virgin olive oil
salt and freshly ground black pepper

Put the breadcrumbs in a bowl and pour the vinegar over them. Set aside.

Peel the garlic clove, cut it in half and remove the hard central core, if necessary. This is the part that has a pungent flavour instead of a sweet flavour.

Squeeze out excess vinegar from the bread and put in a food processor. Add all the other ingredients except the oil, salt and pepper. Process while you add the oil slowly through the funnel. Stop often to scoop the mixture down from the sides of the bowl. At the end add salt and pepper to taste.

BRODO DI CARNE
Italian Meat Stock

Il brodo is typical of Italian cooking, delicate yet full of well balanced and harmonizing flavours, flavours that would never be too assertive. For this reason, none of the ingredients is ever sautéed in butter or oil beforehand.

A good stock depends entirely on the quality of the ingredients. 'A stock that is made with garbage will taste of garbage,' wrote Alice Waters of Chez Panisse fame. The classic brodo di carne is made with three different kinds of meat: veal, beef and chicken – never lamb or pork, which make too strong a stock. Meat must be present as well as bones, to give the stock the right flavour. Too many bones and the stock will have an unpleasant sweetish flavour. The same applies to chicken carcasses. If possible use half, or a quarter, of a boiling chicken, which a good butcher will have or will get for you.

I prefer to add a minimum of salt and then season the stock at the end. This is to avoid producing a stock that is too salty after the reduction.

MAKES 1.5–2L/2½–3½PT [US 1½–2QT]

1.5kg/3¼lb assorted meat, in large pieces
1 onion, cut in half and stuck with 3 cloves
1 or 2 carrots, cut into pieces
2 celery stalks, cut into pieces
1 leek, cut into pieces
a handful of mushroom peelings or stalks
½ dozen parsley stalks
1 bay leaf
2 garlic cloves, unpeeled
1 ripe tomato, cut into quarters
1 tsp salt

Put all the ingredients in a stockpot. Add about 3l/5pt [US 3qt] of cold water, or enough to cover, and bring to the boil. The water must be cold to start with, so that the meat and the vegetables can slowly release their juices. Set the lid very slightly askew so that the steam can escape. Turn the heat down to the minimum for the stock to simmer. The best stock is made from liquid that cooks at a temperature of 80°C/175°F, rather than 100°C/220°F, the boiling point. Using a slotted spoon, or – better still – a skimmer, skim off the scum that comes to the surface during the first quarter of an hour of cooking. Cook for about 3 hours.

Strain the stock through a large strainer lined with muslin or cheesecloth into a large bowl. Leave to cool and then put in the refrigerator.

Remove the fat that will have solidified on the surface. At the end of the operation, when it is hard to remove a few specks of fat, heat the stock a little, then lay a piece of kitchen paper towel on the top of the stock and drag it gently across the surface. Most of the fat 'eyes' will stick to the paper.

Taste and, if you think it is a bit too mild, reduce over high heat, remembering, however, that the stock may taste mild because it contains a minimal amount of salt. Cover with cling film and keep in the fridge for up to 3 days or in the freezer for up to 3 months.

If you want to use the stock for sauces, boil to reduce over high heat until the flavour is very concentrated. Cool, then pour it into ice-cube trays and freeze. When the stock is frozen, unmould the cubes and place them in 2 or 3 plastic bags. Seal tightly and place back in the freezer. These cubes are very handy to use for stewing vegetables, for sauces etc. – whenever only a little stock is needed.

BRODO DI PESCE
Fish Stock

MAKES ABOUT 1.25L/2PT [US 5 CUPS]
1.3kg/3lb heads and bones of white fish, such as
turbot, brill, sole, haddock etc.
1 large onion
1 carrot
1 celery stalk
3 or 4 parsley stalks
a handful of bulb fennel tops, if available
2 tomatoes
3 garlic cloves, peeled
1 dozen peppercorns
1 tsp salt
2 bay leaves
300ml/10fl oz dry white wine

If still there, cut off and discard the gills in the
heads of the fish, as they would give the stock a
bitter taste. Wash the heads and bones and put
them in a stockpot. Cut the vegetables into
chunks and add them to the pot together with all
the other ingredients except the wine. Add
2l/3½pt [US 2qt] of water. Bring to the boil and
simmer for 15 minutes, then add the wine and
simmer for another 15 minutes.

Strain the stock through a large fine sieve into
a clean saucepan. Now you must boil to reduce
this stock by about half, over high heat.

BRODO VEGETALE
Vegetable Stock

A good vegetable stock is just as useful a standby
in the kitchen as a meat stock. It can be used for
many vegetable risottos, for stewing vegetables
and for adding to soups and sauces.

MAKES ABOUT 1.5L/2½PT [US 1½QT]
3 celery stalks
4 carrots
2 leeks, both white and green part
2 tomatoes
1 courgette [US zucchini] (optional)
a bunch of greens, such as beet spinach or lettuce
leaves but not spring [US collard] greens (optional)
1 onion, stuck with 1 clove
2 garlic cloves, peeled
a large bunch of parsley, leaves and stalks
2 bay leaves
6 peppercorns
1 tsp salt

Cut the vegetables into pieces. Put them in a
stockpot with the herbs and the peppercorns.
Cover with 2.5l/4¼pt [US 2½qt] cold water, add
the salt and bring to the boil. Simmer gently for
about 2 hours. Strain and leave to cool, then
refrigerate in a covered container.

Stock keeps in the refrigerator for about 3
days, after which it must be brought back to the
boil and boiled for at least 5 minutes. Or it can be
frozen.

If you want a stronger flavoured stock, boil to
reduce the stock over high heat until the flavour
is more concentrated. This stronger stock is best
for adding in small quantities to vegetable stews
or sauces. Pour the stock into ice-cube trays and
freeze. One cube is equal to about 1 tablespoon.

Home-made Pasta

This is the recipe for home-made pasta as it is made in Emilia. In other regions an egg is often replaced by water or, as in the case of vincisgrassi (page 217), by Vinsanto. The mixture in this recipe makes a good pasta with a delicate flavour and a nice bite. I make pasta with an old-fashioned hand-cranked machine, which is cheap, noiseless and easy to work. It makes very good pasta and it is easy to use and to clean.

I recommend the use of Italian grade 00 flour for making pasta because it absorbs the eggs more evenly, is easier to knead and roll out and, above all, makes pasta with a more fragrant flavour and a more delicate texture. You can buy 00 flour in most Italian food shops and good supermarkets.

MAKES ABOUT 350G/12OZ PASTA, ENOUGH FOR 4 PEOPLE AS A FIRST COURSE OR 3 AS A MAIN COURSE

2 size-2 free-range eggs [US extra-large eggs]
approximately 225g/8oz [US 2 cups] Italian 00
flour or stone-ground plain flour
semolina for dusting

Put most of the flour on the work-top and make a well in the centre; place the rest of the flour to one side. Break the eggs into the well. Beat them lightly with a fork, drawing the flour in gradually from the inner wall of the well. Now use your hands to mix and then knead for 5 minutes or so. The dough should be elastic and soft, but not moist. If necessary add more flour. Wrap in cling film and leave to rest for at least half an hour. This resting is very important because it allows the gluten in the flour to relax.

Knead the dough for 1 or 2 minutes, then divide it into 4 equal portions. Take one piece of dough and re-wrap the other pieces in cling film.

Set the rollers of the pasta machine to the widest opening. Flatten the piece of dough slightly, so that it is nearly as wide as the rollers.

Run it through the machine 5 or 6 times, folding the sheet over and giving it a 180° turn each time. Now run the sheet, unfolded and without turning it, through all the settings, closing the rollers one notch at a time, until you achieve the desired thickness. You may have to dust the dough with flour every now and then. Pasta made in the hand-cranked machine needs more flour than that made by hand.

For tonnarelli (like spaghetti but square in section) stop the rolling out at the second from last setting. For tagliatelle, fettuccine or pappardelle stop at the last but one. For lasagne, ravioli or cannelloni stop at the last setting.

When you make long pasta you must allow the pasta sheets to dry until no longer damp, but not yet leathery, before you cut them, or the strands will stick together. For stuffed pasta, lasagne and cannelloni proceed immediately to the next operation.

Sprinkle semolina in between strands or sheets of fresh pasta to prevent sticking.

If you are making pasta without the help of a machine, you must knead the dough for much longer – no less than 5 minutes. Give it a rest, well wrapped in cling film, and then proceed to roll out. If you do not possess a long Italian rolling pin, divide the dough into 4 portions and work on one at a time, keeping the rest well wrapped. Roll out the piece of dough as thin as you can, especially if you are making lasagne or ravioli.

Polenta

The first people to make polenta with maize flour are said to have been the Friulani, although I am sure that many people who started to grow maize after it first arrived from the New World must have tried using its flour in the way they had always used buckwheat, chick-pea or other kinds of flour. The advantage of maize was that it grew in areas where no other crop would easily grow, so it was soon intensively cultivated in the marsh-lands and elsewhere in northern Italy. Thus polenta soon became a staple, taking its place alongside rice, which grew further south in the Po valley.

The polenta of Friuli and Veneto is softer than that of Lombardy or Trentino. There it is made not only with a smaller proportion of water to flour, but also with a finer maize flour. In Veneto it is often made with a kind of white maize, *polentina bianca*, which makes a deliciously deli-cate polenta.

Polenta is traditionally made in a *paiolo*, a large bucket-shaped pan made of unlined copper, which conducts the heat very rapidly all over the surface. The tool used for stirring is a long wooden stick-like implement, a *bastone*. Failing these, use a large, deep saucepan and stir with a long wooden spoon so that the polenta can boil fast without danger to your hand.

The making of polenta is a task taken very seri-ously by polenta devotees. I sometimes prefer to cut a few corners, depending on how my polenta is going to be used. However, the corner I refuse to cut is that involving the use of pre-cooked polenta flour, which I find is not good enough. But when I am short of time, or especially when I am making polenta for grilling or for a baked dish, I make polenta either in a pressure cooker or in the oven (see recipes below).

When I cook polenta in the traditional way I follow the instructions given to me by a friend who is a seriously good cook, Rosanna Lockhart.

She has devised a method for making a very light polenta, which she finds much preferred in this country. And I totally agree with her. My English husband never really liked plain polenta, until I learnt Rosanna's method. The only drawback to this method is that it needs constant presence and a strong wrist because instead of a spoon you use a balloon whisk.

I use a good brand of polenta flour, like Spadoni polenta bramata, which is available in good supermarkets and in most Italian food shops.

THESE QUANTITIES MAKE ENOUGH POLENTA FOR ABOUT 6 PEOPLE

ROSANNA'S POLENTA
Bring to the simmer – not the boil – 1.8l/3pt [US 7½ cups] of water. Add 2 teaspoons of salt and then add 250g/9oz of maize (polenta) flour [US 2 cups coarse cornmeal], letting the flour fall into the water through the fingers of a clenched fist while with the other hand you beat the mixture in the pan with a large metal balloon whisk. When all the flour has been added, cook at a lively boil for 40 minutes, whisking constantly at first and then as often as you can between one short rest and the next. This whisking aerates the mixture, making it much lighter in texture and more delicate in flavour than polenta stirred with the wooden stick.

Polenta is traditionally served on a wooden board lined with a linen napkin to absorb the excess moisture. But Rosanna's polenta is a bit too floppy, and I prefer to serve it in a deep bowl, preferably earthenware for absorbing the mois-ture.

POLENTA MADE IN THE PRESSURE COOKER
Put 1.8l/3pt [US 7½ cups] of water and 2 tea-spoons of salt in the pressure cooker and bring to the simmer. Draw the pan from the heat and add 400g/14oz of maize (polenta) flour [US 3½ cups coarse cornmeal] in a very thin stream, letting it

run through the fingers of your clenched fist, while with the other hand you stir the mixture in the pan rapidly with a long wooden spoon, always in the same direction. When you have added all the flour, return the pan to the heat and bring to the boil, stirring constantly. Fit the lid on the pressure cooker and bring up to pressure. Put the weight in position and cook for 20 minutes. The polenta is now ready.

POLENTA SENZA BASTONE (POLENTA MADE IN THE OVEN)
Bring 1.8l/3pt [US 7½ cups] of water to the simmering point. Remove the pan from the heat and add 2 teaspoons of salt, then gradually add 350g/12oz of maize (polenta) flour [US 3 cups coarse cornmeal], letting it fall through your fingers while you stir rapidly with a long wooden spoon. Return the pan to the heat and bring slowly to the boil, stirring constantly in the same direction. Boil for 5 minutes, still stirring. Now transfer the polenta to a buttered oven dish. Cover with buttered foil and cook in a preheated oven (190°C/375°F/Gas Mark 5) for 1 hour.

A revolutionary note. Lately, and after much tasting and testing, I have come to the conclusion that – as pointed out to me by Lynda Brown, a friend and colleague – adding the maize (polenta) flour to cold water is much easier than adding the flour to boiling water. You can add the flour all in one go, because, the water being cold, there is no risk of lumps forming, and the final result is just as good.

In Italy maize (polenta) flour is always added to boiling water simply because nobody dared to flout the age-old tradition. In the country kitchens of the 16th century the water was always boiling in the *paiolo* hanging over the open fire, ready for the maize to be added. When the open fire was replaced by gas or electricity, the ritual of polenta making was too deeply ingrained for anyone to dream of suggesting that there might be an easier way.

FRITTATA
Italian Flat Omelette

Although this is not a basic recipe, it belongs to so many regions of northern Italy that there seemed nowhere else to put it. In Tuscany you would add sage or mint, in Lombardy onion, in Umbria a black truffle, in Liguria porcini and in Piedmont sweet peppers. You can add other vegetables, such as left-over sautéed courgettes [US zucchini] or stewed fennel, or even left-over spaghetti or tagliatelle. They all go to make a delicious frittata.

A good frittata should be set and moist, never dry and stiff.

Here is the recipe for cheese frittata. If you are adding vegetables, use only 5 eggs and less Parmesan.

SERVES 4
7 size-2 eggs [US extra-large eggs]
40g/1½oz [US 6 tbsp] freshly grated Parmesan
salt and freshly ground black pepper
30g/1oz [US 2 tbsp] unsalted butter

Break the eggs into a bowl and beat lightly until blended. Add the Parmesan, salt and pepper, remembering not to add too much salt because the cheese is salty. Beat again.

Melt the butter in a heavy-based 30cm/12in frying pan and, as soon as the butter has melted, pour in the egg mixture. Turn the heat down to very low. When the eggs have set and only the top surface is still runny, pass the pan under a preheated grill [US broiler], just for 30 seconds, enough to set the top.

Loosen the frittata with a spatula and cut into lovely wedges. Transfer to a serving dish or individual plates.

Frittata is a perfect dish for picnics or, cut into small pieces, for snacks with a drink.

MARMELLATA DI CIPOLLE
Onion Jam

When you find some sweet onions in the shops,
and you have a little spare time, buy a kilo and
prepare this jam to keep in the fridge. It is a good
starter for stew, sauces and soups. Instead of
having to sauté the onion gently for, say, half an
hour, you just add 1 tablespoon or so of this jam.

MAKES ABOUT 450G/1LB
900g/2lb onions
15g/½oz [US 1 tbsp] butter
2 tbsp olive oil
1 tsp salt

Slice the onions very finely and put them in a
large sauté pan with all the other ingredients. Add
150ml/5fl oz of hot water and cook at the lowest
simmer (I use a flame diffuser), with the lid firmly
on, for about 1 hour, stirring occasionally. At the
end the onion will be very soft but there will
probably still be too much liquid. Take the lid off
the pan and cook very rapidly to reduce. The jam
should be thick and have a lovely golden colour.

Spoon the jam into a jar or a plastic container
and keep in the fridge. It will come in useful
many a time . . . if you manage to make it last! It
is so good that I have also served it around some
meat, made a frittata with it, and eaten it on a
crostino.

INDEX

ACKNOWLEDGEMENTS

I am deeply grateful to many friends and acquaintances who so generously gave me ideas and recipes. My particular thanks go to members of the Accademia Italiana della Cucina: firstly to Massimo Alberini, the Honorary Vice-President, a dear friend who has helped me all through my writing career, and then to Giovanni Capsit, the Vice-President, to Ugo and Teresa Cesaritti, Giovanni Goria, Giuseppe Moraglia and Barth Pallanca.

I am indebted to Romana Bosco, Gianna Modotti and Margherita and Valeria Simili who run cookery schools in Turin, Udine and Bologna respectively.

The following are some of the people in Italy to whom I want to send special thanks:

Dina Alberghini of La Buca di San Petronio in Bologna
Claudio Aliani, chef of Grand Hotel del Mare in Bordighera
Ezio and Maria Anghinetti of the Trattoria La Maesta near Parma
The Ansuini brothers, sausage makers in Umbria
Luigi Aquilante, Mayor of Staffolo in Marche
Pio Bartolini, sausage maker in Marche
Clara Belcapo
Capineta Nodio Benini
Antonietta and Luciano Bertocchi of the Trattoria Da Bussè in Pontremoli
Mariateresa Bestetti
Francesca Bianchi
Luigi Bianchi of the Grand Hotel del Mare in Bordighera
Paola Bini of the Villa Gaidello Club near Modena
Baldo Arno and Ferdinando Anegg of the Albergo Rosa in Alto Adige
Andrea Bordignan and Dante Bernardi of Blasut in Montegliano, Friuli
Dino Boscorato of the Trattoria dall'Amelia in Mestre
Leopoldo e Costanza Budini Gattai
Giovanni Cabani of Miranda in Tellaro near La Spezia
Lina and Giuseppe Campioni of Da Lina in Casteggio near Pavia
Sorelle Carboni of Manuelina in Recco near Genoa
Cinzia Certosini of Vecchia Osteria del Ponte a Bozzone near Siena
Giovanni Colombo, cheese producer near Pavia

Livio Crespi, oil producer in Liguria
Maria Deana
Guido and Bianca Del Conte
Marco Del Conte
Gastone Delio of Gastone in Dolceacqua near Ventimiglia
Antonio Farinella
Giorgio Fini of the eponymous restaurant in Modena
Catia Franci, bread maker in Pitigliano
Ferdinanda Galletti di San Cataldo
Grazia Gay
Marco Ghezzi
Pietro Grecchi of the pasticceria Vigoni in Pavia
Loreta Guastini of Albergo Guastini in Pitigliano
Margherita König of the pasticceria König in Merano
Magda Lucchini
Wilma Magagnato
Tarsilia Mancini
Signor Martinotti, rice producer in Piedmont
Mariella Massola
Elsa Mazzolini
Giulia Mercuri
Geltrude Mitterman of Hotel Bella Vista in Mendola, Alto Adige
Lalla Morassutti
Mara Mori of the Leone in Pomponesco, near Mantua
Giuseppe e Mariadele Muzio of Angiolina in Sestri Levante
Domenico Passero of Trattoria all'Antica in Milan
Annamaria de'Pedrini
Joan Peregalli
Sandra Polo, baker in Turin
Angelina Purin of Crucolo near Trento
Fritz Rabauser, butcher in Alto Adige
Franco Roi, oil producer in Liguria
Giovanna Rosti
Paolo Scarpellini
Heidi Schmidt, baker in Lana, Alto Adige
Lorenzo Secchi of Taverna del Vecchio Borgo in Massa Marittima
Signor Seibstock, salumiere in Merano
Renato Sozzani of Hotel della Posta in Sondrio
Sandro and Paola Spinosi, pasta producers in Marche
Antonio Stoppani of Peck in Milan
Artemio Strazzi
Carla Toffoloni
Francesco Tofoni, buffalo breeder in Marche

Maria Pia and Domenico Triassi of Cral Ferrera in Crema
Alberto Varisco of the Leon d'Oro in La Spezia
Gianfranco Vissani of the Ristorante Vissani near Todi
Guy Waley

In Britain I have special thanks for the following who helped me generously, one way or another, with their expertise:

Anthony Beevor
Vincenzo and Anne Bergonzoli of Al San Vicenzo in London
Mauro Bregoli of The Old Manor House in Romsey
Charles and Julia Cardozo
Gianfranco Carraro
Philippa Davenport
Willi Elsener and Paolo Sari of the Dorchester
Geraldine Gartrell
Albino and Anna Gorini of Salumeria Estense in London
Thérèse Ingram
Gioacchino La Franca
Rosanna Lockheart
George and Betsy Newell
Pietro Pesce
Eve Pollekoff
Andrea Riva and Francesco Zanchetta of Riva in London
Antonello Tagliabue of Bice in London
Ann and Franco Taruschio of The Walnut Tree near Abergavenny
Carla Tomasi
Claudia Wolfers Vasquez
Paul Waley
Lyn Williamson

My deepest gratitude goes to my husband Oliver, who had to go without food, or eat four meals a day, during the long gestation of this book. He has been my adviser, support, constant help and – as always – my word processor.

Finally, I thank everyone at Pavilion who has been involved in producing this book, and particularly the cookery editors Gillian Young, John Midgley and Rachel King. Thanks also to Norma MacMillan, who has been the most thorough yet unassuming copy editor, and to Caroline Liddell for preparing the dishes so beautifully for photography. And, as ever, I owe a great deal to Vivien Green, my agent, who was always at the other end of the telephone to support me and cheer me up.